PENGUIN CLASSICS

THE RAMCHARITMANAS 3

TULSIDAS (c.1532–1632), the most important of the saint-poets of the medieval bhakti movement in northern India, is also Hindi's greatest poet. Though very little is known about Tulsi's personal life, he left behind a considerable body of work, including his epic, the *Ramcharitmanas*, a retelling of the story of Ram in Avadhi. Tulsi was an ardent devotee of Ram, and his works have come to occupy almost a canonical status in the Ram tradition in northern India. His other important works include the *Gitavali*, the *Vinay Patrika* and the *Kavitavali*. In addition, the *Hanuman Chalisa*, a short devotional poem of forty verses in praise of Hanuman, is popularly ascribed to Tulsidas, and is considered by many to be his most important work after the *Manas*. Tulsidas's works continue to remain popular even today, more than four hundred years after their composition.

ROHINI CHOWDHURY is an established literary translator. Her primary languages are pre-modern (Braj Bhasha and Avadhi) and modern (Khari Boli) Hindi, and English. Her translations include the seventeenth-century Braj Bhasha text *Ardhakathanak*, widely regarded as the first autobiography in an Indian language, into modern Hindi and into English. She also writes for children, and has more than twenty books and several short stories to her credit. Her published writing, in English and Hindi, covers a wide spectrum of literary genres including novels, short fiction and non-fiction. Her literary interests include mythology, folklore, mathematics and history. She runs a story website at www.longlongtimeago.com.

THE RAMCHARITMANAS

3

Tulsidas

Translated by Rohini Chowdhury

PENGUIN BOOKS

An imprint of Penguin Random House

PENGUIN BOOKS

USA | Canada | UK | Ireland | Australia
New Zealand | India | South Africa | China | Singapore

Penguin Books is part of the Penguin Random House group of companies
whose addresses can be found at global.penguinrandomhouse.com

Published by Penguin Random House India Pvt. Ltd
4th Floor, Capital Tower 1, MG Road,
Gurugram 122 002, Haryana, India

Penguin
Random House
India

First published in Penguin Books by Penguin Random House India 2019

10 9 8 7 6 5 4 3 2

ISBN 9780143425892

Typeset in Adobe Caslon Pro by Manipal Technologies Limited, Manipal
Printed at Manipal Technologies Limited, India

www.penguin.co.in

MIX
Paper | Supporting
responsible forestry
FSC
www.fsc.org   FSC® C043100

Contents

Contents

Introduction

Amongst the most important of the saint-poets of the medieval bhakti movement in northern India, Tulsidas is also Hindi's most renowned poet. In 1574, he commenced the composition of his *Ramcharitmanas*, a retelling of the story of Ram, the legendary prince of Avadh. Tulsi's epic poem is unanimously regarded as the greatest achievement of Hindi literature, and is a significant addition to the Ramayana corpus. Composed in the vernacular Avadhi—a literary dialect of eastern Hindi—and therefore accessible to everyone without the need for learned intervention by the Brahmin, it became, and remains, the dominant and accepted version of Ram's story in the Hindi-speaking north.

My own engagement with Tulsidas began one crisp autumn night fifty years ago in a small town by the banks of the Ganga, when I saw my first performance of the *Ram Lila*. The sky was sprinkled with stars but I had eyes only for the drama unfolding upon the crude wooden stage before me, where the story had reached a critical point: Hanuman's tail was to be set on fire. The sets were crude, the costumes garish, the acting unsophisticated— but the story transcended all such concerns, such was its magic and power. I did not know it then, but that was also my first intimate encounter with the *Ramcharitmanas*, upon which the *Ram Lila* is based. Growing up, Tulsi's poem was always around me—chanted in the homes of friends or neighbours, sung on the radio, or the

theme of plays and dance dramas. So when the opportunity came
to translate it into English for Penguin India, I accepted it with
alacrity—and the last five years that I have spent walking behind
Tulsi, one of the greatest literary minds of all time, have been
a pleasure and a privilege. My translation does not do justice to
Tulsi's extraordinary poetic genius. His use of wordplay, his rhymes
and alliteration, and the sheer musicality of his poem I have found
impossible to capture in English. I have therefore contented myself
with being as clear and accurate as possible in my translation, and
to convey, to the best of my ability, the scale and grandeur of his
great poem.

The Ramayana tradition

For at least the last two and a half thousand years, poets, writers,
folk performers, and religious and social reformers have drawn upon
the story of Ram as a source of inspiration. It has been told again
and again in countless forms and dozens of languages, making it
one of the most popular and enduring stories in the world. More
than any other hero, Ram has been upheld as dharma personified,
the epitome of righteousness, and his actions as the guide for right
conduct. In recent times, the story has provided inspiration for films,
novels, and in the late 1980s, a weekly television series watched by
more than eighty million viewers.

The oldest and most influential surviving literary telling of the
story of Ram is the Sanskrit epic called the Ramayana. Composed
sometime during the first millennium BCE, and consisting of some
50,000 lines in verse set in seven kands or books, it is attributed
to the poet Valmiki, and is widely regarded as the 'original'.[1] The
influence of Valmiki's Ramayana has been so profound that the title
of his epic has come to denote the entire tradition, from oral and
folk performances to literary texts and translations. Within this rich
and varied tradition also lie the Ramayana songs from Telangana,
the folk performances of the *Ram Lila* in northern India, the

eleventh-century Tamil *Iramavataram* ('The Incarnation of Ram') by Kamban, and Tulsidas's *Ramcharitmanas*.

The rise of bhakti

Scholars of the Ramayana tradition hold the view that Ram was originally a human hero and was only later raised to the status of avatar of Vishnu. In the five central books of Valmiki's epic, Ram is portrayed as an earthly prince: though endowed with godlike courage, fortitude and compassion, his exploits are those of a human being. It is only in the first and last books of the poem—which are considered to be later additions to Valmiki's epic—that Ram is explicitly declared to be an incarnation of Vishnu on earth.

Soon after the beginning of the Common Era, Ram began to be increasingly regarded as an avatar of Vishnu. At about the same time, a new attitude towards the divine began to replace austere monistic meditation, sacrificial rites and polytheistic practices. This was bhakti, or intense emotional attachment and love towards a chosen, personal god and his avatars—particularly Vishnu and his earthly incarnations, Ram and Krishna—and joyous and public worship of that god. Bhakti assumed a dualistic relationship between the devotee and his god, as opposed to the monistic ideal of the Advaita or non-dualistic school of philosophy. Its proponents considered the way of bhakti (bhakti-marg) superior to other means of achieving salvation such as knowledge or good works or ascetic disciplining of the body; it was also open to everyone, regardless of their caste, class or sex. With the advent of bhakti, Ram's transition from godlike prince to God became complete. This was a critical transformation of the Ram story—and it is within this bhakti tradition that Tulsi wrote his *Ramcharitmanas*.

The bhakti movement was characterized by its emphasis on the use of vernacular languages, making its teachings directly accessible to the common people, regardless of class or caste. This was in stark contrast to traditional practice, within which Sanskrit, regarded as the sacred language, was used for all important literary and religious texts. Sanskrit was thus the preserve of an elite few, typically high-caste Brahmins, who would study, interpret and explain the texts to the common people. The earliest bhakti texts to appear were in Tamil—these were devotional poems in praise of Shiv and Vishnu, composed by saint-musicians, the Nayanars and Alvars, of southern India between the seventh and the tenth centuries CE. Also written in Tamil was Kamban's *Iramavataram*. Composed in the eleventh century, it is amongst the earliest vernacular Ramayanas. It became, and still is, the definitive version of the Ram story in the Tamil-speaking areas of the subcontinent. The bhakti movement soon spread northwards, appearing in texts such as the *Bhagavata Purana*, composed in Sanskrit in the tenth century and celebrating devotion to Krishna. More vernacular Ramayanas were composed. Amongst the more noteworthy of these were the thirteenth-century Telugu Ramayana of Buddharaja and the fifteenth-century Bengali *Sriram Panchali* by Krittibas. In Hindi, the bhakti movement reached its zenith in the sixteenth century, with Tulsidas's *Ramcharitmanas*.

The *Ramcharitmanas*: spread and impact

From Tulsi's own writings we infer that his poem, written in the spoken tongue rather than in the sacred Sanskrit, was criticized and ridiculed by the religious establishment of his times. Despite this initial disapproval by the Brahmins (ironically complicated by the fact that the *Ramcharitmanas* itself is so pro-Brahmin), it became hugely popular amongst other groups, especially the merchant caste and lower orders of society, and soon acquired the status and religious authority usually enjoyed only by Sanskrit texts. Within a very short time, carried by wandering sadhus, recited and performed by travelling bards and musicians across towns and villages, it had spread across northern India, from Tulsi's native Banaras in the east to the Rajput kingdoms of Rajasthan in the west. It is worth noting that this initial circulation of Tulsi's poem took place before the advent of printing in India, in areas and times of exceedingly low literacy, its currency strongly dependent on the oral tradition and remarkable feats of memorization by its devotees. Such was the rapid spread and influence of Tulsi's poem that his contemporary, the poet Nabhadas, declares Tulsi to be Valmiki himself, born again to bring his epic once more to the world.[2]

In the late eighteenth century, the *Ramcharitmanas* found royal patronage in the courts of resurgent Hindu kingdoms in northern India who found it a convenient, authoritative and accessible text through which to assert their Hindu identity and legitimize their rule by invoking Ram as the ideal and perfect king. In the nineteenth century, the *Ramcharitmanas* gained even greater currency as north Indian mainstream Hinduism found within it not only an answer to the Christian Bible, but also a nationalistic response to British colonialism. The development of movable type in Indian scripts led to the growth of vernacular presses and the printing of popular books in Indian languages, including, in 1810 in Calcutta, Tulsidas's *Ramcharitmanas*. By the end of the century, printed versions of Tulsi's epic were available all across the north of India—from Calcutta, in Bengali translation, to Gurmukhi-script editions in Delhi and Lahore, and Gujarati and Marathi versions from Bombay.[3] Today, known to its audience as 'Tulsi's Ramayan', or simply the *Manas*, Tulsi's great poem is read, sung, recited and retold in almost every Hindu household in northern India as the accepted and dominant version of the story of Ram. It is also the basis of the *Ram Lila*, a tradition believed to have been started in Banaras almost 500 years ago by Tulsidas himself and still enthusiastically observed.

Tulsidas

We know very little about Tulsidas himself, except what can be pieced together from autobiographical references in his own writings and some contemporary and later, not entirely reliable, accounts of his life. His date and place of birth are uncertain—though it is now generally accepted that he was born in 1532, possibly in the town of

Sukarkhet in the present-day state of Uttar Pradesh. From some of his later works, we know Tulsidas was abandoned in childhood by his parents, and that he was rescued and looked after by sadhus who introduced him to the worship of Ram. Some scholars believe that Tulsidas then took up the life of a sadhu. It is probable, though, that Tulsidas did not become a sadhu at once, but went to Banaras and acquired the traditional Sanskrit education of a Brahmin. He then returned to the village of his birth, where he married. He began to live as a householder, but an altercation with his wife caused him to renounce home and family and take up the wandering life of a sadhu. He lived for a while in Ayodhya, where he composed the initial parts of his *Ramcharitmanas*. Tulsi later settled in Banaras where he wrote most of his other major works; there, he also instituted the *Ram Lila*. He died in Banaras, probably in 1632.[4]

A synopsis

In the beginning sections of his poem, Tulsidas tells us that he commenced this work in Ayodhya, on the ninth day of the Hindu month of Chaitra—the day of Ram's birth—in the year 1631 of the Vikram Era, i.e., 1574 CE.[5] This also makes the *Ramcharitmanas* the earliest of his major works. Consisting of approximately 12,900 lines of Avadhi verse set in seven kands or books, it is also Tulsi's longest work, and its composition probably took him several years. The fourth book of his poem opens with an invocation to the city of Banaras, suggesting that he completed the epic after moving there.

   In the beginning of the *Ramcharitmanas*, Tulsi explains that he first heard the story of Ram from his guru in Sukarkhet when he was still a boy, and that this is the story that he now seeks to set down in the spoken tongue.[6] In outline, the story of the *Ramcharitmanas* is as follows:

   King Dasharath of Koshal rules in splendour from his capital city, Avadh. The king has all that a man could desire, except a son.

So, upon the advice of his guru, the sage Vasishtha, he holds a great fire-sacrifice, as the result of which four sons are born to him: Ram, the eldest, to his chief queen, Kaushalya; Bharat to his favourite wife, Kaikeyi; and the twins Lakshman and Shatrughna to his third queen, Sumitra. Ram is no other than the great god Vishnu, who has become incarnate in human form in order to rid the world of Ravan, the powerful king of the Rakshasas, who cannot be killed except by a mortal man and who has overrun the earth and overwhelmed even the gods.

The four princes grow up to be brave and skilled warriors. One day, when the princes are still youths, the sage Vishvamitra arrives at Dasharath's court and requests that Ram and his brother Lakshman be sent with him to help protect his fire-sacrifices from the depredations of the Rakshasas. Dasharath protests that his sons are still too young, and offers the sage his whole army instead. But Vishvamitra insists that he wants only Ram and Lakshman to help him. Finally, Dasharath agrees.

The two young princes leave with Vishvamitra for the forest, where they successfully kill the Rakshasas disturbing his worship. Vishvamitra then takes the princes to the city of Mithila, to the court of King Janak. There, Ram sees and falls in love with the king's daughter, Sita, and wins her hand in marriage by breaking the great bow of Shiv. The wedding of Ram and Sita is celebrated with great splendour. Lakshman, too, is married to Sita's sister Urmila, and Bharat and Shatrughna to her cousins, the daughters of King Janak's brothers. The four princes and their brides return to Ayodhya, where they continue to live in harmony for several years.

The aging Dasharath then decides to appoint Ram his heir. As preparations for his investiture get under way, Kaikeyi's old nursemaid Manthara convinces her that Ram's investiture would mean the end of her position as the king's favourite, and would cause Bharat to languish in a prison cell while Ram ruled with the help of his favourite, Lakshman. Once, in return for saving his life on the battlefield, Dasharath had given Kaikeyi the gift of two boons: she could ask of him anything that her heart desired and he would fulfil it. Kaikeyi now demands that Bharat be made heir in place of Ram, and that Ram be banished to the forest for fourteen years. Bound by his word, the old king is unable to deny her requests. Realizing the situation, Ram cheerfully accepts his exile and leaves for the forest. Sita and Lakshman, who refuse to stay back, accompany him. Dasharath dies of a broken heart, and all of Avadh is plunged into mourning.

Bharat, who has been away all this while, is summoned back urgently by Vasishtha. He returns and is devastated to find his brother exiled and his father dead. He denounces his mother's actions, refuses the kingship and sets out in pursuit of Ram, determined to bring him back as the rightful king of Avadh. Ram, however, refuses to return, saying that he must honour their father's word, and requests Bharat to go back and rule as their father had desired. Bharat returns heartbroken to Avadh, and taking up an ascetic residence in the nearby village of Nandigram, rules as Ram's regent till the end of his period of exile.

Ram, Lakshman and Sita wander through the forest, encountering demons, ascetics and sages, including the sage Valmiki, who directs them to make their home amongst the hills and forests of Chitrakut. There, Supnakha, the sister of Ravan, sees and falls in love with Ram. Turning herself into a beautiful woman, she approaches Ram, who rejects her advances. Lakshman cuts off her ears and nose in order to teach her a lesson. Mutilated and humiliated, she appeals to her Rakshasa brothers, Khar and Dushan, who attack Ram with their entire army. While Lakshman protects Sita and hides her away in a mountain cave, Ram single-handedly kills the demons and destroys their army. Supnakha then runs in despair to Ravan, who is infuriated by her story, in particular the killing of Khar and Dushan. Ravan decides to kidnap Sita and enlists the help of Marichi, another Rakshasa. Marichi turns himself into a golden deer and manages to lure

Ram and Lakshman into the forest. In their absence, Ravan carries Sita off to his island kingdom of Lanka, where he keeps her prisoner.

The vulture Jatayu sees Sita being carried off and tries to save her, but is fatally wounded by Ravan. Ram and Lakshman return to find the hermitage deserted and Sita missing; as they search for her, they find the wounded Jatayu, who lives just long enough to tell them of her abduction. Ram performs his last rites, and Jatayu receives liberation.

Ram and Lakshman search desperately for Sita, and reach the monkey kingdom of Kishkindha. There, Ram meets Hanuman, who becomes a staunch devotee. He also meets the displaced monkey prince Sugriv, who has also lost both wife and kingdom to his brother Baali. Ram kills Baali and installs Sugriv as king of the monkeys; in return, Sugriv agrees to help him and sends his warriors in every direction in search of Sita. They discover that she is being held prisoner in Lanka.

Hanuman leaps across the ocean, locates Sita and gives her Ram's ring. He lays waste the ashok grove in which Sita is being held, and allows himself to be captured. On Ravan's orders, his tail is set on fire, but Hanuman escapes and, after setting the city of Lanka ablaze, returns to Ram. Meanwhile, Ravan's brother, Vibhishan, who is a devotee of Vishnu and opposed to Ravan's abduction of Sita, also joins Ram's forces. The monkeys build a bridge across the ocean to Lanka, and after a long and bloody battle, Ram kills Ravan. Vibhishan is crowned king of Lanka, and Sita is rescued.

The kidnapped Sita proves to be a shadow replica of herself— Ram, as Vishnu, had foreseen her abduction, and at his behest, the real Sita had stepped into fire, leaving behind a shadow image of herself. It was this shadow Sita that Ravan had kidnapped, while the real Sita had remained hidden, safe from dishonour till Ravan had been killed and the purpose of the gods achieved. Ram now orders Lakshman to light a great fire, and demands that Sita step into it as a test of her chastity. The shadow Sita steps into the fire and is destroyed, and the real Sita steps out, unharmed.

The period of his exile almost over, Ram returns to Ayodhya with
Sita and Lakshman. There, he is crowned king amidst much joy
and celebration, and so begins his long reign, during which pain
or unhappiness were unknown, and all beings lived in harmony
and joy.

The influence of Valmiki's epic upon Tulsi cannot be denied:
in the initial verses of the *Ramcharitmanas*, Tulsi salutes Valmiki
as the author of the Ramayana,[7] thus acknowledging him as one
of the important sources for his own poem. Tulsi's epic, however,
differs from Valmiki's in one very important particular: Valmiki's
Ramayana was a secular text, whilst Tulsi's *Ramcharitmanas* is,
without question, a devotional text. Tulsi's Ram is unequivocally
divine. He is also Tulsi's chosen god, in whose worship the poet
is totally, completely and blissfully immersed—as he tells us in the
invocatory verses of the first book, he composed this story of Ram
for 'his own delight and satisfaction'.[8]

Tulsi's telling of the Ram story in the *Ramcharitmanas* is very
close to the version contained in the Sanskrit text known as the
Adhyatma-ramayana (or 'spiritual' Ramayana). Composed sometime
between 1450 and 1550, the *Adhyatma-ramayana* identifies Ram not
only as an incarnation of Vishnu, but also as the personification of
brahm, the ultimate Absolute of the Upanishads and the Advaita
school of philosophy. It also emphasizes bhakti rather than
knowledge, and recommends meditation on Ram's name as a means
to salvation. It is only through intense devotion to Ram, says the
Adhyatma-ramayana, that knowledge of the non-dual Self can arise
in the individual soul. This is reflected in Tulsi's own, more skilful,
amalgamation of the dualism of Vaishnav bhakti with Advaita
monism in the *Ramcharitmanas*, particularly in the sections where
Tulsi explains the reasons for Ram's actions and their significance.
Tulsi's Ram, as the avatar of Vishnu, also has the attributes of the
Supreme God—he is all-knowing and all-seeing, so that his actions
are predetermined by him to suit his purpose and all that he does or

causes to happen in his incarnate form is merely his *lila*, his divine play or pastime.

Tulsi's replacement of the kidnapping of Sita by the abduction of a 'shadow' or illusory Sita whilst the real Sita remains concealed in the abode of Agni, the fire god, is a major deviation from Valmiki and in keeping with the demands of bhakti. The idea of an illusory Sita arose as early as the eighth century and was further developed in the *Adhyatma-ramayana* where it became an integral part of the plot. Along with Ram's transformation from earthly prince to avatar of Vishnu, Sita acquired the status and attributes of Shri, Vishnu's divine consort. As the incarnation of the goddess upon earth, it became unacceptable that she be kidnapped and imprisoned by Ravan and defiled by his touch. Tulsi's substitution of the real Sita with a shadow replica of herself solved this problem and kept safe the purity and chastity of the goddess. In addition to protecting the sacred person of the goddess, it also justified Ram's demand that Sita prove her chastity after her long imprisonment in Lanka by stepping into the sacred fire. Sita's trial by fire thus becomes a device for the return of the real Sita rather than an unwarranted and unjust test of her purity as in Valmiki's epic.[9] Tulsi's poem ends on a 'happily-ever-after' note, with Ram ruling gloriously in Ayodhya, his beloved Sita by his side. Valmiki's epic does not stop there, but continues in the last book to describe Ram and Sita's later years, in particular the aspersions cast on Sita's chastity by the people of Ayodhya, and her consequent banishment by Ram to the forest. Though Tulsi does refer to this in passing in the first book—Ram, he says, has great affection for the people of Ayodhya, 'for although they maligned Sita, he freed them from all their sins and sorrows'[10]—his device of the shadow Sita precludes the need for him to include this in his version of the story.

Tulsi pays homage to the great and eminent poets who preceded him, as well as to the vernacular poets who told of the deeds of Ram in the spoken tongue.[11] The influence upon him of texts other than Valmiki's is evident in passages such as his delightful descriptions of Ram's childhood, which were probably inspired by the *Bhagavata Purana* and contemporary bhakti poetry in praise of Krishna, both of which celebrate the child Krishna. Tulsi's charming description of Sita's first meeting with Ram[12]—in a garden, where Ram has gone with Lakshman to gather flowers for his morning worship and Sita with her handmaidens to offer worship at a temple of the goddess Parvati—was possibly inspired by the fourteenth-century Sanskrit drama, *Prasannaraghava*, by Jaidev.[13]

In the *Ramcharitmanas*, Tulsi successfully brings together the many contrasting ideologies of his time—joyous, unrestrained Vaishnav bhakti and austere Advaita meditation, the worship of Vishnu and the worship of Shiv, the worship of the abstract, nirgun ('without attributes') Absolute and the adoration of the sagun ('with attributes') Incarnate endowed with form and beauty. Tulsi's Ram is the Supreme Being personified, and Sita is his Shakti, or primal energy. From Ram and Sita spring all the other gods, including Shiv and Parvati (whom Tulsi elsewhere calls 'the father and mother of the Universe'), and even Lakshmi and Vishnu. For Tulsi, Ram is the Supreme God, yet throughout the poem, Tulsi's Ram declares that without the worship of Shiv, no one can attain to his bhakti. Yet, the name of Ram is the high mantra chanted by Shiv, who declares it necessary for salvation even in his own holy city of Banaras. Tulsi takes every opportunity to describe the beauty of Ram's incarnate form in loving detail—his body dark as a rain-laden cloud, his radiant face and lotus eyes, the tilak upon his forehead—but reminds us at once that he is the all-pervading Spirit of the Universe, unborn, uncreated, without flaw, without form. Tulsi prostrates himself at the lotus-feet of the incarnate Ram and adores the name of Ram as borne by his chosen god. This integration of different ideologies in the *Manas* is one of Tulsi's most significant achievements.

Tulsi has been criticized in modern times for his apparent support of the caste system, his reverence for Brahmins and his characterization of women as inherently inferior to men. However, here too he brings together opposing views. While paying homage to

Brahmins as 'gods upon earth', he upholds the tribal woman Shabari, who waited in the forest for Ram, as the epitome of devotion and virtue.[14] So, while the social order must be upheld, within bhakti, the boundaries of caste, class and gender disappear. Tulsi's institution of the *Ram Lila* may be seen as an attempt at a degree of social integration, albeit within the Hindu framework—for everyone, regardless of caste, class and religion, was invited to take part in these performances, whether as actors or audience. This inclusivity remains, by and large, a feature of the *Ram Lila* even today.

Structure

The titles and line counts of the seven books of the *Ramcharitmanas* are as follows:

1. *Balkand* (Childhood)   4200 lines
2. *Ayodhyakand* (Ayodhya)   3300 lines
3. *Aranyakand* (The Forest)   750 lines
4. *Kishkindhakand* (Kishkindha)   400 lines
5. *Sundarkand* (The Beautiful)   750 lines
6. *Lankakand* (Lanka)   1700 lines
7. *Uttarkand* (Epilogue)   1800 lines

Each book begins with a *mangalacharan*, the traditional worship or salutation at the commencement of a written work, in which Tulsi calls upon various gods to bless his endeavour. In order to underline the sacred nature of what was to come, Tulsi chose to write these invocatory passages in Sanskrit.

Tulsi presents his story through a series of interwoven conversations between four narrator–listener pairs, whom he introduces at the beginning of his poem:[15]

- Shiv, and his wife, the goddess Parvati—the story arose in Shiv's heart and he revealed it to Parvati

- Kak Bhushundi, a sage in a crow's body, and Garud, king of the birds and Vishnu's divine steed—Shiv gave the same story to Bhushundi, who related it to Garud
- The sages Jagbalik and Bharadvaj—Jagbalik obtained the tale from Bhushundi and recited it to Bharadvaj
- And finally, Tulsidas and his audience—Tulsi heard the story from his guru and set it down in common speech for his audience

The narrative moves deftly, often unexpectedly, from one narrator to another and back again. The conversation between Bhushundi and Garud is contained mainly in, and takes up most of, the seventh book. Tulsi indicates the narrator–listener pairs sometimes directly, explicitly naming either the speaker or the listener ('Then said Mahesh [Shiv] with a smile . . .'),[16] or by frequent interjections that identify the listener ('O king of the birds' or 'O muni') and so, by extension, the speaker (Bhushundi in the first instance, and Jagbalik in the second). A fifth narrator is implied—just as Tulsi is relating the story to his listeners, in the same way, they too may tell this story to others.

The title of Tulsi's work deserves some attention.[17] The name 'Ram' needs little explanation. Not only is it the name of the hero of the epic, but it is also the name of Tulsi's chosen god, who is none other than the personification of the Supreme Spirit of the Universe. The word *charit* (from the root *char*, 'to move') means 'going, moving' and becomes by extension, 'movement or deeds'. Thus *Ram+charit* means 'the movements or doings of Ram'. The word *manas* is derived from the root word *man*, usually translated into English as 'heart' or 'mind', and means 'belonging to, or born from, the heart or mind'. 'Manas' is also the name of a lake in the Himalayas; lying at the foot of Mount Kailash, the abode of Shiv, the Manas lake, or Manasarovar, is considered to be sacred by many faiths and is used as a metaphor for the mind in its highest state of pure bliss. In the early sections of the first book, Tulsi tells us that this work arose in the mind of Shiv, who kept it within his heart, till, finding an auspicious moment, he revealed it to his wife, the goddess Parvati. And that is why, having seen this sacred story of the doings of Ram within his mind, Shiv called it '*Ramcharitmanas*'. Inspiration, by the grace of Shiv, then gladdened his own mind, says Tulsi, and he composed his great work, making it as pleasing to the heart as his wit allowed.[18]

Tulsi also compares his epic, the *Manas*, to the holy Manas lake—it is the reservoir that contains within it the sacred story of the doings of Ram. Its four narrators are the four ghats that surround it, and the seven books seven staircases that lead down to the clear waters of Ram's fame.[19] He introduces the imagery of the lake in Stanza 36 of the first book and builds it up over the next seven stanzas. He describes the clusters of waterlilies and many-coloured lotuses that grow upon the lake—these are the poetic metres he has used in his poem, and their fragrance the elegant language. Swans of wisdom and detachment float upon the tranquil surface of the lake, while the fish that are wordplay and allusion shimmer beneath its clear waters. The songs in praise of Ram are rare and wonderful water birds, while lustful and evil men are storks and crows that dare not come near the lake. The pleasure derived from this tale, says Tulsi, is a garden watered by the heart with tears of love, and the bliss that wells up in his heart and pours out in a flood of love and joy is the Sarju, Ayodhya's sacred river. This stream of love flows into the glittering Ganga of devotion to Ram, and is joined by the majestic Sone, the great river that is the splendour of Ram and Lakshman in battle. Together, these three streams flow into the ocean that is Ram himself. Tulsi reaffirms the imagery of the Manas lake through his entire work. He calls each of the seven books a 'sopan' or 'descent' into the lake, and reintroduces the imagery of the lake in the seventh book, in the conversation between Bhushundi and Garud.[20]

Tulsi wrote for an audience which was familiar not only with the story of Ram, but also knew the dozens of 'backstories' that weave in and out of the main narrative, or to which Tulsi refers, either directly or obliquely. I am aware that many of those who read my translation will not have the same familiarity with these tales, and so I have attempted, in footnotes, endnotes and a glossary, to give as much background information as I could. Also, the Hindu gods all have more than one name, and Tulsi refers to them by these different names, with which, once again, his audience would have been familiar. Each distinct name or epithet for a god or goddess refers to a quality, characteristic or action of that deity. So, for instance the god of love, Kamdev, or 'lord of passion', may also be referred to as Hridayniket, 'one whose abode is the heart', Manmath, 'he who churns the heart', or Manobhav, 'mind-born'. Similarly, the god Shiv ('the auspicious, the fortunate'), the Destroyer, the great and powerful third deity in the Hindu triad, is, as the lord of all creation, also called Akhileshvar, and as the Destroyer, he is also called Har. While I am aware that these different names for the same deity may be confusing to modern readers, reducing the gods to a single name would, I felt, take away from the meaning and atmosphere of Tulsi's poem. So, for the most part I have kept the names as Tulsi has used them; to make it easier, I have given the most familiar name of the deity as a footnote at the first occurrence of another name for the same god or goddess (for instance, 'Hridayniket' has been footnoted as 'Kamdev'; 'Har' has been footnoted as 'Shiv'). I have also included the various names with their meanings under the glossary entry for the relevant god or goddess (so all of the names of Kamdev used in the text are given under the entry 'Kamdev' in the glossary).

Tulsi may have composed his poem in the 'common tongue', but his control of language, his mastery of rhythm and his deliberate and skilful use of literary devices throughout display a literary virtuosity that is nothing short of genius. He composed his poem mainly in two alternating metres, the *chaupai* and the *doha*. A chaupai is a quatrain consisting of four parts or 'feet'; each quarter verse is made up of sixteen *matras* or 'instants', which is the time required to pronounce a short vowel (a long vowel is twice the length of a short vowel, and thus is equal to two matras). A doha is a couplet, each line of which consists of two unequal parts, usually of thirteen and eleven matras respectively, separated by a caesura; the rhyme occurs at the end of the lines. Thus the doha, though a couplet, may also be thought of as consisting of four, even if unequal, parts. Sometimes Tulsi uses the *sortha* instead of, or along with, the doha. Also consisting of two lines, a sortha is a mirror image of the doha, with its half-lines transposed so its lines are divided into eleven- and thirteen-matra segments separated by a caesura; the rhyme falls at the caesura in the middle of the line. I have rendered each metre in four lines in English translation: each quarter part of a chaupai translates into a single line of verse in English as does each part of a doha or sortha; the lines of the doha and sortha are usually shorter than those of the chaupai.

Tulsi uses the measured and regular chaupai metre in which to tell his story and take it forward. Each series of four to eight chaupais is followed by a doha or dohas (or sometimes a sortha or doha/sortha mix). Many oral performances of the epic take the doha/sortha as a unit of closure. I have followed the same approach, and for the sake of easy reference, taken each chaupai set along with its concluding dohas/sorthas to represent a stanza—though the term 'stanza' has no equivalent in medieval Hindi poetry and Tulsi's text shows no such divisions. I have numbered only the concluding couplets, and matched this numbering to my source text, the popular and widely available Gita Press edition of the *Ramcharitmanas* with a commentary by Hanuman Prasad Poddar. A stanza could just as well be defined as beginning with a doha and some commentators prefer this approach.

A fourth metre that occurs with some frequency in the *Ramcharitmanas* is the *chhand*.

The most musical of the metres used by Tulsi, a chhand consists of four equal lines of twenty-six to thirty matras, with the rhyme at the end of each line. Tulsi uses the chhand to highlight moments of intense emotion, or to further describe and thus emphasize critical scenes or events. The chhand's flowing lyrical nature makes it particularly well suited for such use. Chhands are usually inserted between chaupais and their concluding dohas/sorthas, and so appear within 'stanzas' as defined above.

Other metres used by Tulsi include the hymns of praise or *stutis* spoken by various characters, and the invocatory Sanskrit shlokas of the mangalacharan at the beginning of each book.

It is impossible to reproduce the beat and rhyme schemes of these metres in English, and I have not attempted to do so. However, I have attempted to give the reader some idea, at least visually, of the structure of the poem. Therefore, the dohas/sorthas are indented; chhands, stutis and shlokas are in italics; and the chaupais form the main body of the text.

Other works

Tulsidas has left behind a considerable body of work. However, of the twenty-two works popularly attributed to him, only twelve, including the *Ramcharitmanas*, can be ascribed to him with certainty. The story of Ram is a recurring theme in Tulsi's writings and his works have come to occupy almost a canonical status in the Ram tradition in northern India. The *Gitavali* is his second-longest work; it presents incidents from the life of Ram in 328 songs. The *Vinay Patrika*, considered Tulsi's second-most important work after the *Ramcharitmanas*, consists of some 280 songs, in the form of a personal petition to Ram asking for deliverance from the age of Kali. Both these works are in the western-Hindi Brajbhasha, and were composed in the middle years of the poet's life. A major work of Tulsi's later years is the *Kavitavali*. Also in Braj, it tells the Ram story in some 325 verses. Other, lesser, works include two poems on mythological weddings: the *Parvati-mangal*, a description of the marriage of Shiv and Parvati, composed in 1586, and the *Janaki-mangal* on the marriage of Ram with Sita, which is undated; both these poems are in Avadhi. Another minor work is the *Barvai-ramayan*, an abridged rendition of the Ram story in sixty-nine stanzas in the barvai metre; this is also in Avadhi. A large collection of verses in the doha and sortha metres, called *Dohavali*, is also ascribed to Tulsidas.

In addition, the *Hanuman Chalisa*, a short devotional poem of forty verses in praise of Hanuman, is popularly ascribed to Tulsidas. Though the poem begins with a doha from the second book of the *Ramcharitmanas*[21] and contains several lines that seem to have been taken from the epic, it remains doubtful that it was composed by Tulsidas. However, it is considered by many to be his most important work after the *Manas*. It is recited daily by millions of Hindus and is one of the most popular devotional poems of all time.

Tulsidas was a man of deep spiritual insight and a poet of extraordinary talent. His bhakti is joyous and intense, and very soon, his audience too is drawn into exuberant devotion to the 'feet of Ram'. He charms and moves his audience with his delicate descriptions and enthrals them with the intellectual force and clarity of his discourses on points of doctrine. His achievements are significant: not only did he successfully recast the ancient story of Ram in the mould of bhakti, but by composing it in the vernacular he took away forever the need for its interpretation by the Brahminical elite. His synthesis of contrasting ideologies and points of view in the *Manas* made it acceptable to a wider audience and led to greater integration within the Hindu community. Nothing that can be said about the beauty of his great poem or the significance of its contribution to the religious and social landscape of northern India is enough. Thus, it is perhaps best that we now 'listen' to this great story in the manner that Tulsi asks—with our full attention. I hope, despite its many shortcomings, my translation will give my readers an appreciation of this great work.

Book IV

KISHKINDHAKAND
(KISHKINDHA)

Mangalacharan

Beautiful as the jasmine flower and the blue lotus,
Of great strength, abodes of wisdom,
Graceful and comely, accomplished bowmen,
Praised by the Vedas, holding cows and Brahmans dear,
Who appeared in the form of men through their maya as the two
*   noble sons of Raghu,*
Protectors of true religion,
Wayfarers intent on their search for Sita—
May they grant me devotion. (1)

Fortunate are the wise who incessantly sip
The life-giving nectar that is Ram's name,
Produced by the churning of the ocean that are the Vedas,
That annihilates the impurities of the age of Kali in every way,
The imperishable,
That ever shines in the beautiful and glorious moon of divine
*   Shambhu's lips,*
The remedy for the diseases that are life and death, that imparts
*   happiness,*
And is divine Janaki's life. (2)

How is it possible not to worship Kashi,
The abode of Shambhu and Bhavani,
Knowing it to be the birthplace of salvation,
A treasury of spiritual knowledge and the
      destroyer of sin?   (0A)

Foolish is the one who does not worship
Shankar, who drank the deadly poison
That was burning the host of gods,
For who is as merciful as Shankar?   (0B)

Once more, Raghurai set forth,
And drew near the mountain Rishyamuk.
There lived Sugriv with his ministers.
Seeing them, the two brothers of immeasurable might, approach,
Sugriv was greatly afraid and said, 'Listen, Hanuman,
Those two men are abodes of strength and beauty.
Assume the form of a young Brahman student and go take a look,
And when you have ascertained who they are, let me know by a sign.
If they have been sent by the evil-hearted Baali,
I will flee and at once leave this mountain.'
Taking on the form of a Brahman, the monkey went up to them
And, bowing his head, he thus questioned them:
'Who are you, one dark-complexioned, the other fair,
Who roam this forest in the guise of Kshatriyas?
Walking upon the hard ground with your soft feet,
Why do you wander in the forest, masters?
Your bodies are delicate, charming and beautiful,
Yet you suffer the intolerable sun and wind of the forest.
Are you any of the three great gods?[i]
Or are you Nar and Narayan?

---

[i]   The Hindu triad of Brahma the Creator, Vishnu the Preserver, and Shiv
    the Destroyer

Or are you the original cause of the universe,
The lords of all the worlds,
Become manifest in human form
To help us cross the ocean of this existence and to
      destroy the burdens of this earth?'   (1)

'We are the sons of Dasharath, the king of Koshal,
And have come to the forest in obedience to our father's command.
Our names are Ram and Lakshman, we are two brothers,
And with us was my young and beautiful wife.
But some night-wandering demon here has carried Vaidehi off,
And it is in search of her, Brahman, that we roam the forest.
We have told you about us,
Now, Brahman, tell us your story.'
Recognizing the Lord, Hanuman fell and embraced his feet—
His bliss, Uma, cannot be described.
His body trembled with joy and no words came to him
As he gazed at the lovely guise the Lord had assumed.
Then, collecting himself, he sang a hymn of praise,
His heart full of joy at having recognized his own Lord.
'That I questioned my Lord was as it should be,
But why do you ask, like a mere man?
I wander lost in the power of your maya,
And, therefore, I did not recognize my Lord.

    First, I am dull-witted and deluded,
    Sinful at heart and ignorant,
    And then you, my master, forgot me,
    You who are the divine Lord, friend of the lowly.   (2)

Though my faults are many, master,
Let not the servant be apart from his Lord.
Master, the soul is deluded by your maya,
And can find release from rebirth only by your grace.

And what's more—I swear upon you, Raghubir—
I know neither worship nor any other way of pleasing you.
A servant relies on his master, a child on its mother,
And thus both remain free of care, but a master must take care of
      his servant.'
Thus saying, Hanuman fell at the Lord's feet, deeply agitated,
And his heart, filling with love, revealed his own true form.
Then Raghupati raised him and clasped him to his heart,
And soothed him with his own tears.
'Listen, O monkey, do not feel small in your heart,
You are twice as dear to me as Lakshman.
All say that I am impartial,
But a devotee is especially dear to me, for he has no other refuge
      but me.

      And he alone is exclusively devoted to me,
      Who never wavers from the belief, Hanuman,
      That he is the servant and this creation, animate and
            inanimate,
      Is the manifest form of God, his master.'   (3)

When Hanuman, son of the Wind, saw the Lord so pleased
      with him,
His heart rejoiced and all his anguish disappeared.
'Master, upon the mountain lives the chief of the monkeys—
His name is Sugriv, and he is your servant.
Make friends with him, master,
And knowing him to be in distress, render him free of fear.
He will have a search launched for Sita
By sending millions of monkeys in every direction.'
In this way, explaining everything to them,
Hanuman took both the brothers upon his back.
When Sugriv saw Ram,
He thought his birth greatly blessed.

Bowing his head at his feet, he met him with reverence,
And Raghunath and his younger brother embraced him in return.
The monkey king wondered to himself,
'Will they, dear God, offer me their friendship?'

> Then Hanuman related the full circumstances
> Of both sides,
> And making the sacred fire bear witness,
> He united them in firm friendship. (4)

Once they became allies, they kept nothing back,
And Lakshman related all of Ram's adventures.
Said Sugriv, his eyes full of tears,
'Lord, the daughter of Mithila's king will be found.
Once, I was sitting here with my ministers,
Deep in thought,
When I saw, flying through the sky,
A woman helpless in an enemy's power, wailing piteously,
And calling out, "Ram! Ram! O Ram!"
Seeing us, she threw down her veil.'
Ram asked for the veil, Sugriv gave it to him at once—
Ram pressed it to his heart, sorrowing deeply.
Said Sugriv, 'Listen, Raghubir,
Don't be so sad, but take courage in your heart.
I will help you in every way
To find Janaki and bring her back.'

> Upon hearing his friend's words,
> Ram, ocean of compassion and might embodied, rejoiced.
> 'Tell me, Sugriv, the reason why
> You are living in this forest.' (5)

'Lord, Baali and I are two brothers,
There was so much love between us that it defied description.

Once, the son of the demon Mai—Mayavi was his name—
Came to our town, Lord.
In the middle of the night, he shouted at the city gates.
Baali could not suffer this challenge from an enemy,
And rushed out, and, seeing him, Mayavi fled.
Now I, too, had gone with my brother.
Mayavi ran into a mountain cave—
Then Baali said to me,
'Wait for me for a fortnight,
If I do not return by then, assume that I have been killed.'
I waited there for a month, Kharari,
And then there came from that cave a great stream of blood.
I thought he had killed Baali and now would come and kill me,
So I blocked the mouth of the cave with a boulder and left.
When the ministers saw the city without a master,
They forced the kingdom upon me.
Meanwhile, Baali slew the demon and returned home,
And seeing me upon the throne, he took me as his enemy,
And, like an enemy, he beat me severely
And took my wife and all that I had.
For fear of him, compassionate Raghubir,
I wandered the whole world utterly wretched.
He cannot come here because of a curse,[1]
But even so I remain afraid in my heart.'
When the compassionate Lord heard his devotee's distress,
His two mighty arms began to tremble.

    'Listen, Sugriv, I will kill
    Baali with a single arrow.
    Even if he takes refuge with Brahma or Rudra,
    His life will not be saved.   (6)

Those who are not distressed at a friend's sorrow,
Merely to look upon them incurs great sin.

The mountain of one's own troubles should appear as trifling as a
    speck of dust,
While a friend's sorrows, though small as a speck of dust, should
    appear as great as Meru.
Those who do not inherently understand this,
Why do such fools insist upon friendship?
To stop from treading the wrong path, and help to walk the path
    of virtue,
To make manifest good qualities and conceal the flaws,
To give and take without doubt or suspicion in one's mind,
To always help with all one's power,
And, in times of misfortune, to be a hundred times more loving—
These, declare the Vedas, are the qualities of a good friend.
He who falsely speaks sweet words to one's face,
But, deceitful and duplicitous, harms one behind one's back,
He whose heart is as crooked as a snake's movement, brother—
It is best to leave such an evil friend.
A foolish servant, a miserly king, a bad wife,
And a deceitful friend—as painful as thorns are these four.
Dear friend, on the strength of my support, give up sorrow,
For I will serve your cause in every way.'
Said Sugriv, 'Listen, Raghubir,
Baali is very strong and exceedingly steadfast in battle.'
He showed him Dundubhi's bones and the palm trees.[2]
Effortlessly, Raghunath hurled the bones away and with a single
    arrow split the trees in two.
Seeing his immeasurable strength, Sugriv's friendship grew,
And he was confident now that Ram would slay Baali.
Again and again the monkey chief bowed his head at Ram's feet,
And recognizing the Lord, he rejoiced in his heart.
When this knowledge came upon him, he said these words,
'Master, with your grace, my heart is now still.
Renouncing all luxury, wealth, family and fame,
I will serve only you.

All these are obstacles that hinder devotion to Ram—
So say the holy men, the worshippers of your feet.
In this world, friends or enemies, joy or sorrow
Are created by maya, they are not the real truth.
Baali is my greatest benefactor, for by his favour
I met you, Ram, the destroyer of sorrow—
When we battle someone in a dream,
We are abashed when we understand the truth on waking.
Now, Lord, show me your grace in this one way,
That, abandoning all, I worship you day and night.'
Hearing the monkey's words of renunciation,
He who holds a bow in his hand[ii] laughed and said,
'All that you say is true—
My friend, my words are never proved false.'
O Khagesh, Ram makes us all dance
Like a conjurer's monkey—so the Vedas declare!
Taking Sugriv with him, Raghunath
Set forth, bow and arrows in hand.
Then Raghupati sent Sugriv ahead,
Who, made bold by Ram's presence, went up to Baali and roared
    a challenge.
Hearing him, Baali sprang up in fury,
But Tara, his wife, clasped his feet with her hands, and, reasoning
    with him, said,
'Listen, my husband, the ones with whom Sugriv has allied himself
Are two brothers of immense strength and power.
They are Lakshman and Ram, the sons of the king of Koshal,
And can vanquish even death on the field of battle.'

> Said Baali, 'Listen my fearful and beloved wife,
> Raghunath looks upon all impartially,
> So even if he were to kill me,
> I would still have found my Lord.'   (7)

---

ii   Ram, who is armed with a bow and arrows

So saying, proud and haughty Baali set forth,
Considering Sugriv of as little account as a blade of grass.
The two closed in combat. Baali ridiculed and threatened Sugriv,
And, with a great roar, struck him a blow with his fist.
Sugriv fled in dismay—
Baali's fist had struck him like a thunderbolt.
'It's as I had said, merciful Raghubir—
He is not my brother, he is death!'
'You two brothers look the same,
For fear of mistaking you for him I did not shoot.'
Ram touched Sugriv's body,
So that it became as hard as adamant and all his pain disappeared.
He then placed a garland of flowers around his neck
And sent him back, endowing him with enormous strength.
Again they closed in combat and battled each other in many ways
While Raghurai watched from behind a tree.

> Sugriv tried every deceit and trick, and put forth all
>   his strength,
> But he was afraid and finally accepted defeat in his heart.
> Then Ram drew his bow,
> And struck Baali in the heart with his arrow.   (8)

Struck by the arrow, he fell in distress to the ground,
But sat up again when he saw the Lord before him,
Dark of form, with his matted hair coiled upon his head,
His eyes aflame, and an arrow fitted to his bow.
Gazing on him again and again, Baali laid his heart at his feet,
And, recognizing his Lord, felt he had received the reward of
     his birth.
In his heart was love, but his words were harsh
As he looked at Ram and said,
'You have descended to earth for the sake of righteousness, master,
But you have killed me as a hunter would.
I am your enemy, and Sugriv your dear friend!

For what fault, Lord, have you killed me?'
'A younger brother's wife, a sister, a son's wife and a daughter—
Hear me, you blockhead, these four are all alike.
There is no sin in killing him
Who looks upon them with a wicked eye.
You fool, you have too much pride,
Your wife tried to warn you, but you did not listen to her.
You knew that Sugriv was protected by the might of my arm,
But you, wicked and arrogant, you still wished to kill him!'

'Hear me, Ram—my cunning
Is of no use against my master.
But am I still a sinner, Lord,
Even though I have found refuge in you in my dying hour?'   (9)

Upon hearing these most gentle words, Ram
Touched Baali's head with his own hands and said,
'I make your body immortal—retain your life's breathe.'
But Baali replied, 'Listen to me, abode of compassion,
Munis strive birth after birth,
Yet at the last moment, they fail to utter the name of "Ram".
He, on the strength of whose name Shankar bestows
Salvation in Kashi upon all,
That same Ram has appeared before me, visible to my eyes—
Lord, will I ever get such a chance again?

He has appeared before my eyes, he whose qualities
The Vedas ever praise as "Not this, not this",
Whom the munis scarcely glimpse even in deep meditation despite
Controlling breath and mind, and freeing their senses from passion.
Knowing me to be in the grip of excessive pride,
The Lord said to me, "Keep your body",
But who is such a fool as to insist upon cutting down
The celestial Kalpataru, and planting a fence of babul[3] instead?

Now, Lord, look upon me with compassion,
And grant me the boon I ask.
In the grip of karma, whatever the womb in which I be born,
May I ever be devoted to the feet of Ram.
My son Angad is equal to me in humility and strength—
O bestower of blessedness, my divine Lord, take him,
And, holding him by the arm, O Lord of gods and men,
Make him your own servant.'

> Showing intense love for Ram's feet,
> Baali gave up his body
> As a garland of flowers falls from an elephant's neck
> Without its knowing it.   (10)

Ram sent Baali to his own ultimate abode.
The townsfolk rushed out, distraught,
And Tara—her hair loose, and barely able to hold herself upright—
Wailed and lamented.
Seeing Tara distracted with grief, Raghurai
Gave her wisdom and took away delusion.
'This vile and wretched body has been fashioned
From earth, water, fire, sky and air.
It is that body that lies asleep before you,
While the soul is eternal—so for whom do you weep?'
Then wisdom sprang up in her mind and she fell at Ram's feet,
And asked for the boon of supreme devotion.
Uma, Ram the master makes everyone dance
Like wooden puppets!
Then Ram gave Sugriv the command,
And he performed all his funeral rites as prescribed.
Ram then instructed Lakshman and said,
'Go, give Sugriv the kingdom.'
Bowing their heads at Raghupati's feet,
All set forth as commanded by Raghunath.

Lakshman at once summoned
The townsfolk and the Brahmans,
And gave Sugriv the crown,
And Angad the title of crown-prince.   (11)

Uma, there is no benefactor like Ram in this world,
Not guru, father, mother, brother, or master.
Whether gods, men or munis, it is the natural disposition of all
To make friends for selfish reasons.
Sugriv, who trembled day and night in fear of Baali,
Whose body was covered with sores, and whose heart burnt
        with anxiety—
That same Sugriv was made king of the monkeys!
Raghubir's disposition is generous indeed!
Those who, knowing this, abandon such a Lord,
Deserve to be caught in a net of troubles.
He then summoned Sugriv,
And instructed him in the principles of statecraft.
Said the Lord, 'Listen, Sugriv, lord of the monkeys,
I may not enter a town for four and ten years.
But summer is spent and the season of rains has arrived,
So I will encamp upon this mountain close by.
Rule your kingdom with Angad,
And ever keep my purpose in your heart.'
When Sugriv returned to his own home,
Ram made his abode on the Pravarshana mountain.

    The gods had already made and kept ready
    A beautiful mountain cave
    Knowing that Ram, abode of compassion,
    Would come and live there for a few days.   (12)

The lovely forest was resplendent with flowers,
Swarms of honeybees hummed in their greed for honey,

And ever since the Lord arrived there,
Beautiful bulbs, roots, fruits and leaves grew in profusion.
Seeing the incomparably enchanting mountain,
The Lord of the gods dwelt there with his brother.
Assuming the forms of bees, birds and deer,
Gods, Siddhas and munis served the Lord.
From the moment that Ramaa's lord made it his home,
The forest took on the form of joy itself.
There, upon a brightly shining crystal rock,
The two brothers sat at ease,
And Ram discoursed to his younger brother
On bhakti, dispassion, statecraft and spiritual wisdom.
As it was the season of rains, clouds covered the sky—
Their rumbling was exceedingly pleasing.

> 'Lakshman, look! See how the peacocks
> Dance upon seeing the clouds—
> Like a householder devoted to dispassion would rejoice
> Upon seeing a devotee of Vishnu somewhere!   (13)

Dark clouds gather in the sky, rumbling and thundering,
But without my beloved, my heart is afraid.
Lightning flashes fitfully amidst the clouds
As fickle as a villain's affection.
The pouring clouds descend close to the ground
As, upon gaining wisdom, the wise bow down.
The mountain endures the buffeting of the raindrops
As a holy man endures the taunts of the vile.
Little rivulets overflow and rush forth breaking their banks,
Like rogues who strut and swagger with a little wealth.
The water becomes muddy as soon as it falls upon the ground,
Like the soul that becomes wrapped in maya as soon as it
    is born.
Drop by drop the rainwater gathers and fills the pond,

Like good qualities gather in a good man.
The water of the river flows into the ocean
And becomes still, like the soul when it finds Hari.

> The earth is green and covered with grass,
> So paths can no longer be discerned,
> Like holy books obscured
> By discourses on false doctrine.   (14)

In all directions is the croaking of frogs, as pleasing
As the chanting of the Vedas by a group of students.
The many trees have put forth new leaves,
Like the minds of aspirants upon acquiring spiritual wisdom.
The ark and javas are without their leaves
As in a well-governed kingdom the efforts of the wicked
     come to nothing.
Dust cannot be found even upon searching,
Just as wrath does away with righteousness.
The earth, rich with grain, looks as lovely
As a philanthropist's estate.
In the deep darkness of the night fireflies gather,
Arrogant in their belief that they can dispel it.
The banks of the fields have broken with the heavy rain
In the same way that women go astray with freedom.
Wise farmers weed their fields
Like the wise discard attachment, passion, and pride.
Chakravaks are nowhere to be seen,
Just as righteousness disappears in the age of Kali.
It rains upon barren land, but not a blade of grass takes
     root there,
Just as lust never grows in the heart of a servant of Hari.
The bright earth teems with creatures of every kind,
Just as, under good government, a kingdom's population grows.
Here and there rest many weary travellers,
Like the senses when spiritual wisdom comes.

Sometimes a strong wind blows
And scatters the clouds here and there,
Like the birth of a wicked and immoral son
Destroys the family virtues.   (15A)

Sometimes there is deep darkness in the daytime,
Sometimes the sun comes out,
Just as wisdom is obscured in bad company,
But appears in the company of the good.   (15B)

The season of rains has gone and autumn has arrived.
Look Lakshman, it is the most beautiful season of all.
The kash is in flower and covers the whole earth
As though the rainy season has revealed its decrepitude.[4]
Agastya[5] has risen and dried up the water on the paths
In the same way that contentment dries up greed.
The clear water of rivers and lakes shines
Like the heart of a holy man free of pride and attachment.
The water of the streams and ponds is drying up drop by drop,
Just as a wise man gradually gives up possessiveness and attachment.
Knowing that it is autumn, the wagtails have appeared,
Just as the fruits of our good deeds appear at their appointed time.
There is neither mud nor dust, and the earth looks as clean
As the actions of a king skilled in statecraft.
With the shrinking of the waters, the fish are as distraught
As a foolish householder without money.
The cloudless, clear sky is as bright
As a devotee of Hari who has given up all worldly desires.
Here and there fall light autumn showers,
Like the few who attain bhakti in me.

Now kings and ascetics, merchants and mendicants,
Rejoicing, leave the city
In the same way that men in all the four stages of life
Give up striving as soon as they attain faith in Hari.   (16)

The fish in deep water are happy,
Like those taking refuge in Hari have not a single worry.
The lake with its flowering lotuses is as beautiful
As the immaterial Absolute upon taking material form.
Countless swarms of honeybees hum,
And beautiful birds call and sing in many tones.
The chakravak, upon beholding the night, is as sorrowful
As a bad man at the sight of another's wealth.
The chatak calls again and again that it is very thirsty,
Like one hostile to Shankar never finding bliss.
The moon at night takes away the heat of the autumn sun,
Just as the sight of a holy man drives away sin.
At the sight of the moon, the flocks of chakors
Gaze at it as unblinkingly as Hari's worshippers upon Hari.
Gnats and mosquitoes have been destroyed by the fear of winter,
Just as hostility to Brahmans brings ruin upon a family.

> The creatures that had thronged the earth in the rains,
> Disappeared with the coming of autumn,
> Just as doubts and errors disappear
> Upon finding a true guru.   (17)

The rains have gone, autumn with its clear skies has come,
But, dear brother, we have received no news of Sita.
If I could, even once, somehow get news of her,
I would bring her back in an instant, even from death itself.
Wherever she may be, if she be still alive,
I would, dear brother, make every effort and bring her back.
Sugriv has forgotten all about me,
Now that he has got a kingdom, a treasury, a city, a wife.
I will slay that fool tomorrow
With the same arrow with which I killed Baali!'
He, whose grace sets one free from pride and attachment,
Can he ever be angry, Uma, even in dream?

Enlightened munis who have attached themselves to Raghubir's feet
Alone understand the mystery of this act.
Lakshman, believing the Lord to be angry,
Strung his bow and picked up his arrows.

> Then Raghupati, the pinnacle of compassion,
> Explained to his younger brother,
> 'Sugriv is our ally, dear brother,
> So merely scare him and bring him here.' (18)

Meanwhile in Kishkindha, the Wind god's son reflected,
'Sugriv has forgotten about Ram's work.'
So, going up to Sugriv, he bowed his head at his feet,
And, using all the four methods of persuasion, reminded him of
     his promise.
Sugriv grew terribly afraid upon hearing Hanuman's words.
'The pleasures of the senses have robbed me of my wisdom!
Now, son of the Wind, send out messengers
To wherever there be monkey bands,
And let it be proclaimed that anyone who does not come here to
     me within a fortnight,
Shall meet his death at my hands.'
Then Hanuman summoned the messengers,
And received them with great courtesy.
Using intimidation, graciousness and statesmanship, he impressed
     upon them their task.
Bowing their heads at his feet, the messengers all set forth.
At that very moment, Lakshman entered the city,
And the monkeys, seeing his anger, scattered in all directions.

> Lakshman then strung his bow and said,
> 'I will burn this city to ashes!'
> Then, seeing the city distraught,
> Baali's son, Angad, came. (19)

Bowing his head at Lakshman's feet, he pleaded with him,
At which Lakshman assured him of his protection.
When the king of the monkeys heard of Lakshman's wrath,
He said, distracted with fear,
'Listen, Hanuman, take Tara with you,
And, with humble supplications, placate the prince.'
Hanuman then took Tara with him,
And, bowing at Lakshman's feet, recounted the Lord's glory.
Pleading with him, he led him to the palace,
And, washing his feet, seated him upon a couch.
Then the king of the monkeys bowed his head,
And Lakshman took him by the arm and embraced him.
'Lord, there is no intoxication like sensual pleasures,
They delude even the minds of munis in an instant.'
Lakshman was pleased to hear this humble apology,
And instructed and reassured him in many ways.
The Wind's son told him all that had been done,
And how the many messengers had already left.

> Then, rejoicing, Sugriv set forth
> With Angad and the other monkeys,
> And, with Lakshman leading the way,
> Came to where Raghunath was.   (20)

Bowing his head at his feet, and folding his hands, he said,
'Master, it is not my fault.
Exceedingly powerful, divine Lord, is your maya—
It may be shaken off only when you, Ram, show your grace.
Gods, men and munis are all under the sway of sensual pleasure,
And I am but a wretched animal, a monkey most dissolute
          and debauched.
He who is not wounded by the arrow of a woman's eyes,
Who can see even in the dark night of anger,
Who has not let his neck be caught in the noose of greed—

That man is your equal, Raghurai.
These qualities cannot be attained by practice or endeavour—
It is only through your favour that a very few receive them.'
Then Raghupati, smiling, said,
'You are as dear to me as Bharat, brother.
Now apply your mind and so contrive
That we get some news of Sita.'

> While they were thus talking,
> The monkey bands arrived,
> So that in every direction could be seen
> Crowds of monkeys of every colour.   (21)

I saw that army of monkeys, Uma—
Only a fool would have tried to count them!
They came and bowed their heads at Ram's feet,
And gazing upon his face, they all found in him their true Lord.
In that army there was not one monkey
About whose well-being Ram did not inquire.
This was no great miracle for my Lord,
For Raghurai exists in every form and pervades all.
They stood as ordered all about,
And Sugriv instructed them all,
'For Ram's work, and at my request,
Go forth, monkey bands, in all four directions.
Search for Janak's daughter
And return within a month, my brothers.
Whoever returns at the end of that time without any news,
Shall meet his death at my hands.'

> At his words, all the monkeys
> Immediately set forth in every direction.
> Then Sugriv called
> Angad, Nal and Hanuman.   (22)

'Listen to me, Nil, Angad, Hanuman
And Jamvant, of resolute minds and wise—
Go all you valiant warriors together to the south,
And ask everyone for news of Sita.
With thought, deed and word devise a way
To accomplish Ramchandra's work.
The sun may be served with one's back to it, and fire with one's
    face towards it,
But a master must be served with one's whole being, without deceit.
Wait upon the next life, abandoning delusion,
So that all the sorrows born of this existence disappear.
The culmination of a corporeal existence, brothers,
Is the worship of Ram, forsaking all worldly desires.
He alone truly recognizes virtue, he alone is fortunate,
Who is devoted to Raghubir's feet.'
Taking their leave of Sugriv, and bowing their heads at his feet,
They set off joyfully, invoking Raghurai.
The last to make obeisance was the Wind's son.
Knowing that his work would be accomplished by Hanuman, the
    Lord called him near.
He touched his head with his lotus hands,
And, knowing him to be his devotee, gave him the ring from his
    finger and said,
'Say all you can to comfort Sita,
Tell her of my great anguish at being separated from her, and
    return quickly.'
Hanuman considered his birth rewarded
And set off, holding the compassionate Lord in his heart.
Though the Lord knows everything,
He, protector of the gods, followed the rules of statesmanship.

    The monkeys all set forth, searching
    Every forest, river, lake and mountain cave.
    Forgetting the needs of their own bodies,
    They were completely engrossed in Ram's work.   (23)

If, somewhere, they ran into a Rakshasa,
They took his life with a single blow.
They carefully searched every mountain and forest,
And if they met a muni, they would all crowd around him for news.
Soon they were overcome by thirst and grew greatly distressed,
But could find no water and lost their way in the dense forest.
Hanuman reflected to himself,
'Without water to drink, we shall all die.'
He climbed a mountain peak and, looking all around,
Saw a strange spectacle around a cavern in the ground.
Chakravaks, herons and swans hovered above it,
While many other birds made their way into it.
The Wind's son came down from the mountain,
And took them all and showed them that cavern.
Placing Hanuman at their head,
They entered the cavern without delay.

> Entering, they saw a lovely garden,
> And a lake upon which bloomed countless lotuses,
> And in a beautiful temple there
> Sat a woman, penance incarnate.[6]   (24)

From a distance they all bowed their heads to her,
And explained their situation when she asked.
She then said, 'Drink some water,
And eat of these delicious and lovely fruits.'
They bathed and ate of the sweet fruits,
And then they returned, all of them, to her.
She then told them her whole story, and said,
'I will now go to Raghurai.
Close your eyes and so leave this cave—
You will find Sita, so do not despair.'
The warriors closed their eyes, and when they opened them again,
They were all standing by the ocean shore.
But she, meanwhile, went to Raghunath,

And bowed her head at his lotus feet.
She paid him great homage,
And the Lord granted her unceasing devotion to him.

> In obedience to the Lord's command,
> She left for the Badri forest,
> Holding in her heart Ram's two feet
> Worshipped by Brahma and Shiv.   (25)

Meanwhile, here, the monkeys thought to themselves,
'The given time is past but we have accomplished nothing.'
Gathering together, they said to each other,
'Without news of Sita, what is the point of returning, brother?'
Said Angad, his eyes filling with tears,
'Both ways we die, brothers—
Here, we have failed to get news of Sita,
There, the king of the monkeys will kill us.
He would have killed me when my father was slain.
It is Ram who protected me, so I owe Sugriv nothing.'
Again and again Angad said to the others,
'Our death has come, of that there is no doubt.'
Upon hearing Angad's words, the monkey warriors
Could not utter a word, and their eyes streamed with tears.
For a moment, they were plunged into worry,
But then all began to speak thus:
'Unless we find news of Sita,
We will not go back, wise prince.'
So saying, the monkeys went down to the salt sea's shore,
And, spreading some darbh[iii] grass, sat down.
Jamvant, seeing Angad's grief,
Related many instructive tales.
'Son, do not take Ram to be a mortal man,

---

iii   kush grass

Know him to be the nirgun brahm, without attributes,
    unconquerable, unborn.
We, his servants, are greatly blessed,
Ever devoted to the Absolute made Incarnate.

    The Lord becomes incarnate of his own will
    For the good of gods, the earth, cows and Brahmans.
    Then the worshippers of his embodied form, giving up
        salvation,
    Descend and remain with him here on earth.'   (26)

As Jamvant thus discoursed on many things,
Sampati heard him in his mountain cave.
He came out, and, seeing the crowd of monkeys, said,
'The Lord of the world has sent me a feast!
I will eat them all up today—
I have been dying for want of food for many days.
Never before have I had enough food to fill my belly,
But today God has given it to me all at once!'
The monkeys were terrified to hear the vulture's words—
'Our death is certain, now we know for sure!'
Seeing the vulture, the monkeys all stood up,
And even Jamvant grew deeply worried.
But Angad, thinking to himself, cried out,
'There is no one as blessed as Jatayu,
Who gave up his body for Ram's purpose,
And, supremely blessed, ascended to Hari's abode!'
Hearing these words that brought both joy and sorrow,
The bird drew near to the monkeys, who grew afraid.
Assuring them of their safety, he asked them about Jatayu,
And they told him the whole story.
When Sampati heard of his brother's heroic deed, and how Ram
    had honoured him,
He sang of Raghupati's glory.

'Take me to the seashore,
So I may make him the last offering of sesame seeds.
In return for this service, I will help you with words
And you will find her whom you seek.'   (27)

He performed his younger brother's last rites on the seashore,
And then, relating his own story, said, 'Listen, monkey warriors,
Once, in our youth, we two brothers
Flew up into the sky so that we drew near the sun.
Jatayu could not tolerate its fierce heat and returned,
But I was arrogant and flew closer to the sun.
My wings were burnt by the intense heat,
And I fell to the ground with terrible screams.
A muni called Chandrama
Took pity on me when he saw me.
He instructed me in many kinds of knowledge,
And rid me of my pride in my body.
He said, "In the Treta age, the Supreme Spirit will assume the
          body of a man,
And the king of the demons will steal away his wife.
The Lord will send out spies to search for her,
And, when you meet them, you will be purified,
And your wings will grow again—so do not worry,
But show them where Sita will be."
The muni's words have come true today,
So listen to what I say and accomplish the Lord's purpose.
Upon the Trikut mountain stands the city of Lanka,
Where lives Ravan, free from fear.
There, in a grove of ashok trees,
Sits Sita, plunged in sorrow.

I see her, though you cannot,
For a vulture's eyesight is unparalleled.
I have grown old, or else
I would have helped you.   (28)

One who can leap a hundred yojans across the ocean,
And is endowed with intelligence—he alone can accomplish
    Ram's purpose.
Look upon me and take courage in your hearts—
See how Ram's grace has restored my body.
By invoking his name even a sinner
Can cross the vast and boundless ocean of this existence—
And you are his envoys. So abandon fear,
And, with Ram in your hearts, make your plans.'
After speaking thus, Garud, when the vulture left,
They felt great dismay in their hearts.
Each monkey stated his own strength,
But doubted that he could leap across the sea.
'I have grown old,' now spoke the king of the bears,
'And not a trace of my earlier strength remains in my body.
When the slayer of Khar had taken the form of Tribikram,[7]
I was young and very strong.

As he took the Daitya Bali captive, the Lord grew to
    such an enormous size
That it cannot be described,
But in less than an hour
I ran around him seven times.'   (29)

Angad said, 'I will leap across,
But I am not sure I will be able to get back again.'
Jamvant said, 'You are capable of it,
But how can we send you? You are our leader!'
The lord of the bears then said, 'Listen, Hanuman,
Why are you silent, mighty one?
You are the son of the Wind, and your strength is equal to that of
    the Wind.
You are also a mine of intelligence, discernment and knowledge.
What task in the world is so difficult
That you, dear son, cannot accomplish it?

It is to serve Ram's purpose that you have descended to this earth.'
As soon as he heard these words, Hanuman grew as large as a mountain,
Golden-hued, his body shining with power,
As though he was another Sumeru, king of all the mountains.
Roaring like a lion again and again, he declared,
'I can leap across this salt ocean as easily as in play,
Kill Ravan himself and all his army,
And tearing out Trikut by its roots, bring it here!
But, Jamvant, I ask you what I must do—
Please give me appropriate instructions.'
'Do just this, dear son—go
And see Sita, and come back with news of her.
Then, by the strength of his own arm will the lotus-eyed one rescue her,
Taking with him as mere spectacle the monkey army.

With the monkey army, Ram will destroy
The demon host and bring back Sita,
And gods, Narad and other munis
Will sing his glorious fame that purifies the three spheres.
He who hears, sings, recites, or meditates upon this glory—
Which Tulsidas, the honeybee to the lotus feet of Raghubir,
Sings—
Will attain the supreme state.

Raghunath's fame is the remedy for all the ills of this life.
He, slayer of the demon Trishira,
Fulfils every wish
Of the men and women who listen to his glory.   (30A)

He, whose body is as dark as the blue lotus,
Who is more beautiful than countless Kamdevs,
And whose name is the huntsman to the birds of sin—
Listen, then to his praises.'   (30B)

Thus ends the fourth descent into the Manas lake of Ram's acts that
destroys all the impurities of the age of Kali.

Book V

SUNDARKAND
(THE BEAUTIFUL)

Mangalacharan

Serene, eternal, beyond proof, without sin,
Bestower of the supreme peace that is salvation,
Unceasingly worshipped by Brahma, Shambhu, and Shesh,
Knowable through Vedant, all-pervading,
The lord of the universe who is called Ram,
The greatest of the gods, visible in human form because of his maya,
    remover of all sins,
He who is the noblest of the Raghu clan, a mine of compassion,
    and the crest-jewel of kings—
I worship him.   (1)

There is no other longing, Raghupati,
In my heart—
I speak the truth and you know the inner hearts of all—
O most excellent of the Raghus, grant me deep and ardent
    devotion to you,
And make my heart free of lust and all other faults.   (2)

The abode of immeasurable strength,
His body shining like a mountain of gold,
The fire in the forest of demons,
First amongst the wise,
The repository of all virtues,
Raghupati's beloved devotee, the son of the Wind,
The monkey chief, Hanuman—
I bow to him.   (3)

Hearing Jamvant's encouraging words,
Hanumant was greatly heartened.
'Wait for me, brothers, and watch for me,
Enduring hardship and eating wild tubers, roots and fruit,
Till I return after seeing Sita.
I am certain our work will be done, for I feel great happiness.'
Saying this, he bowed to them all
And joyfully set forth, with Raghunath in his heart.
By the shore of the sea was a majestic mountain—
He sprang lightly to its peak.
Invoking Raghubir again and again,
The mighty son of the Wind leaped forth.
That mountain, upon which Hanumant had stood,
Was pushed down at once into the nethermost world.
Like Raghupati's own unerring arrow,
Flew Hanuman.
The ocean, realizing that he was Raghupati's envoy,
Said to Mainak, 'Go, rise up, and offer him some rest.'[1]

> But Hanuman merely touched the mountain
> With his hand, and then, paying it homage, said,
> 'Until I have accomplished Ram's purpose,
> There can be no rest for me.'   (1)

The gods saw the Wind's son flying by,
And to test his extraordinary strength and intelligence,
They sent the mother of serpents, Surasa,
Who came and said to him,
'Today the gods have sent me a meal!'
The Wind's son replied,
'Let me return after fulfilling Ram's work,
And give news of Sita to my Lord—
Then I will enter your mouth.
I speak the truth, now let me go, Mother.'

But when, despite all his efforts, she would not let him go,
Hanuman said, 'Then why not swallow me?'
She opened her jaws a full yojan wide,
But the monkey made his body twice that size.
She spread her mouth sixteen yojans wide,
And at once the Wind's son became thirty-two!
As Surasa spread her jaws wider and wider,
The monkey kept making his body twice as large.
But when she made her mouth a hundred yojans wide,
The Wind god's son assumed a tiny form,
And entered her mouth and came out again at once.
Then, bowing his head to her, he asked leave to depart.
'I have done what the gods had sent me for—
To try your strength and wisdom.

> You will accomplish all Ram's work,
> For you are a treasure-house of strength
>   and wisdom.'
> Thus giving him her blessing, she left,
> And Hanuman continued through the air, rejoicing.   (2)

A she-demon lived in the sea,
Who, through her magic, caught the birds of the air.
She would see the shadows cast on the water
By the creatures that flew across the sky—
These shadows she would grasp, so they could not fly.
In this way she would devour flying creatures every day.
She tried the same trick upon Hanuman,
But the monkey saw through it at once.
The valiant son of the Wind killed her,
And then that steadfast hero reached the ocean's other shore.
There he saw the beauty of the forest,
With bees buzzing in their greed for honey,
And trees of many kinds, beautiful with fruits and flowers,

And multitudes of birds and deer pleasing to behold.
Seeing a high mountain ahead,
He ran and fearlessly climbed to its top.
Uma, this was not the monkey's greatness,
But the glory of the Lord who devours death itself.
From the top of that mountain, he gazed upon Lanka,
A magnificent fortress that cannot be described—
Towering walls, encircled by the ocean on all sides,
And golden ramparts of dazzling brilliance.

Golden ramparts inlaid with rare and precious jewels,
And within them, numerous magnificent mansions,
Squares and marketplaces, and lovely lanes and alleyways—
A beautiful city, cleverly laid out.
Who could count the multitudes of elephants, horses and mules,
The crowds on foot, the chariots,
The troops of shape-shifting demons—
A mighty army that defied description?

Here were forests, orchards, groves and gardens,
Lakes, wells, ponds and pools, all lovely to behold.
Daughters of men, Nagas, gods and Gandharvas,
Captivated the hearts of munis with their beauty,
And mighty wrestlers as vast as mountains
Bellowed and thundered,
As they grappled in the many wrestling-grounds,
Wrathfully challenging each other.

Countless warriors, hideous and formidable,
Carefully guarded the city in every direction,
While here and there vile demons gorged themselves
On buffaloes, men, cows, donkeys and goats.
Tulsidas has told a little of their story
Because they will give up their bodies

At the pilgrimage site of Raghubir's arrow
And so most certainly attain salvation.

> Seeing the numerous city guards,
> The monkey thought to himself,
> 'I will take a very tiny form
> And enter the town by night.'   (3)

The monkey took on a form as small as a gnat,
And set off for Lanka, invoking the Lord in human form.
At the city gates, a Rakshasi called Lankini, stood guard.[2]
She called out, 'Where are you going, disregarding me?
Don't you know my speciality, fool?
Every thief here is my food!'
The mighty monkey punched her with a fist,
So that she staggered and fell to the ground, vomiting blood.
Then, recovering from the blow, Lankini stood up,
And full of fear, folded her hands and humbly said,
'After giving the boon to Ravan,
Brahma told me before he left,
"When you reel from a monkey's blow,
Know that the destruction of the demons is at hand."
Sire, I must have done many good deeds,
That I can see Ram's envoy with my own eyes.

> Place all the joys of heaven and the bliss of salvation
> In one scale of the balance, sire—
> But they cannot, even all together, equal
> The bliss of a moment's communion with the good.   (4)

Enter the city, and accomplish your task,
Keeping the king of Koshalpur[iv] in your heart.'

[iv] Koshal's city, i.e., Avadh; and Ram, the king of Avadh.

Poison turns into nectar, an enemy becomes a friend,
The ocean reduces to a small puddle, fire becomes cold,
And Sumeru becomes like a grain of dust, Garud,
For him upon whom Ram looks with favour.
Assuming a tiny form, Hanuman
Entered the city, invoking the divine Lord.
He searched each and every mansion,
And saw countless warriors everywhere.
He then entered Dashanan's palace,
So exceedingly marvellous, it defied description.
The monkey saw Ravan sleeping there,
But could not see Vaidehi anywhere in the palace.
He then saw another lovely mansion,
Which had its own temple to Hari set apart.

> The house had painted upon it Ram's weapons—
> Its beauty was more than words can tell.
> Seeing there a cluster of tender, young tulsi plants,
> The monkey chief rejoiced.[3]   (5)

'Lanka is the abode of countless demons,
How could a good man make a home here?'
As the monkey began thus pondering to himself,
Vibhishan awoke,
And began repeating 'Ram, Ram' in prayer.
With a joyful heart, the monkey recognized a true devotee.
'I will most certainly make his acquaintance,
For a good man will not hurt my mission.'
Taking on a Brahman's form, he called out,
And, hearing him, Vibhishan at once rose and hurried out.
Paying him homage, he asked after his well-being, and said,
'O Brahman, tell me your story.
Are you one of Hari's servants,
For my heart is filled with love at sight of you,

Or are you Ram himself, loving friend of the lowly,
Who has come here to make me deeply blessed?'

> Then Hanumant told him all—
> Ram's story, and his own name.
> Hearing Ram's story, their bodies trembled
>   with joy,
> And their hearts grew absorbed in remembering
>   his virtues.   (6)

'Listen, son of the Wind, I live here
Like the poor tongue in the midst of teeth.
Revered sir, knowing that I have no master,
Will the master of the solar dynasty ever show me his favour?
My impure, Rakshasa body is not fit for spiritual endeavours,
Nor is there love for his lotus feet in my heart.
But now I have hope, Hanuman,
For without Hari's grace, one can never meet a saint.
It is only because Raghubir has showed me his favour,
That you, of your own accord, revealed yourself to me.'
'Listen, Vibhishan, it is the Lord's way—
He is ever loving towards his servants.
Tell me, what noble descent can I claim?
I am just a frivolous monkey, deficient in every way.
Why, he who takes our name in the morning,
Gets no food through the rest of the day!

> This is how vile I am! But listen, my friend,
> Raghubir has been gracious even to me!'
> Remembering the Lord's virtues,
> Hanuman's eyes filled with tears.   (7)

'Is it any wonder then that those who, knowing this, forget
      such a master

And wander in pursuit of sensual pleasures, should be unhappy?'
In this way he related Ram virtues,
And found inexpressible peace.
Then Vibhishan related the whole story
Of the manner in which Janak's daughter was living there,
And Hanumant said, 'Listen, brother,
I want to see mother Janaki.'
Vibhishan explained how he might do so,
And the Wind's son left, bidding him farewell.
Assuming his earlier, tiny form he went
To the ashok grove where lived Sita.
Beholding her, he paid her homage in his heart.
She spent the watches of the nights sitting up,
Her body thin and wasted, a single braid of matted hair wound
    upon her head,[4]
Repeating to herself the list of Raghupati's virtues.

    Her eyes were fixed upon her own feet,
    But her heart was absorbed in the contemplation of
        Ram's lotus feet.
    The son of the Wind grew exceedingly sorrowful
    Upon seeing Janaki so sad.   (8)

He remained hidden amongst the leaves of a tree,
And wondered to himself, 'What shall I do?'
At that very moment, Ravan came—
With him were many women in rich attire.
The scoundrel tried every means to win Sita over—
Sweet words, gifts, threats, and even distrust of her Lord.
Said Ravan, 'Listen, wise and beautiful one,
I will make Mandodari and all these other queens
Your handmaidens, I promise,
If you will look at me but once.'
Placing a blade of grass between herself and Ravan,

And remembering her most beloved lord of Avadh,
    Vaidehi replied,
'Listen, ten-faced one, can a firefly's glimmer
Ever make a lotus bloom?
Think about this!' Janaki continued,
'Have you no idea of Raghubir's arrows, wretch?
You deceitful scoundrel! You carried me away when I was alone!
You have no shame, you brazen cad!'

    Hearing himself likened to a firefly,
    And Ram to the sun,
    Ravan, deeply humiliated by her harsh words,
    Drew his sword and roared in rage.   (9)

'Sita, you have insulted me!
I will cut off your head with my sharp sword!
Obey me this instant,
My pretty one, or else lose your life!'
'Lovely as a garland of blue lotuses is my Lord's arm,
And as mighty as an elephant's trunk, Dashkandhar!
Only that arm will touch this neck, or else your cruel sword!
Listen well, fool—this is my solemn vow!
O glittering Chandrahas,[5] take away the searing anguish
Of my separation from Raghupati!
Your noble blade is cold and sharp—
Relieve me, then, of my burden of sorrow,' cried Sita.
Hearing her words, Ravan rushed again to kill her,
But Mai's daughter[v] intervened with prudent counsel.
So he summoned all the demon women and said,
'Go, scare Sita in every way.
If she does not yield to me in a month's time,
I will draw this sword and kill her!'

———————————
[v]   Mandodari, Ravan's chief queen

Dashkandhar then returned to his palace,
While the horde of demon women
Assumed hideous forms of every kind
To frighten Sita.   (10)

But amongst them was a Rakshasi called Trijata—
She was devoted to Ram's feet, and was discerning and wise.
She gathered them all and told them her dream.
'Serve Sita, for your own sakes.
In my dream, I saw a monkey set fire to Lanka,
And the entire demon army killed.
The ten-headed one was mounted, naked, upon an ass,
With shaven head, and all his twenty arms broken.
In this manner, he went towards the south,[6]
And it seemed that Vibhishan got Lanka.
Raghubir's victory was proclaimed in the city,
And then the Lord sent for Sita.
This dream, I solemnly declare,
Will come true in a few days.'
Hearing her, they all grew afraid,
And fell at the feet of Janak's daughter.

They then went off here and there,
While Sita thought anxiously to herself,
'A month must pass before
This vile Rakshasa will kill me.'   (11)

Folding her hands, she implored Trijata,
'Mother, you are my friend in adversity.
Now quickly find a way for me to leave this body,
For I cannot bear this intolerable pain of separation any more.
Fetch some wood and build a pyre,
And then, Mother, set it on fire,
So that it may prove my love to be true, wise one—

For who can bear to hear Ravan's sharp and painful words?'
Hearing her words, Trijata clasped her feet and comforted her,
Reminding her of the Lord's majesty, might and glory.
'Listen, beautiful princess, it is night and there is no fire to be had.'
So saying, she left for her own home.
Said Sita, 'Even providence has turned against me!
No fire to be had, so no end to my anguish!
I see bright sparks of fire in the sky,
Yet not a single star falls to earth.
The moon, though burning brightly, refuses to rain fire,
As if he knows what a luckless one I am.
Ashok tree, listen to my prayer. Your name means "without
    sorrow"—
Be true to it and take away my grief.
Your tender new leaves are red like flames,
So give me fire and do not prolong my agony any further.'
Watching Sita so distraught with the grief of separation,
Each instant passed like a kalpa for Hanuman.

> The monkey reflected to himself,
> And then threw down the ring
> Like a falling spark from the ashok tree.
> Joyfully she rose and caught it in in her hand.   (12)

Then she saw that lovely ring,
Beautifully inscribed with Ram's name.
Recognizing the ring, she gazed at it in wonder,
Her heart turbulent with joy and sorrow.
'No one can conquer the invincible Raghurai,
Nor can such a ring be made through maya!'
As Sita was reflecting upon the various possibilities,
Hanuman began to speak sweet words,
Recounting Ramchandra's virtues.
The instant she heard him, her sorrow fled,

And she listened with all her heart
As Hanuman told the whole story from the start.
'You who tell this tale which is nectar to my ears—
Why do you not show yourself?'
So Hanuman climbed down and approached her,
But Sita, startled, turned away.
'I am Ram's messenger, Mother Janaki,
I swear it truly by that ocean of mercy.
I am the one who has brought this ring, Mother—
Ram gave it as his token for you.'
'Tell me, how can men keep company with monkeys?'
So he told her the story of how their alliance was formed.

> Hearing the monkey's affectionate words,
> Trust arose in her heart,
> And she recognized him as a servant of the merciful Lord,
> In thought, word and deed.   (13)

Knowing him to be one of Hari's followers, she felt great affection
    for him.
Her eyes filled with tears, and her body trembled with emotion.
'I was drowning in the ocean of separation, Hanuman,
But now, dear son, you have become my raft.
Tell me now of their welfare, I beseech you—
How is he, that abode of bliss, Khar's enemy, and his
    young brother?
Raghurai is soft-hearted and kind, monkey,
So why is he being so cruel?
His innate nature is to please his devotees—
But does Raghunayak ever remember me?
Will my eyes ever be soothed, dear Hanuman,
By looking upon his dark and tender form?'
She could speak no more, and her eyes filled with tears.
'Ah, my Lord, you have completely forgotten me!'

Seeing Sita so distraught by separation,
The monkey replied in sweet and respectful tones,
'Mother, the Lord and his younger brother are both well,
Except that the abode of mercy is sorrowful in your sorrow.
Do not be so sad, Mother,
For Ram loves you twice as much as you love him.

> Now compose yourself, Mother,
> And hear Raghupati's message.'
> But even as he said these words, the monkey's
>   voice faltered,
> And his eyes filled with tears. (14)

'Ram says, "Ever since I have been separated from you, Sita,
All things have become contrary for me.
Tender new leaves upon the trees are like tongues of fire,
The night like the night of all-destroying time, and the moon is as
    scorching as the sun.
Clusters of water-lilies seem like forests of spears,
While rain clouds shower boiling oil.
Things that used to soothe now give pain—
Soft, cool and fragrant breezes now are like a serpent's breath.
Sorrow lessens by speaking of it—
But whom can I tell? There is no one who will understand.
The secret of such love as mine and yours,
My beloved, only my heart knows,
And this heart remains always with you.
Know this to be the essence of my love."'
Hearing her Lord's message, Vaidehi
Lost herself in love.
Said the monkey, 'Take courage, Mother,
And remember Ram, the bringer of joy to his servants.
Reflect upon Raghupati's majesty,
And listening to my words, discard all fear.

The demon hordes are like moths,
Raghupati's arrows the flame.
Consider the demons reduced to ashes,
Mother, and take courage in your heart!   (15)

Had Raghubir but known where you were,
He would not have delayed.
When the sun of Ram's arrows rises, O daughter of Janak,
Can the darkness of the demon hordes remain?
I would have taken you away this instant, Mother,
But, I swear upon Ram, I have not received his command to do so.
Be patient for a few days more, Mother,
Till Raghubir arrives with the monkeys.
Slaying all the demons, he will take you away,
And Narad and the other munis will sing his fame in all the
        three worlds.'
'Son, are all the monkeys like you?
The demon warriors are mighty and strong,
And I have grave misgivings in my heart.'
Hearing this, the monkey revealed his true form,
His body as vast as a golden mountain,
Terrible in battle, mighty and valiant.
Then Sita believed in her heart and was comforted,
And the Wind god's son took on his tiny form once more.

'Listen, Mother, we creatures of the trees
Have no great strength or intelligence of our own,
But by the Lord's power, even the tiniest snake
Can eat Garud himself.'   (16)

The monkey's words, steeped in devotion, majesty, glory and power,
Soothed Sita's heart.
Recognizing him as being beloved of Ram, she blessed him,
'Dear son, be ever an abode of strength and virtue.

Be ever free from old age and death, my son, and a treasure-house
     of good qualities,
And may Raghunath ever shower you with his grace.'
The instant he heard her blessing 'May the Lord shower you with
     his grace',
Hanuman became utterly immersed in love.
Again and again the monkey bowed his head at her feet,
And then, folding his hands, he said,
'I have now accomplished all my purpose, Mother,
For your blessing never fails, as everyone knows.
But listen, Mother, I am feeling very hungry
At the sight of those trees laden with delicious fruit.'
'Son, this grove is guarded
By the most mighty demon warriors.'
'I am not afraid of them, Mother,
If you approve.'

     Knowing the monkey to be wise and strong,
     Janaki said, 'Go then, my son—
     Holding Raghupati's feet in your heart,
     Eat and enjoy the sweet fruits.'   (17)

He bowed his head to Sita, and entered the orchard,
And after eating the fruit, he began breaking the trees.
Many warriors had been placed there as guards—
Some he killed, some ran to call for help.
'Lord, an enormous monkey has come
And laid waste the ashok grove!
He has eaten the fruits, uprooted the trees,
And, beating and pounding the guards, he has hurled them to
     the ground!'
Hearing this, Ravan sent several mighty warriors—
Seeing them, Hanuman roared like thunder.
The monkey killed all the demons,

Except a few who, half-dead, fled back, shrieking.
Ravan then sent his eldest son, Prince Aksh,
Who took with him an immense number of his best warriors.
Seeing him approach, Hanuman seized a tree,
And killed Aksh with a tremendous roar.

> Some he killed, some he crushed to pulp
> And some he ground into the dust.
> Some escaped and returned, crying,
> 'Lord, the monkey is much too strong!'   (18)

When he heard of his son's killing, the king of Lanka was furious,
And sent the strong and powerful Meghnad.
'Don't kill him, my son, but bind him.
Let us see this monkey and find out from where it has come.'
Indrajit, that matchless warrior, set forth,
Full of fury at his brother's death.
The monkey saw a fearsome warrior approach—
Gnashing his teeth, he rushed to meet him with a roar.
He uprooted an enormous tree,
And smashed the prince of Lanka's chariot.
As for the great warriors with him,
The monkey seized them one by one and crushed them against his body.
After killing them, he turned to battle Meghnad—
They clashed like two king elephants.
Striking him with a fist, Hanuman ran up a tree,
And, for an instant, Meghnad lost consciousness.
He rose up again and tried many delusive tricks,
But the son of the Wind could not be vanquished.

> When Meghnad readied Brahma's weapon,
> The monkey thought to himself,
> 'If I do not yield to Brahma's arrow,
> Its infinite glory will be destroyed.'   (19)

Brahma's arrow struck the monkey,
But even as he fell, he killed a legion.
Meghnad saw that the monkey had become unconscious,
And, binding him with Varun's serpent snare,[7] carried him off.
Now consider, Bhavani—he, by repeating whose name,
Discerning men cut the bonds of this existence—
Can his messenger ever be bound?
It was for the Lord's purpose that the monkey allowed himself to
    be tied up!
Hearing that the monkey had been caught and bound,
    the demons rushed
To see the spectacle and came crowding into the court.
The monkey arrived and beheld ten-headed Ravan's court,
So magnificent that it cannot be described,
Where even the gods and guardians of the eight quarters stood
    humbly with folded hands,
All fearfully watching the play of his brows.
But even at this sight of Ravan's power, the monkey's heart knew
    no fear,
And he remained as undismayed as Garud amongst a nest of snakes.

    Seeing the monkey,
    Dashanan laughed and cursed,
    But then he remembered the killing of his son,
    And his heart grew sad.   (20)

Said the king of Lanka, 'Who are you, monkey,
And by whose might did you destroy and lay waste my grove?
What, have you not heard of me,
That I see you standing there, fool, utterly unafraid?
For what offence did you kill the demons?
Tell me, fool, are you not afraid to die?'
'Hear me then, Ravan,' replied Hanuman. 'He, by whose might
Maya brings forth countless universes,

By whose might, O ten-headed one, Viranchi, Hari and Ish
Create, preserve and destroy them,[8]
By whose might the thousand-headed serpent, Shesh, bears upon
    his head
The whole world with its mountains and forests,
Who assumes diverse forms to protect the gods
And to teach rogues like you a lesson,
Who broke Har's unbending bow,
And with it the pride of the assembled kings,
Who slew Khar, Dushan, Trishira and Baali,
All of immeasurable strength,

> He, by the tiniest trace of whose might
> You vanquished all creation, moving and unmoving,
> And whose beloved wife you have stolen away—
> I am his messenger.   (21)

I know all about your great power—
You fought Sahasrabahu,
And in your battle with Baali you won great renown!'[9]
Ravan heard the monkey's words but, laughing uneasily, brushed
    them away.
'I ate the fruits, lord, because I was hungry,
And because I am a monkey and it is my nature, I began
    breaking boughs.
Everybody loves their own life more than anything else, master—
Yet those wicked fellows began beating me up.
Those who hit me, I hit them back,
And then your son tied me up!
But I am not ashamed of being tied up,
For I only want to accomplish my Lord's purpose.
I beseech you with folded hands, Ravan,
Abandon your pride and listen to my advice.
Have some consideration for your own family,

And, abandoning delusion, worship him who removes the fear of
   his devotees.
He who terrifies death itself,
That devourer of gods and demons and all creation, moving or unmoving,
Never fight him.
Listen to me and return Janaki to him.

> Raghunayak, slayer of Khar,
> Is the protector of suppliants and an ocean of compassion—
> Go to him for shelter, and he will protect you,
> Forgetting your transgressions.   (22)

Hold Ram's lotus feet in your heart,
And rule unhindered in Lanka.
Rishi Pulastya's fame is a spotless moon—
Do not be the blemish on that moon.
Speech lacks all beauty without Ram's name—
Think, and see this for yourself, abandoning pride and attachment.
A beautiful woman, O enemy of the gods, though adorned with
   every jewel,
Lacks all charm without clothes.
With hostility to Ram, wealth and power
Eventually disappear, their acquisition as if they had never been acquired.
Rivers that have no perennial source of water,
Dry up the instant the rains cease.
Listen, O ten-headed one, I solemnly swear,
There is none to protect one hostile to Ram.
Even a thousand Shankars, Vishnus and Brahmas
Cannot save you, Ram's enemy.

> Abandon the darkness that is arrogance—
> It is rooted in delusion, and gives much pain—
> And worship Ram, lord of the Raghu clan,
> Ocean of compassion, supreme God.'   (23)

Though the monkey spoke words that were for his good,
Of devotion, wisdom, dispassion and prudence,
That most arrogant Ravan laughed disdainfully and said,
'What a wise guru I have found in this monkey!
Your death is close at hand, villain,
Yet you try to instruct me, scoundrel!'
'I can clearly see this is your mind's delusion,
For just the reverse will happen,' replied Hanuman.
Hearing the monkey's words, Ravan flew into a rage,
And roared, 'Someone, quickly, put an end to this fool's life!'
At this, the demons rushed to kill him,
But at that very moment, Vibhishan arrived with his counsellors.
Bowing his head, he humbly entreated,
'It is against all morality—do not kill an envoy.
Give him some other punishment, lord.'
'This is sound counsel, friends,' said all.
At this, Dashkandhar laughed and said,
'All right, let's break his limbs and send the monkey back!

> A monkey is most attached to its tail—
> I tell you this with authority—
> So bind his tail in oil-soaked rags,
> And then set it on fire!   (24)

The tail-less monkey will return,
And then the fool will bring his master back with him,
Whom he has praised so much—
I will see his master's power then!
Hearing his words, the monkey smiled to himself,
'I believe Sharada has helped me by playing with his mind!'
But the stupid demons, hearing Ravan's words,
Began to prepare the rags.
There remained not a piece of cloth in the city, nor a drop of ghee
       or oil,
For the monkey had playfully made his tail very long.

The citizens came flocking to see the show,
And kicked him and laughed and jeered at him.
Beating their drums and clapping their hands,
They led him through the city, and then set his tail alight.
Seeing the burning flames, Hanumant
Immediately assumed his tiny form—
Slipping out of his bonds, he sprang onto the golden roofs,
Terrifying the demon women.

> At that very moment, impelled by Hari,
> The forty-nine winds began to blow.[10]
> The monkey roared with laughter,
> And grew so he touched the sky.   (25)

His body, though enormous, was exceedingly light and nimble.
He ran and sprang from house to house,
Till the whole city was ablaze and its people distraught.
A million fierce flames leapt up,
And cries and shouts were heard everywhere,
'Ah Father! O Mother! Who will save us now?
Did we not say this was no monkey,
But some god in monkey's guise?
Such is the fruit of insulting the good—
The city burns like it has no master.'
He burnt down the city in the blink of an eye,
Except only Vibhishan's house.
Hanuman was the messenger of the one who created fire,
That is why he himself did not burn, Girija.
He turned all Lanka upside down and reduced it to ashes,
And then jumped into the middle of the ocean.

> He put out his burning tail and recovered from his fatigue,
> And then once more assuming his tiny form,
> He went and stood in front of Janak's daughter
> With folded hands.   (26)

'Mother, give me some token,
Like Raghunayak had given me.'
So Sita unfastened the jewel she wore in her hair and gave it to him,
And the Wind's son received it with joy.
'Convey my obeisance to him, dear son, and say,
"My Lord, you lack for nothing and are fulfilled in every way,
Yet remembering your vow of kindness to the afflicted,
Take away my great distress, master."
Dear child, repeat to him the incident with Indra's son,
And remind him of the might of his arrows.
If my Lord doesn't come here within a month,
He will not find me alive.
Tell me, monkey, how do I stay alive?
You too, dear son, now speak of leaving.
Seeing you, my heart had been soothed,
Now I face again those days, those nights.'

> Reassuring Janak's daughter,
> And doing all he could to give her courage,
> The monkey bowed his head at her lotus feet,
> And set forth to rejoin Ram.   (27)

As he left, he gave a thunderous roar,
So that the demon women miscarried.
Leaping across the ocean he arrived on this shore,
And greeted the other monkeys with a cry of joy.
The monkeys all rejoiced to see Hanuman,
And felt as though they had been reborn.
His face was joyous, his body radiant,
So that they knew he had accomplished Ramchandra's work.
They greeted him with great delight,
Like floundering fishes restored to water.
Rejoicing, they set out to rejoin Raghunayak,
Talking, as they went, of the latest events.

When they reached Madhuvan, Sugriv's forbidden orchard,
    they entered
And, together with Angad, began eating the sweet fruit.
When the guards tried to stop them,
They beat them with their fists till they fled.

    The guards ran to Sugriv and cried,
    'Prince Angad has laid waste your entire orchard!'
    Hearing this, Sugriv rejoiced,
    'My monkeys return, having accomplished the
        Lord's work!   (28)

Had they not found news of Sita,
Would they have dared eat the fruits from my orchard?'
The king was thus reflecting to himself
When Hanuman and the monkeys arrived.
They came and all bowed their heads at his feet,
And the king of the monkeys embraced them all with great affection,
And asked after their well-being. 'We are well, now that we have
    seen your feet,' they replied.
'With Ram's grace, our task has been completed very successfully.
Master, it is Hanuman who fulfilled the mission,
And saved the lives of all the monkeys.'
Hearing this, Sugriv embraced Hanuman again,
And went with all the monkeys to Raghupati.
When Ram saw the monkeys approaching,
Their mission accomplished, his heart filled with joy.
The two brothers were seated upon a crystal rock,
And all the monkeys went and fell at their feet.

    Raghupati, that accumulation of compassion,
    Embraced them all with affection,
    And asked after their well-being. 'Lord,
    All is well, now that we have seen your lotus feet.'   (29)

Jamvant said, 'Listen, Raghurai,
He upon whom, Lord, you bestow your mercy,
Is always blessed and forever fortunate,
And gods, men and munis ever pleased with him.
He alone is victorious, modest and an ocean of virtue,
And his bright renown illuminates the three worlds.
By the Lord's grace, all has been accomplished,
And our birth has been made fruitful today.
Master, what the Wind's son has done,
Even a thousand tongues cannot describe.'
Then Jamvant related to Raghupati
The glorious deeds of the Wind god's son.
Hearing of his doings, the treasure-house of compassion was
    greatly pleased,
And once more clasped Hanuman to his heart.
'Tell me, dear son, how does Janaki
Endure her days and stay alive?'

    'Your name guards her day and night,
    Her contemplation of you is a door, closed tight,
    Her eyes, fixed on her own feet, are the fetters—
    So by what path can her life's breath flee?   (30)

As I was leaving, she gave me the jewel from her hair—'
Raghupati took it from him and held it to his heart.
'Lord, her two eyes were full of tears
As Janak's daughters spoke these words:
"Clasp the feet of the Lord and his brother,
Saying to him, 'O friend of the lowly, remover of the
    suppliant's distress,
In heart, word and deed I am devoted to your feet.
For what offence, Lord, have you abandoned me?
Yes, I have one fault, I admit—

That my life's breath did not leave the moment I was separated
    from you.
But this, my Lord, is the fault of my eyes,
That do not let my life depart.
In this fire of separation, fanned by the wind of my sighs,
My body is a heap of cotton fibres that could burn in an instant.
But my eyes, in their selfish interest to see you again, rain such a
    flood of tears
That my body burns not even in this fire of separation.'"
The immensity of Sita's grief is overwhelming,
And is best not told, merciful one.

> Each and every instant, abode of compassion,
> Passes like an aeon for her.
> Go quickly, Lord, and bring her back,
> Vanquishing that evil horde by the might of your arms.'   (31)

Hearing of Sita's anguish, the lotus eyes of the Lord,
That abode of bliss, filled with tears,
'Can one who depends completely on me, in speech, body and mind,
Ever know suffering even in dream?'
Said Hanuman, 'Lord, suffering is
When you are not remembered or adored.
Of what account are those demons to you, Lord?
You will vanquish the enemy, and bring back Janaki.'
'Listen, monkey, there is no benefactor equal to you,
No god, man, muni or any creature endowed with a body.
What service can I do you in return?
I cannot think of any, and my inadequate heart cannot face you.
Listen, my son, I can never repay your debt—
I see that upon reflecting in my heart.'
Again and again the protector of gods looked at the monkey,
His eyes full of tears, his body trembling with emotion.

Listening to the Lord's words, and gazing upon
His grateful face and trembling body, Hanumant
Fell at his feet overcome with love,
Crying, 'Save me, save me, divine Lord!'   (32)

Again and again the Lord tried to raise him up,
But Hanuman, immersed in love, did not want to rise.
The Lord's lotus hands lay upon the monkey's head,
And remembering that state, Gauri's lord too, was drowned
      in bliss.[11]
Then steadying his mind, Shankar
Resumed telling this most lovely tale.
The Lord raised the monkey and clasped him to his heart,
And taking his hand, seated him by his side.
'Tell me, monkey, how were you able to burn down
Lanka, Ravan's own stronghold, and its magnificent fort?'
Hanuman saw that the Lord was pleased,
And spoke words utterly devoid of pride.
'A monkey's greatest accomplishment
Is to leap from branch to branch.
So that I crossed the ocean, burnt down the golden city,
Killed the demon host, and laid waste the ashok grove,
It was all the manifestation of your majesty, Raghurai,
And no great power of mine, master.

Nothing is unattainable, Lord,
For him whom you favour.
Through your might even a wisp of cotton wool
Can extinguish the mighty fire beneath the sea.   (33)

Lord, show me your grace and grant me
Unceasing devotion, that giver of extreme bliss.'
Hearing the monkey's simple and artless speech,
Bhavani, the Lord, replied, 'So be it!'

Uma, he who realizes Ram's true nature,
Takes pleasure in nothing but his worship,
And he who takes into his heart this conversation,
Attains devotion to Raghupati's feet.
Hearing the Lord's words, the assembled monkeys cried,
'Victory, victory, victory to the merciful Lord, root of all bliss!'
Then Raghupati summoned Sugriv, king of the monkeys,
And said, 'Make ready to set forth,
What reason now for delay?
Order the monkeys at once to march.'
The gods, upon seeing this spectacle, showered flowers,
And returned, rejoicing, from the sky to their own abodes.

> The lord of the monkeys quickly summoned them,
> And his commanders arrived in crowds,
> Of various colours, all unequalled in strength,
> A vast multitude of monkeys and bears.   (34)

All bowed their heads at the Lord's lotus feet,
And roared, those mighty bears and monkeys.
Ram beheld the whole monkey army,
Gazing kindly upon them with his lotus eyes.
Made stronger by Ram's grace, the monkey chiefs
Became like the chief of mountains regaining its wings.[12]
Pleased, Ram then marched forth
Amidst good omens, beautiful and auspicious.
It was only fitting that good omens accompany the departure
Of the one whose glory embodies all blessings.
Janaki understood that her Lord had set forth,
For her left side trembled, as though telling her.
Every good omen that occurred for Janaki,
Became a bad omen for Ravan.
The army marched forth—but who can describe it?
The countless bears and monkeys bellowed,

And, with claws as their weapons, bearing boulders and trees,
They went—in the sky, on the earth, as they pleased.
The bears and monkeys roared like lions,
And the elephants of the eight quarters staggered and screamed.

The guardian elephants trumpeted, the earth trembled,
Mountains shook, and the seas grew rough and turbulent.
Gandharvas, gods, munis, Nagas and Kinnaras
All rejoiced in their hearts, knowing their troubles were over.
Countless millions of formidable warrior monkeys
Rushed on, gnashing their teeth, calling
'Glory to Ram, the mighty and powerful Lord of Koshal!'
And singing his praises.

Unable to bear the weight of the army,
Shesh, mighty king of the serpents, staggered again and again,
And again and again steadied himself by clutching with his fangs
The hard shell of the tortoise that bears the world upon its back.
As the serpent-king's fangs scored the tortoise's shell, he looked as beautiful
As though he had understood the supreme beauty of Raghubir's glorious
       setting-forth,
And was inscribing his eternal and sacred story
Upon the tortoise's shell.

In this way, the abode of compassion marched on
And arrived at the ocean's shore,
Where his bear and monkey warriors
Began devouring the abundant wild fruits that grew
       all about.   (35)

Meanwhile, in Lanka, the demons lived in apprehension,
Ever since the monkey had burnt down their city and left.
Each in their own home, they all worried,
'There is no deliverance for the demon tribe.'

The might of whose messenger defies description,
Can there be any good in his coming himself to our city?'
When she heard from her informers what the townsfolk were saying,
Mandodari grew extremely distraught.
Alone with him, she fell at her husband's feet with folded hands,
And implored him in words steeped in prudence,
'Beloved, abandon enmity to Hari—
Know my words to be for your well-being and hold them in your heart.
Remembering the doings of whose messenger,
The wives of night-wandering demons miscarry—
Summon your ministers, my husband, and send back
His wife, if you want your own welfare.
To blight the lotuses that is your lineage,
Sita comes like a winter's night.
Listen, my lord, unless you give up Sita,
Neither Shambhu nor Brahma can help you.

> Ram's arrows are like serpents,
> And the demon host, like frogs.
> So give up your obstinacy and resolve the situation,
> Before they swallow us all.'   (36)

When he heard her words, the foolish Ravan,
Renowned in the world for his arrogance, laughed.
'A woman is truly fearful by nature and timid,
Afraid even when all fares well, and weak-hearted too!
Should the monkey army come,
Our poor demons will sustain themselves by eating them.
Even the guardians of the eight quarters tremble in fear of me—
That you, my wife, should be afraid—that is quite absurd!'
So saying, he laughed and embraced her,
And left for his council-chamber, full of conceit.
But Mandodari was deeply troubled in her heart,
'Now fate has turned against my lord.'

As he sat down in the council-chamber, he received the news
That the whole enemy army had arrived on the opposite shore of
    the sea.
He asked his ministers, 'Tell me what you think is best to be done.'
They laughed and replied, 'What's to be said?
You vanquished gods and demons without effort—
Of what account then are men and monkeys?'

> When these three—a minister, a physician and a guru—
> Speak sweet words from fear or hope of reward,
> Dominion, dharma and health,
> All three are rapidly destroyed.   (37)

Such was the help that Ravan received—
Only praise and flattery to his face.
Perceiving his opportunity, Vibhishan came,
And bowed his head at his brother's feet.
Bowing his head again, he took his own seat,
And receiving permission, spoke these words:
'Since, gracious lord, you ask my advice,
I give it, dear brother, to my ability and for your good.
He who desires his own welfare,
And seeks fame, wisdom, felicity and joys of many kinds,
Turns away from the face of another man's wife
As from the waxing moon on its fourth day, lord.
Though he be lord of the fourteen spheres,
One who turns against creation will not endure.
Even if a man is an ocean of virtue, and accomplished in every way,
No one speaks well of him if he shows even the slightest greed.

> Lust, anger, arrogance and greed,
> Lord, are all roads that lead to hell.
> Abandon them all, and worship
> Raghubir, whom the saints revere.   (38)

Dear brother, Ram is no mere mortal king,
But the sovereign of the universe, the death of death itself.
He is brahm, the Supreme Absolute, the unchanging, unborn God,
All-pervading, invincible, without beginning or end.
For the good of the earth, Brahmans, cows and gods,
The ocean of mercy has assumed the body of a man.
Listen, brother, he delights his devotees, destroys the wicked,
And is the protector of the Vedas and dharma.
Abandon enmity and bow your head to him,
For Raghunath destroys the sorrows of those who seek
        refuge in him.
My king, give Vaidehi back to the Lord,
And worship him—Ram, who loves without motive.
The Lord will not abandon one seeking shelter,
Though he be guilty of the sin of enmity against the world.
He whose name destroys the anguish of the triple fires,
That same Lord has become manifest—understand this in your
        heart, Ravan.

        Again and again I fall at your feet
        And implore you, Dashashish,
        Abandon arrogance, delusion and pride,
        And worship the king of Koshal.   (39A)

        Our grandfather, sage Pulastya,
        Sent this same message through a pupil,
        And I have at once repeated it to you, my lord,
        Deeming this to be the right moment, sire.'   (39B)

One wise minister, called Malyavant,
Was extremely pleased to hear Vibhishan's words.
'Son, your younger brother is the very ornament of prudent counsel,
So take what Vibhishan says to heart.'
'My enemy is superior, say these two fools!

Is there no one here to remove them?'
At this, Malyavant returned home,
But Vibhishan spoke again with folded hands.
'Lord, wisdom and folly reside in everyone's heart—
So say the Vedas and Puranas.
Where there is wisdom, there is prosperity too,
But where there is folly, there is calamity in the end.
Perverse folly has taken up residence in your heart,
So you take good as bad, and your foes as friends,
And are so excessively fond of this Sita
Who is the night of ultimate destruction for the demon clan!

> Dear brother, I clasp your feet and beg you,
> For the love you bear me—
> Return Sita to Ram,
> So that no harm comes to you.'   (40)

In words supported by the authority of the wise, the Puranas and
    the Vedas,
Vibhishan gave him prudent counsel,
But upon hearing them, Dashanan leapt up in fury, crying,
'Villain, your death approaches!
You have always lived, wretch, under my patronage,
But now, fool, you prefer to take my enemy's side!
Tell me, you scoundrel, who in this world
Have I not conquered with the might of my arms?
You live in my city but love some ascetics—
So go to them, idiot, talk to them about prudence!'
So saying, he kicked his younger brother,
Who clasped his feet again and again.
Uma, this is the greatness of saints,
That they return good for evil.
'You may strike me, for you are like my father,
But it is in worshipping Ram, my lord, that your well-being lies.'

Taking his counsellors with him, Vibhishan left, flying through
    the air,
Proclaiming aloud to them all,

'Ram is true to his resolve and the master of all,
While your assembly is in the grip of doom.
I now go to take refuge with Raghubir—
Lay no blame upon me!'   (41)

The moment Vibhishan left with these words,
The doom of the rest of them became assured.
Disrespect to a good man, Bhavani, immediately
Destroys all well-being.
The moment he abandoned Vibhishan,
The unfortunate Ravan lost all his glory.
But Vibhishan went rejoicing to Raghunayak,
With many hopes and expectations in his mind.
'On reaching there I will see the lotus feet,
Rosy, soft, which give bliss to the devotee,
The feet whose touch saved the rishi's wife,
And which made holy the Dandak forest,
The feet which Janak's daughter holds in her heart,
Which ran to capture the false kurang deer,
The feet which are the lotuses upon the lake of Har's heart—
What good fortune that I will behold them!

The feet, whose wooden sandals
Bharat holds in his heart—
Those feet I will now see,
With these my eyes, today!'   (42)

In this manner, lovingly reflecting,
He quickly reached this shore of the ocean.
The monkeys, seeing Vibhishan approach,

Took him to be a special messenger of the enemy.
They stopped him and went to their king,
And told him the situation.
Said Sugriv, 'Listen, Raghurai,
Dashanan's brother has come to see you.'
Said the Lord, 'Friend, what do you think?'
The king of the monkeys replied, 'Listen, king of men,
The deceitful magic of these night-wanderers cannot be understood.
Why should this shape-shifting demon come here?
It seems the villain has come to learn our secrets—
So I think it best we take him prisoner and bind him.'
'Friend, you have reasoned prudently and well,
But my vow is to dispel fear from the minds of those who come to
    me for refuge.'
Hanuman rejoiced to hear these words from the Lord,
The God who loves as his children all those who seek his protection.

'The men who abandon those seeking refuge,
Suspecting their own harm,
Are vile and sinful,
And even to look upon them is harmful.   (43)

Though he be guilty of killing ten million Brahmans,
I will not abandon one who turns to me for shelter,
For the instant a soul comes before me,
Its sins of countless lives are destroyed.
A sinner's natural disposition is such
That to worship me never pleases him.
If Vibhishan were truly evil-hearted,
Would he have come into my presence?
Only one who is pure of heart can find me,
For I do not like hypocrisy, deceit and duplicity.
The ten-headed one may have sent him to find out our secrets,
But even so, king of the monkeys, we have nothing to fear or lose—

All the demons, dear friend, that this world contains,
Lakshman can destroy in the blink of an eye.
And if he has come out of fear to seek shelter with me,
I will protect him as I would my own life.

In either case, bring him here.'
So said the abode of compassion with a smile.
'Victory to the merciful Lord,' said the monkey,
And set off with Angad and Hanuman. (44)

The monkeys respectfully escorted him
To Raghupati, the all-compassionate.
Vibhishan saw from a distance the two brothers,
The givers of the gift of bliss to all eyes.
Then, looking again at Ram, that abode of beauty,
He stood stock still, gazing unblinkingly
At his long arms, and red-lotus eyes,
His dark-hued body that destroys the fear of the suppliant,
His lion shoulders, magnificent broad chest,
And his face that captivates the heart of Madan himself.
His eyes full of tears, his body trembling with love,
Vibhishan steadied his heart, then softly said,
'Lord, I am Dashanan's brother.
I have been born in the demon-lineage, protector of the gods,
And my body, imbued with ignorance and vice, loves evil
    as naturally
As an owl loves the night.

I have heard with my own ears of your glorious fame
As the destroyer of the fear of rebirth, Lord, and so I have
    come to you.
O save me, save me, Raghubir, you who are the destroyer
    of distress,
And the giver of bliss to those who seek refuge!' (45)

Seeing Vibhishan prostrating himself after speaking thus,
The Lord, greatly delighted, stood up at once.
His humble words had pleased the Lord,
And enfolding him in his mighty arms, he clasped him to his heart.
Then with his younger brother, he seated him by his side,
And spoke words to remove his devotee's fear.
'Tell me, lord of Lanka, is all well with you and your family?
Your home is in an evil place,
Day and night you live surrounded by the wicked—
So, my friend, how do you hold to dharma?
I know all your ways and your disposition—
You are committed to what is moral and right, and dislike injustice
     and wrong.
May providence never give us the company of the wicked—
It is better to live in hell, my son.'
'Now that I have seen your feet, Raghurai, all is well with me,
Since you have recognized me as your devotee and shown me
     your mercy.

     There is no well-being for the soul,
     Nor any peace even in dream,
     Till it abandons desire, that abode of sorrow,
     And worships Ram.   (46)

Greed, delusion, envy, arrogance, pride—
These evils continue to dwell in the heart
Until Raghunath, with bow and arrow and a quiver at his waist,
Takes up his abode there.
The utterly dark night of self-interest and pride
Delights the owls of anger and hate,
And continues to abide in the hearts of living beings
Until the sun of the Lord's glory rises there.
Now I am truly well, my fear and delusion destroyed,
Now that I have seen your lotus feet, Ram.

The three kinds of afflictions cannot affect him,
Gracious Lord, to whom you show your favour.
I am a demon, my nature is utterly vile,
And I have never done anything good.
Yet the Lord whose beauty even the minds of munis cannot perceive
Has gladly taken me to his heart.

> Ah Ram, my good fortune is beyond measure,
> O accumulation of compassion and joy,
> That I beheld with my eyes the two lotus feet
> That Viranchi and Shiv adore!'   (47)

'Listen, my friend, I will tell you my ways and my disposition,
Known to Bhushundi, Shambhu and Girija.
Though a man be hostile to all creation, moving and unmoving,
If in fear he comes to me, seeking my protection,
And abandoning all pride, delusion, deceit and duplicity,
I instantly make him equal to a saint.
Mother, father, friend, sons and wife,
Body, wealth, house, friends and kinsfolk—
He who gathers up these strands of attachment
And twisting them into a rope, ties with it his heart to my feet,
Who views all alike and is free of desire,
Whose heart remains unmoved by joy, grief, or fear—
That good man resides in my heart,
Like treasure in the heart of a miser.
Virtuous men like you are dear to me,
And I take bodily form from no other obligation.

> Those who worship my embodied form, who are intent on the
>   good of others,
> Firm in the practice of righteousness,
> And revere the feet of Brahmans—
> Such men are as dear to me as my own life's breath.   (48)

Listen, prince of Lanka, all these virtues are yours,
Which is why you are very dear to me.'
Hearing Ram's words, the assembled monkeys
All cried, 'Victory to the all-merciful!'
Vibhishan, hearing the Lord's speech,
Found it to be nectar for his ears, and could not have enough.
Again and again he clasped Ram's lotus feet,
Unable to contain the boundless love in his heart.
'Listen, Lord, master of all creation, moving and unmoving,
Protector of the suppliant, who pervades the hearts of all,
In my heart some desires did exist,
But they have now been washed away in the stream of devotion to
       your feet.
Now, merciful Lord, grant me that pure devotion to you
That ever delights Shiv's heart.'
'So be it,' said the Lord, the steadfast in battle,
And called at once for some water from the sea.
'Dear friend, though you have no wish for this,
Yet the sight of me brings reward in this world.'
So saying, Ram set the royal tilak upon his forehead,
As an endless rain of flowers fell from the sky.

> Thus, from the fire of Ravan's wrath,
> Fanned by the mighty wind of Vibhishan's own words,
> Did Ram save Vibhishan,
> And give him complete and secure dominion.   (49A)

> The fortune that Shiv had given Ravan
> Upon him offering his ten heads in sacrifice,
> That same fortune did Raghunath
> Modestly give Vibhishan.   (49B)

Forsaking such a Lord, men who worship another
Are but beasts without tails and horns.

Recognizing Vibhishan to be his servant, the Lord made him
    his own.
His gracious nature delighted the hearts of his monkey troops.
Then the omniscient one, who lives in all hearts,
Manifest in all forms though without form, indifferent,
The destroyer of the demon race, and who had become a man
    for a reason,
Spoke words upholding righteousness.
'Listen, king of the monkeys and valiant lord of Lanka,
How are we to cross the deep ocean?
Full of crocodiles, serpents and fish of many kinds,
It is bottomless and impossible to cross in every way.'
Said Lanka's king, 'Listen, Raghunayak,
Though a single arrow of yours can soak up a million seas,
It would be prudent and right policy
That you first approach the ocean and humbly ask its help.

Lord, the ocean is an ancestor of yours,[13]
So he will certainly think and tell you a way
By which the whole army of bears and monkeys
Will be able to effortlessly cross without trouble.'   (50)

'Dear friend, you have suggested a good plan,
Let us try it, and see if providence favours us.'
But this plan did not appeal to Lakshman at all,
And he was greatly distressed to hear Ram's words.
'Don't depend on providence, Lord,
But give vent to your wrath and dry up this ocean.
Providence is but a crutch for the coward's heart,
And it is only the lazy who cry out, "Fate! Fate!"'
At this, Raghubir laughed and said,
'That is what I will do, but be patient.'
Saying this, the Lord reassured his younger brother,
And went to the ocean's edge.

First, he made obeisance, bowing his head,
And then, spreading some darbha grass on the shore, sat down.
Now, when Vibhishan had come to the Lord,
Ravan had sent his spies behind him.

> Deceitfully assuming the form of monkeys
> They watched all that Ram did,
> And began praising in their hearts the Lord's virtues
> And his love for those who came to him for refuge.   (51)

As they praised Ram's gracious nature, they revealed their
     true forms—
Full of love, they forgot concealment!
The monkeys then recognized them as enemy spies,
And tying them up, brought them to their king.
Said Sugriv, 'Listen, all you monkeys,
Send back these night-wanderers after breaking their limbs.'
At Sugriv's words, the monkeys rushed
And paraded them in bonds all around their camp.
The monkeys began to beat them in every possible way,
And refused to let them go despite all their wretched calls
     for mercy.
'He who cuts off our ears and noses,
Let him answer to Koshal's king!'
Hearing this, Lakshman called them to him,
And feeling sorry for them, he laughed and had them released
     at once.
'Give this letter to Ravan, and say to him,
"Read Lakshman's words, destroyer of your own line!"

> And repeat to that fool's face
> My generous message,
> "Give back Sita and make peace,
> Or else your death approaches!"'   (52)

Bowing their heads at Lakshman's feet, the spies
Set off at once, praising his mercy.
Recounting Ram's glory, they entered Lanka,
And bowed their heads at Ravan's feet.
Dashanan laughed and asked for news,
'Why do you not speak, Shuk,[vi] telling me how you are?
Also give me news of that Vibhishan
Whose death approaches.
That fool abandoned Lanka, where he ruled,
Now the unfortunate wretch will be crushed with Ram's army as a
    weevil is with grain.
Tell me, too, about that army of bears and monkeys,
Being impelled to come here by cruel Fate,
The protector of whose lives is now
Only the poor, soft-hearted ocean.
And then tell me about the two ascetics,
Whose hearts tremble in fear of me.

Did you meet them, or did they turn back
Hearing of my great renown?
Why aren't you saying anything about the enemy army's
    power and strength?
Your mind seems utterly dazed!'   (53)

'My lord, as you so graciously ask,
So believe what I say without anger.
When your younger brother left to join him,
Ram put the tilak of sovereignty upon his forehead the moment
    he arrived.
Hearing that we were Ravan's spies,
The monkeys tied us up and tormented us in many ways.
They were about to cut off our ears and noses,

_____
vi   The chief of Ravan's spies

But when we invoked Ram, they let us go.
You ask, my lord, about Ram's army,
But ten million mouths could not describe it.
It is a vast multitude of bears and monkeys of innumerable hues
And frightful faces, huge and terrifying.
The one who burnt your city and killed your son,
His strength is the least amongst all the monkeys.
Heroes with countless names, they are unyielding and
    formidable,
With the strength of countless elephants, and of enormous size.

Dwivid, Mayand, Nil, Nal
Angad, Gad, Bikatas,
Dadhimukh, Kehari, Nishath,
Shath and Jamvant—all imbued with
    enormous strength.   (54)

Each of these monkeys is equal to Sugriv,
And there are uncountable millions like them.
By Ram's favour, their strength is boundless,
And they consider the three worlds as of little account as
    blades of grass.
And, Dashkandhar, I heard with my own ears,
That the monkey commanders alone number
    eighteen thousand billion.
Lord, there is no monkey in that army
Who cannot vanquish you in battle.
They are all wringing their hands in greatest fury,
But Raghunath does not give them the order.
"We will drink up the ocean with its fish and serpents,
Or fill it up with massive mountains,
And crush Dashashish and grind him into the dust."
Such were the words that all the monkeys utter,
By nature fearless, they roar and thunder,
As though they would swallow Lanka.

All the bears and monkeys are born heroes,
And then they have Lord Ram at their head.
Ravan, I tell you, they could vanquish death
Ten million times in battle.   (55)

Even a thousand Sheshnags cannot describe
The greatness of Ram's bright glory, might and wisdom.
With a single arrow, he can dry up a hundred seas,
Yet so righteous is he that he asked your brother for advice,
And hearing his words, went to the sea
And asked him for passage, compassion in his heart.'
Hearing his words, Dashashish laughed.
'If such is his intelligence, no wonder he made monkeys his allies!
He trusts the words of a born coward,
And pleads with the ocean like a wayward child!
Fool, why do you bestow false praise on him?
I have already fathomed my enemy's wit and strength.
How can triumph and glory in this world be his,
Who has as his counsellor the cowardly Vibhishan?'
The villain's words made the messenger angry,
And he thought it a good time to produce the letter.
'Ram's brother gave me this letter,
Have it read, my lord, and calm your anger.'
Laughing, Ravan took it in his left hand,
And summoning his minister, the villainous fool had it read out.

"'Beguiling your mind with mere talk, fool,
Do not destroy your line.
If you oppose Ram, you will not be saved
Though you seek refuge with Vishnu, Brahma, Shiv.   (56A)

Either abandon pride, and, like your brother,
Become a bee at the lotus of the Lord's feet,
Or, in the fire of Ram's arrows, villain,
Perish like a moth with your clan.'"   (56B)

Though his heart filled with fear at the words,
Dashanan smiled and said for all to hear,
'Like one lying prostrate upon the ground, yet reaching for
    the sky—
So does this little ascetic grandly plays on words!'
Said Shuk, 'My lord, every word of this message is true—
Set aside your natural arrogance and understand that.
Give up anger and listen to my advice—
Sire, abandon opposition to Ram.
Raghubir's disposition is exceedingly gentle,
Though he is the master of all the worlds.
The moment you approach him, the Lord will show you his grace—
He will not hold a single offence of yours in his heart.
Return Janak's daughter to Raghunath—
Just do this much, my lord, I ask.'
When Shuk spoke of giving up Vaidehi,
The villain kicked him hard.
But Shuk bowed his head at his feet,
And left to join that ocean of compassion, Raghunayak.
There, making obeisance, he told him his story,
And by Ram's grace recovered his own true state.
He had been a wise and learned muni, Bhavani,
And it was by Rishi Agastya's curse that he had become a Rakshasa.
Prostrating himself again and again at Ram's feet,
The muni returned to his own hermitage.

    Meanwhile, three days had passed,
    And the stubborn ocean had not granted Ram's request.
    Then said Ram in anger,
    'There is no love given without fear!'   (57)

Lakshman, fetch my bow and arrows,
That I may dry up the ocean with arrows of flame.
To entreat a fool, show affection to a rogue,

Preach generosity to a born miser,
Discourse on wisdom to one steeped in attachment,
Explain dispassion to one exceedingly greedy,
Speak of reconciliation to one who is angry, or tell Hari a
    tale of lust,
Is all as hopeless as planting seeds in barren ground.'
So saying, Raghupati strung his bow.
This approach pleased Lakshman.
As the Lord fitted his dreadful arrow to his bow,
A fierce fire erupted in the ocean's heart.
And the crocodiles, serpents and schools of fish grew distraught.
When Ocean himself realized his creatures were burning,
He filled a golden salver with all kinds of precious jewels,
And, abandoning pride, appeared in the form of a Brahman.

A plantain bears fruit only upon being pruned,
Though one may take infinite trouble to water it.
In the same way, O king of the birds, a wretch pays no
    heed to prayers,
But yields only when reprimanded. (58)

Terrified, Ocean clasped the Lord's feet.
'Forgive all my faults, Lord.
Air, wind, fire, water and earth
Are all inherently inert and slow to change.
Impelled by you, your maya brought them forth
For the purpose of creation—so declare all the scriptures.
Each finds happiness in remaining
As it has been commanded by the Lord.
The Lord did well in teaching me this lesson,
But fixing my bounds was also your doing.
A drum, a fool, a Shudra, a beast and a woman,
All deserve to be beaten.
By the Lord's blazing splendour I will be dried up,

And his army will cross over, and my glory will be at an end.
But the Lord's command is inexorable, so sing the Vedas,
So I shall do at once whatever pleases you.'

> Hearing his exceedingly humble words,
> The merciful Lord smiled and said,
> 'Sire, tell me how
> The monkey army may cross.'   (59)

'Lord, the two monkey brothers, Nil and Nal,
Were blessed in their childhood by a rishi.
If touched by them, even the mightiest mountains
Will, by your favour, float upon the sea.
Keeping the Lord's sovereignty in my heart, I, too,
Will help you in accordance with my strength.
In this manner, Lord, subdue the waves,
So that the three worlds may sing of this glorious deed.
With this very arrow, Lord, destroy the evil men,
Those accumulations of sin, who dwell on my northern shore.'
Hearing Ocean's pain, the compassionate
And valiant Ram removed it at once.[14]
Seeing Ram's mighty strength and valour,
Ocean rejoiced and was happy.
He related all the doings of those villains to the Lord,
And then, after prostrating himself at his feet, Ocean departed.

Ocean returned to his own abode,
And Lord Raghupati heeded well his advice.
This story removes the impurities of the Kali age,
And Tulsi has sung it in accordance with his own understanding.
The multitude of Raghupati's virtues is the abode of bliss,
And the destroyer of all sorrows and doubt.
Forsake hope and faith in all others, foolish heart,
And listen to and sing unceasingly of his perfections.

The singing of Raghunayak's virtues
Gives every blessing,
And those who listen with reverence
Will cross, without a boat, the ocean of this existence.   (60)

Thus ends the fifth descent into the Manas lake of Ram's acts, that destroy all the impurities of the Kali age.

Book VI

LANKAKAND
(LANKA)

Aisa Sar rucha, caho prarat rhea prna vat dec adore vaat clare B.

S. Mippadp a adatte.

Appasang parishe the afftlet—

At lehe alme Sdankar gita, aug a pparip

Mangalacharan

The adored of Shankar, Kamdev's foe,
The dispeller of the fear of rebirth, the lion that destroys the fierce
    elephant of death,
The lord of the yogis, accessible through knowledge, the storehouse of
    all virtues,
The invincible, the unchangeable, the formless,
The sovereign of the gods, beyond maya, intent upon the destruction of
    the wicked,
The Brahmans' only god,
Dark and beautiful as a rain-laden cloud, lotus-eyed,
The Supreme Lord incarnate as king of the earth—Ram,
    I worship him.   (1)

His body as beautiful as the radiance of the conch and the moon,
Clad in tiger's skin,
Adorned with serpents as terrible and black as death,
Beloved by Ganga and the moon,
The lord of Kashi, the destroyer of the sins of the age of Kali,
The Kalpataru of every blessing,
Girija's lord, the repository of every virtue, the vanquisher of
    Kandarp[vii]—
Shankar, I pay him homage.   (2)

[vii] Kamdev

May Shambhu, who grants the virtuous liberation from rebirth,
So difficult to attain,
And who punishes the wicked—
May that same Shankar grant me prosperity.   (3)

O heart, why do you not worship
Ram, whose
Bow is Time,
And its divisions his fierce arrows?   (0A)

Heeding Ocean's words, Ram
Summoned his counsellors and said,
'Now why the delay?
Make that bridge so the army may cross over.'   (0B)

Jamvant, folding his hands, said,
'Listen, pride of the solar line,
Lord, your name is the bridge by which
Men cross over the ocean of this existence.   (0C)

So how long, then, can it take you to cross this little sea?'
Hearing this, the Wind's son said,
'The Lord's glory is like a mighty fire beneath the sea—
It had, before now, dried up the ocean's water.
Then it was filled again by the streams of tears
Shed by the wives of your enemies—and that's why it came to
      be salt.'
Upon hearing Hanuman's ingenious explanation,
The monkeys gazed in rapture at Raghupati.
Jamvant summoned the two brothers,
Nal and Nil, and explained the whole situation to them.
'Invoking Ram's majesty in your heart,
Build the bridge—you will find it to be effortless.'
He then summoned the monkey troops and said,
'Listen, all of you, I have one request—
Hold in your hearts Ram's lotus feet,
And together, bears and monkeys, put on a show!
Rush away, you formidable monkey host,
And bring back great piles of trees and mountains.'

At this, the bears and monkeys set off with a great noise, whooping
    and shouting,
'Victory to Raghubir, the all-powerful!'

> Huge trees and mighty mountains
> They uprooted as though in play,
> And bringing them back, gave them to Nal and Nil,
> Who began to build the bridge.   (1)

The monkeys brought and handed to them enormous mountains,
And Nal and Nil took them as though they were balls to play with.
Seeing the exceedingly beautiful construction of the bridge,
The all-merciful Lord smiled and said,
'Most excellent and supremely delightful is this place,
Its immeasurable glory defies description.
I will set up here an image of Shambhu—
I have this great plan in my heart.'
Hearing this, the king of the monkeys sent out several messengers,
Who invited and brought back with them all the great munis.
Installing the shivaling in the manner prescribed and duly
    worshipping it,
The Lord declared, 'There is no one as dear to me as Shiv.
A man who is Shiv's enemy may be called my devotee,
But he will never find me, even in dream.
One opposed to Shankar but aspiring to serve me
Is bound for hell, and is a fool with little understanding.

> Those who love Shankar but are my foes,
> Those who oppose him but wish to be my servants—
> Such men shall abide
> For a full cycle of creation in the deepest hell.   (2)

Those who will pay homage to my Lord, in this shivaling installed
    by me,

Will, upon quitting the body, depart for my abode.
He who brings and pours upon it water from the Ganga,
Will attain salvation and become one with me.
He who worships it selflessly and without deceit,
Shankar will grant him faith in me.
He who beholds this bridge built by me—
Will effortlessly cross the ocean of this existence.'
Ram's words pleased all,
And the great munis returned, each one to his own ashram.
Girija, this is Ram's way—
He is ever loving to those who seek refuge in him.
Clever Nil and Nal built the bridge,
And by Ram's grace, their fame spread far and wide.
Those rocks, which themselves sink and cause other things to sink,
Became as buoyant as boats.
This is not a description of the sea's greatness,
Nor of a quality of the stones, nor of the doing of the monkeys,

> For it was by Raghubir's power
> That stones floated across the sea.
> They are fools indeed, who, leaving Ram,
> Worship another god.   (3)

They completed the bridge and made it strong and secure,
And, beholding it, the compassionate Lord was delighted.
The army began to cross, a sight that defied description—
The host of monkey warriors roared and bellowed as they went.
Raghurai climbed up to the side of the bridge,
And gazed out at the vastness of the ocean.
In order to behold the compassionate Lord,
All the creatures of the sea appeared—
Crocodiles, sharks, many kinds of fish and serpents
With enormous bodies a hundred yojans long,
Others that could devour them,

And still others of whom even these latter were afraid.
Beholding the Lord, they would not leave—
Their hearts were joyous and all grew blissful.
So thickly did they cover it, the water could not be seen,
And they gazed, enraptured, upon Hari's beauty.
The army marched forth at the Lord's command—
Who can describe the vast size of the monkey host?

> There was a huge crowd upon the bridge,
> So that some of the monkeys took to the air,
> While many others climbed on to the backs of
>   the sea creatures
> And crossed over.   (4)

The two brothers gazed at this spectacle,
And then the merciful Raghurai set forth with a smile.
Raghubir crossed over with the army—
It is impossible to describe the monkey legions and their
    commanders.
The Lord set up camp across the sea,
And ordered all the monkeys,
'Go, eat the delicious fruits and roots!'
At this, the bears and monkeys ran off here and there.
All the trees bore fruit for Ram's sake,
Disregarding the time of year and whether it was the right season
    or not.
They ate the sweet fruit and shook the trees,
And hurled the tops of mountains at the city of Lanka.
While wandering here and there, if they found a demon,
They would all surround him and tease and harass him,
Bite off his nose and ears with their teeth,
Relate to him their Lord's great renown, and only then let him go.
Those who had lost their nose and ears,
Told Ravan all that had happened.

Hearing with his own ears that the ocean had been bridged,
He rose up in alarm, and cried out with all his ten tongues,

'What! Has he truly bridged the sea, into which fall all the
     streams and rivers,
The deep, the vast ocean, the lord of all the waters,
The holder of the tides, with its surging waves,
The receptacle of the floods, the repository of the waters,
     the lord of all the rivers?'   (5)

Then, becoming aware of his own agitation,
He put away his fears with a laugh and left for his palace.
When Mandodari heard that the Lord had arrived
And had bridged the ocean as though in play,
She took her husband by the hand and led him into her
     own apartments,
And spoke to him in sweet and gentle tones.
Bowing her head, she most humbly pleaded,
'Listen to my words, beloved, without anger.
Lord, you should antagonize only those
Whom you can vanquish through wit or might.
But the difference between you and Raghupati
Is like that between a firefly and the sun.
He, who slew the most mighty Madhu and Kaitabh,[1]
And killed Kanakakasipu and Hataklochan, the valiant sons of Diti,
Who subdued the Daitya Bali, and killed Sahasrabahu,
Has become incarnate to relieve the earth of her burden.
Oh my lord, do not oppose him
In whose hands lie Time and Fate and all individual souls.

Surrender Janaki to Ram,
Bowing your head at his lotus feet,
And handing over your kingdom to your son,
Retire to the forest and worship Raghunath.   (6)

My lord, Raghurai is merciful to the meek—
Even a tiger does not devour one who goes humbly before him.
All that you had to do, you have already done.
You have vanquished gods, Asurs, and all creation, moving
    and unmoving.
Holy men, Dashanan, have laid down this rule,
That in his fourth stage of life, a king must retire to the forest.
There, my husband, adore him
Who is the Creator, Preserver and Destroyer.
Abandoning ego and all attachment, my lord, worship him,
That same Raghubir, who ever cherishes the humble,
For whom the greatest munis strive,
And kings give up their kingdoms to become ascetics.
That same Raghurai, king of Koshal,
Has come to shower his mercy upon you.
If, my beloved, you listen to my advice,
Your fame, pure and glorious, will spread throughout the
    three spheres.'

    So saying, and with eyes full of tears
    And trembling in every limb, she clasped his feet,
    'Lord, worship Raghunath,
    So that my wedded state never changes.'   (7)

Then Ravan raised up Mai's daughter,
And began, that villain, to boast of his own power.
'Listen, my beloved, you are being needlessly afraid.
Is there any warrior in this world my equal?
Varun, Kuber, Vayu[viii], Jam,
And all the other guardians of the quarters I have vanquished by
    the might of my arms.
Gods, demons and men are all under my sway,

---

viii The Wind god

So why are you afraid ?'
Ravan, having said all he could to comfort her,
Went and sat once again in his council-chamber.
Mandodari now knew in her heart,
His doom had made him arrogant.
Entering his council chamber, he asked his ministers,
'How shall we engage with the enemy?'
Said the ministers, 'Listen, king of the demons,
Why do you ask us thus again and again, lord?
Tell us, what is there to be afraid of that we must reflect upon?
After all, men, monkeys and bears are food for us!'

But, after listening to the words of all,
Prahast, Ravan's son, folded his hands and said,
'Do not act against what is moral and right, lord!
Your ministers have little understanding!   (8)

Your fawning ministers say only what pleases their master,
But success cannot be achieved in this way, my lord.
A single monkey leapt across the sea and came here,
And all the people still praise his doings in their hearts.
Were none of you hungry then?
Why didn't you catch and eat him when he set fire to the city?
Pleasant to hear but leading to trouble later—
That is the kind of advice that these ministers have given you, my lord.
He who has bridged the ocean in play,
And has crossed over with all his army to Mount Suvela—
Tell me, is he a mere man whom you say you will devour?
Your ministers merely vaunt and vapour.
Father, listen to my words with deep attention,
And do not think me to be a coward.
There are plenty of men in this world
Who make and listen only to pleasant speeches,
But very few, my lord, who are willing to hear or to give

Beneficial advice if it sounds harsh and unpleasant.
Listen to my prudent counsel, and first send an envoy,
And after you have given Sita back to Ram, make friends with him.

> If, having recovered his wife, he withdraws,
> Do not continue the quarrel;
> If not, meet him face to face on the battlefield, Father,
> And, standing firm, fight him with determination
>   and resolve.   (9)

If you follow this advice of mine, my lord,
In either case you will have glory in the world.'
The ten-headed one said to his son in fury,
'Who has taught you, fool, to give such advice?
Is your heart already full of doubt?
You have proved to be prickly ghamoi, son, sprung from a
    bamboo root!'[2]
At his father's harsh and brutal speech,
Prahast went off home with these hard and bitter words,
'Good advice is as lost upon you
As medicine upon one in the grip of death.'
Seeing that it was now evening, ten-headed Ravan
Set off towards home, glancing with pride at his twenty arms.
On Lanka's highest peak there stood a wonderful palace
Where musicians and dancers used to gather—
Ravan went and took a seat in that palace.
Kinnaras began to sing his praises,
As cymbals, drums and vinas played,
And graceful apsaras danced before him.

> Here, he enjoyed unceasingly pleasures
> A hundred times more delightful than those of Indra's court.
> Though the most powerful enemy stood at his door,
> He was disturbed by neither worry nor fear.   (10)

Meanwhile, upon Mount Suvela, Raghubir
Had arrived with his vast army.
There, Lakshman saw a high and lofty peak,
Exceedingly lovely, level, and particularly shining and bright.
Upon it, he spread
Tender young leaves and pretty flowers from the trees,
Which he covered with a soft and lovely deer's skin.
Upon this seat the compassionate one sat down.
The Lord's head rested in the monkey-king, Sugriv's, lap,
And to his left and right lay his bow and quiver.
With his two lotus hands he trimmed his arrows,
As Vibhishan, king of Lanka, whispered some counsel in his ear.
The most fortunate Angad and Hanuman
Assiduously massaged his feet,
While behind him stood Lakshman in warrior stance,
With a quiver at his waist and a bow and arrows in his hands.

　　Thus sat Ram,
　　Abode of mercy, grace and virtue.
　　Blessed are those men who ever remain absorbed
　　In contemplation of him in this form.   (11A)

　　Looking towards the east, the Lord
　　Saw the risen moon,
　　And cried to them all, 'Look at the moon,
　　Fearless as the king of the beasts!   (11B)

Dwelling in the mountain cave that is the east,
Supremely glorious, the aggregation of splendour and might,
This lion that is the moon roams freely in the forest of the sky
Having sundered the forehead of the mast elephant[ix] that is darkness.
And strewn across the sky are the stars, like pearls

[ix]   An elephant in rut, fearsome and out of control

Adorning beautiful Night.'
Then said the Lord, 'But the blackness upon the moon's face—
What is it? Tell me, each one, what you understand.'
Said Sugriv, 'Listen, Raghurai,
It is the earth's shadow upon the moon's face.'
'Rahu struck the moon,' said another,
'And the darkness is the bruise upon its chest.'
A third said, 'When Vidhi made Rati's face,
He stole a part of the moon's essence.
That hole is present on the moon's breast,
And through it can be seen the shadow of the sky.'
The Lord said, 'Poison is the moon's dear friend,
So beloved that it has given it a place in its heart.
Spreading its innumerable poison-imbued rays,
It tortures men and women already suffering the anguish of
    separation from their beloved.'

But Hanuman said, 'Listen, Lord,
The moon is your beloved servant.
Your dark form resides in its heart,
And it is that which gives this impression of blackness.'   (12A)

Hearing the words of the Wind god's son,
The all-wise Ram smiled.
Then looking towards the south,
The compassionate Lord spoke again.   (12B)

'Look, Vibhishan, towards the south,
At the gathering clouds and flashing lightning.
The dark clouds rumble gently—
Let there be no fierce shower of hail!'
Said Vibhishan, 'Listen, merciful one,
That is not lightning, nor gathering clouds.
On Lanka's peak there stands a palace,

Where Ravan watches musicians and dancers perform.
Above him is the canopy of the royal umbrella—
It is that which seems like a mass of black clouds.
The glittering ornaments in Mandodari's ears—
Those are the lightning flashes, Lord.
And the incomparable music of drums and cymbals—
That is the gentle rumble that you hear, king of the gods.'
Perceiving Ravan's arrogance, the Lord smiled,
And stringing his bow, he fitted an arrow to it.

    Then royal umbrella, crown and earrings,
    He struck with a single shaft.
    They fell to the ground in the sight of all,
    But no one could explain the mystery. (13A)

    After performing this astonishing show,
    Ram's arrow returned to his quiver.
    But in Ravan's assembly, all were overcome by fear
    Upon witnessing this spectacular interruption to
        their revels. (13B)

'The earth did not tremble, there was no wind to speak of,
Nor did our eyes see any weapon or missile,'
They anxiously pondered in their hearts.
'This is a terrible and frightening ill omen.'
Dashanan saw that the gathering was afraid,
So he laughed and reassured them cleverly,
'How can the tumbling of crowns be an ill omen
For whom the falling of heads has ever been auspicious?
Go, each to your own home, and sleep.'
Bowing their heads, they all went home.
But worry had taken up its abode in Mandodari's heart
From the moment her ear ornament had dropped to the ground.
With eyes full of tears, and folded hands, she wept,

'Lord of my life, listen to my prayer.
Beloved, give up this hostility to Ram,
Do not persist in it, with the idea that he is an ordinary man.

> Believe me when I say
> The jewel of the Raghu line is the omnipresent God,
> Whose every part, the Vedas declare,
> Is a distinct world.   (14)

His feet are the netherworld, his head Brahma's abode,
And in every limb there is some separate sphere.
The play of his brows is dreadful death,
His eyes are the sun, his hair the massing clouds.
His nostrils are the twin sons of Ashvini,ˣ
The constant blinking of his eyes, night and day,
And his ears the ten directions—so the Vedas declare.
His breath is the wind, his own speech the Vedas,
His lips are greed, and Jam, god of death, his fearsome teeth.
His laughter is Maya, his arms the guardians of the quarters,
His face is Fire, and Varun, lord of the waters, his tongue.
Creation, preservation and dissolution are his movements.
The hairs on his chest are the countless trees and shrubs,
His bones the mountains, and the network of his veins the rivers.
His belly is the ocean, and his nether regions hell.
The world is a manifestation of the Lord—what is the need for
    more discussion?

> His ego is Shiv, his intellect the unborn Brahma,
> His heart the moon, and his mind the great Lord Vishnu.
> Ram, the Supreme God, existing in all the forms of
>   this creation,
> Moving and unmoving, lives like a man amongst us.   (15A)

ˣ   The sons of the nymph, Ashvini are the Ashvins, the physicians of the gods.

Considering this, listen to me, lord of my life,
And set aside enmity with the Lord.
Devote yourself to Raghubir's feet,
So that my wedded state may never end.'   (15B)

Ravan laughed when he heard his wife's words, and said,
'Ah, great indeed is the power of worldly attachment!
Truly do they say of a woman's nature
That eight faults ever abide in her heart—
Foolhardiness, falsehood, fickleness, deceit,
Cowardice, ignorance, impurity and callousness.
You have praised the enemy's form as manifest in the glory of
     the universe,
And told me terrifying tales.
But all that embodied in his cosmic form, beloved, is inherently
     under my sway—
I understand it now by your grace.
I know well your cleverness, my beloved—
This is how you proclaim my power.
Your words, my doe-eyed one, are abstruse—
Pleasing once understood, though causing fear when
     heard.'
Mandodari came to the firm conclusion
That her husband, in the grip of fate, had lost his mind.

While Ravan was thus engaged in various pleasures,
Dawn came.
The inherently fearless king of Lanka then
Went to his council chamber, blinded by pride.   (16A)

The cane neither flowers nor bears fruit,
Though the clouds rain nectar upon it.
So a fool never knows wisdom,
Though he find a guru like Viranchi.   (16B)

Here, at dawn, Raghurai awoke,
And summoning all his counsellors, asked their opinion,
'Tell me quickly, what must we do now?'
Jamvant, bowing his head at his feet, said,
'Listen, all-knowing one, you who reside in the hearts of all,
The aggregation of wisdom, strength, majesty, righteousness and virtue,
I advise you according to my understanding—
Send Baali's son, Angad, as your messenger.'
'This is good counsel,' agreed all,
And the abode of mercy said to Angad,
'Son of Baali, abode of wisdom, might and virtue,
Go to Lanka, my son, for my purpose.
What lengthy instructions can I give you?
I know that you are extremely clever and wise.
Speak with the enemy in such a way
That our purpose is accomplished and he benefits too.'

> Obedient to the Lord's command,
> Angad touched his feet and stood up.
> 'He alone is an ocean of virtue
> Upon whom you shower your grace, divine Ram.   (17A)

> Your every purpose is accomplished of its own accord, Lord—
> Yet you have given me this honour!'
> Thinking thus, Prince Angad
> Was overwhelmed with joy.   (17B)

Paying homage to his feet, and holding the Lord's majesty in heart,
Angad bowed his head to all and went forth,
The Lord's glory in his heart, innately fearless,
Skilled in battle, Baali's valiant son.
As he entered the city, he ran into Ravan's son,
Prahast, who was playing there.
In an instant, their hostility flared up—

Both were of unequalled strength and also youthful.
Prahast raised his foot to kick Angad,
Who grabbed him by it, swung him round and dashed him to
    the ground.
The crowd of demons, seeing a formidable hero,
Scattered and ran, too afraid to even give the alarm.
They did not speak to each other of what had happened,
But remained silent, knowing that the prince had been killed.
A great cry arose in the city,
'The monkey who set Lanka ablaze has come again!'
Deeply afraid, all wondered
What providence would do next!
They showed him the way without his asking,
And those he glanced at turned pale with fright.

    Then, thinking of Ram's lotus feet,
    He reached the door of Ravan's council chamber,
    And with a lion's swagger, he glanced here and there,
    That mighty and steadfast hero.   (18)

He at once sent one of the demons
To give Ravan the news of his coming.
On hearing it, Dashashish laughed and said,
'Go, bring him here—let's see where this monkey is from.'
At his command, several messengers rushed away,
And fetched the monkey, huge as an elephant, into his presence.
Angad saw Dashanan seated
Like a black mountain imbued with life.
His arms were as massive as trees, his heads like mountain peaks,
The lines of hair on his chest like numerous vines,
And his lips, nose, eyes and ears
Like mountain caves and caverns.
He entered Ravan's court without the slightest hesitation,
That mighty and valiant son of Baali.

The assembled ministers all stood up at the sight of the monkey,
And Ravan's heart filled with immense anger.

> Just as a lion walks fearlessly into the midst
> Of a herd of elephants in rut,
> So did Angad, invoking Ram's glory in his heart,
> Bow to the assembly and take a seat there.   (19)

Said Dashkanth, 'Who are you, monkey?'
'I am Raghubir's envoy, Dashkandhar.
My father and you were friends,
And so it is for your good, brother, that I have come.
Yours is a noble family, and you are Pulastya's grandson.
You have worshipped Shiv and Viranchi in many ways,
Obtained boons from them, and accomplished all your objectives.
You have conquered the guardians of the quarters and all the
      earthly kings.
Through kingly arrogance, or in the grip of delusion,
You have stolen away Sita, the mother of the world.
Now listen to my advice, which is for your benefit,
And the Lord will forgive all your offences.
Hold a twig in your teeth and an axe to your throat,
And with your kinsmen and your own wife,
Placing Janak's daughter respectfully at your head,
Go to him, abandoning all fear, and say,

> "Protector of those who seek refuge with you, O jewel of the
>   Raghu line,
> Save me, save me, now!"
> The Lord, upon hearing your words of distress,
> Will relieve you of your fear.'   (20)

'Ho, you son of a monkey, be careful what you say!
Fool, did you not recognize me, the enemy of the gods?

Tell me your own name and your father's, fellow.
Through what relation do you claim friendship?'
'My name is Angad, and I am Baali's son—
Have you ever met him?'
Ravan flinched upon hearing Angad's words, but said,
'There was a monkey called Baali, I recall,
But Angad, are you Baali's son?
Destroyer of your clan, you are the fire that will burn down the
     bamboo grove of your lineage!
Why did you not perish in the womb? You have been born in vain—
That you, with your own mouth, should call yourself an
     ascetic's envoy!
Now tell me, is all well with Baali, and if so, where is he?'
Then Angad, laughing, replied,
'Ten days from today, go yourself to Baali,
Clasp your friend to your heart, and ask him about his well-being.
He will tell you all about the kind of
Well-being that results from opposition to Ram.
Listen, fool, dissension can be caused only in the minds of those
Who have no love for Lord Raghubir in their hearts.

     In truth, I am the destroyer of my clan,
     And you, Dashashish, the preserver of yours!
     Even the blind and the deaf don't say this—
     And you have twenty eyes and ears!   (21)

He whose feet Shiv, Viranchi, and the company
Of gods and munis wish to serve—
Have I, by being his messenger, disgraced my family?
Despite holding such notions, why does your heart not burst?'
Upon hearing the monkey's harsh and fierce words,
Dashanan glared at him and said,
'Wretch, I endure all your rough and insolent words,
For I know the rules of statecraft and decorum.'

The monkey replied, 'Yes, I have heard of your statesmanship
    and decorum—
You have stolen away another man's wife!
And I have seen with my eyes how you safeguard messengers!
How have you not died of shame yet, you upholder of
    righteousness?
You saw your sister without her ears and nose,
And forgave, with righteousness in mind!
Your piety and virtue are known throughout the world,
And I am exceedingly blessed in having seen you!'

    'Do not talk nonsense, you stupid animal!
    Foolish monkey, look at my arms,
    All Rahus that have eclipsed the full moons
    That are the mighty guardians of the quarters!   (22A)

    And resting upon the palms of my many lotus hands,
    Kailash with Shambhu
    Had looked as lovely as a swan
    Upon the lake of the sky!   (22B)

Tell me, Angad, in all your army,
Which warrior will dare confront me?
Your master has lost his strength in his grief of separation from
    his woman,
And his younger brother is sad and sorrowful in his grief.
You and Sugriv are like two trees on the banks of a river, and will
    be easily washed away.
As for my younger brother, he is an utter coward.
The minister, Jamvant, is very old—
He cannot stand in battle now.
And Nal and Nil are mere masons.
Yes, there is one monkey of great power and might—
He who came first and set fire to the city.'

Hearing his words, the son of Baali replied,
'Speak the truth, king of the demons,
Did a monkey really burn down your city?
"A little monkey burnt down Ravan's city"—
Who will say these words are true?
The one you praise as a great and noble champion, Ravan,
Is only one of Sugriv's insignificant runners.
He runs long distances, but he is no warrior—
We only sent him to get news.

Did that monkey truly burn down your city
Without receiving any orders from his master?
This is why he did not return to Sugriv,
But remained hidden out of fear.   (23A)

All that you say, Dashkanth, is true,
And I am not at all angry upon hearing it.
There is no one in our army
Who will find glory in fighting you.   (23B)

Make friends and enemies only with your equals—
That is prudent and right.
If the king of beasts were to slay frogs,
Would anyone speak well of him?   (23C)

Even if it be inglorious of Ram to kill you,
And he incurs great blame,
Even then, listen O Dashkanth,
The wrath of the Kshatriyas is terrible.'   (23D)

With sarcasm as his bow and words for his arrows,
The monkey set ablaze the enemy's heart.
With the pincers of his retorts and rejoinders
The ten-headed hero pulled out the barbs.   (23E)

Then, laughing, ten-headed Ravan said,
'A monkey has one great quality—
It will do everything it can to serve
The man who nurtures and protects it.   (23F)

Fortunate is the monkey who, for his master's purpose,
Dances here, there and everywhere without shame.
Prancing and leaping to entertain people,
It serves its master. This is the culmination of its duty.
Angad, your kind are devoted to their masters,
So how could you not have praised your lord as you have done?
I appreciate merit and am exceedingly good-natured,
So I pay no heed to your rude and bitter chatter.'
Said the monkey, 'Your appreciation of merit—
The Wind's son told me the truth of that.
He laid waste your grove, killed your son, burnt down your city,
But even then you believed he did you no harm.
It was considering this generous nature of yours,
Dashkandhar, that I have been so bold and impudent.
I have now seen for myself what Hanuman had told me—
You feel no shame, no anger, nor any resentment.'
'It is because you think this way, monkey, that you proved to be
          your father's death.'
Saying these words, the ten-headed one laughed.
'Having consumed my father, I would have killed you next,
But another thought has just occurred to me—
Knowing you to be the cause of Baali's untainted fame,
I will not kill you, you arrogant wretch.
Tell me, Ravan, how many Ravans are there in this world?
Or listen while I tell you the ones I have heard of—
One went to Patal to conquer Bali, king of the underworld,
Where children tied him up and kept him in the stables.
The boys beat him in play,
Till Bali took pity on him and let him go.

Another one was spotted by Sahasrabahu,
Who ran and captured him as though he were a strange animal,
And finding him to be a curious spectacle, took him home—
The sage Pulastya then went and had him released.

> And one, I feel greatly abashed to say,
> Was held tight under my father, Baali's, armpit.
> Which amongst these are you, Ravan?
> Tell me the truth, without anger.'					(24)

'Listen, fool, I am that same mighty Ravan,
The miraculous doings of whose arms is known to Har's mountain,
Whose valour is known to Uma's beloved lord,
In whose worship I have offered my heads as flowers.
I have, with my own hands, taken off the lotuses of my heads
Countless times to worship Tripurari.
The guardians of the quarters know the might of my arms,
Which is like a thorn in their hearts even today, you fool.
The elephants who hold up the earth know the hardness of my chest,
Whose formidable tusks, whenever I closed with them in combat,
Made not the slightest impression upon it,
But snapped off like radishes as they struck against it.
He, at whose moving the earth rocks
Like a small boat when a mast elephant steps into it,
I am that same Ravan, whose glory is famed throughout the world!
Did you never hear of him, you lying chatterer?

> That is the Ravan you belittle
> And exalt a mere man!
> You savage, rude, vile and wicked monkey,
> Now I understand your wisdom!'					(25)

Hearing these words, Angad angrily replied,
'Speak with care, you vile braggart.

How can he be a mortal man, you ten-headed wretch,
Beholding whom Parashuram's arrogance fled—
That same Parashuram whose axe was like a fire
That burnt down the boundless forest of Sahasrabahu's arms,
Or like the sharp, swift tide of the sea
In which countless kings drowned again and again?
How can Ram be a mere man, you arrogant fool?
Is Kamdev a mere bowman, or the Ganga only a river?
Is the divine Kamadhenu a mere beast, and the Kalpataru only a tree?
Is the gift of food just any gift, or nectar an ordinary drink?
Is Vainateya just a bird, thousand-headed Shesh only a snake,
And the wish-granting Chintamani merely a stone, Dashanan?
Listen, you dull-witted fool, is Vaikuntha just any world,
And unceasing devotion to Raghupati an ordinary blessing?

> And Hanuman, who trampled your pride and that of
>   your army's,
> Laid waste your grove, burnt down your city—
> Is he, fool, a mere monkey,
> Who returned home unharmed after killing your son?   (26)

Listen, Ravan, give up deceit.
Why do you not worship the ocean of mercy, Raghurai?
If you, wretch, remain Ram's enemy,
Neither Brahma nor Rudra can protect you.
Fool, do not brag and boast in vain.
If you fight with Ram, this will be your state—
Struck by Ram's arrows, your multiple heads
Will fall to the ground in front of the monkeys,
And using your heads like so many balls,
The bears and monkeys will play chaugan[3] with them.
When Ram grows wrathful in battle,
His arrows fly thick and terrible.
Will your boasting then still prevail?

Reflect on this and worship Ram, who is generous and forgiving.'
Hearing Angad's words, Ravan flared up anew,
Like a blazing fire upon which ghee has been poured.

> 'I have a brother like Kumbhakaran,
> And my son is the renowned Meghnad, vanquisher of Indra!
> And have you not heard of my valour,
> By which I conquered all creation, moving and
>   unmoving?   (27)

With the help of tree-dwelling monkeys, fool,
Ram bridged the sea—and that is his power and glory?
Countless birds also cross the ocean,
But listen, monkey, that doesn't make them heroes!
My arms are seas brimming over with the tides of strength,
In which have drowned innumerable gods, men and demons.
Who is there so valiant who can cross
These twenty oceans, deep and vast?
I have made the guardians of the quarters draw water for me,
And you tell me about some mere mortal king's glory, wretch?
If that master of yours, whose glory you recount again and again,
Is truly valiant in battle,
Then why does he need to send a messenger?
Is he not ashamed to make alliance with his enemy?
Look at my arms, which lifted and shook Har's mountain,
And then, foolish monkey, praise, if you will, your master to me!

> What hero is as valiant as Ravan,
> Who cut off his heads with his own hands,
> And joyously gave them as offerings to the sacrificial fire
> Countless times—as Gauri's lord is witness!   (28)

When, as my heads burnt, I saw
The letters written upon my brow by Vidhi,

And read that I would be killed by a man,
I laughed, knowing that Vidhi's words were untrue.
Remembering this, I have no fear—
Old Viranchi wrote this with his mind confused by age.
And yet, fool, casting aside all modesty and decorum,
You praise again and again another hero's might in my
    presence!'
Replied Angad, 'In this world, Ravan,
There is none so modest as you.
Modesty is innate in you—
Never do you, with your own tongue, praise yourself.
The story of your heads and the mountain is constantly in
    your mind,
Which is why you have told it me twenty times!
And the strength of your arms by which you defeated Sahasrabahu,
    Bali, and Baali—
Those tales you have kept hidden in your heart.
Listen, dimwit, now end this.
Does one become a hero by cutting off one's head?
No one calls a magician brave,
Though he cuts up his whole body with his own hands!

    Moths, overcome by delusion, burn themselves to death
    And herds of donkeys carry heavy loads,
    But they are not called heroic or valiant—
    Think, idiot, and understand!   (29)

Now stop arguing, wretch,
And listen to my words without arrogance.
Dashmukh, I have not come here as an envoy to propose
    an alliance.
Raghubir has sent me here with a different motive.
The merciful one often says
That a lion earns no glory by killing a jackal.

Keeping those words of my Lord in my heart,
I have tolerated, fool, your rude and discourteous words.
Otherwise I would have broken your head,
And forcibly taken away Sita.
I had the measure of your might, vile enemy of the gods,
When you stole away another's wife when she was all alone.
You are the king of the demons and very haughty,
While I am only a messenger of one of Raghupati's servants.
But if I were not afraid of displeasing Ram,
I would have wrought this wonder even as you watched.

> After dashing you to the ground, routing your army,
> And destroying your town, fool,
> I would have taken away Janak's daughter,
> With all your women and wives. (30)

Were I to do so, though, I would gain no glory,
For there is no valour in killing those already dead.
One of heretical views, one in the grip of lust, a miser, or a fool,
One exceedingly poor, of bad repute, or extremely aged,
One who is always ill, or perpetually angry,
One hostile to Vishnu, or opposed to the Vedas and the saints,
One who pampers only his body, or defames others, or in whom
    resides every sin—
These fourteen kinds of beings are like corpses even when alive.
Reflecting thus, I do not kill you, wretch.
So now don't make me angry.'
On hearing this, the lord of the demons grew furious—
He bared his teeth and rubbed his hands, and snarled,
'You wretched monkey! It seems you are now determined to die,
For you speak big words from a tiny mouth!
He, by whose strength, stupid monkey, you so fiercely gibber
    and chatter,
Has no might, no power, no wit, nor glory.

Finding him bereft of good qualities or self-respect,
His father exiled him to the forest.
This sorrow and the grief of separation from his young wife
    weigh heavily upon him—
And then, terror of me oppresses him night and day.   (31A)

He of whose might you are so proud,
There are many men like him—
We demons devour them day and night.
Stop being so stubborn, fool, and understand what
    I say.'   (31B)

When he thus disparaged Ram,
The monkey prince was furious.
He who listens to attacks upon Hari and Har,
Incurs sin equal to that of killing a cow.
The monkey, huge as an elephant, gnashed his teeth in fury,
And, flying into a terrible rage, struck the earth with both his
    mighty arms.
The earth swayed and shook. The ministers, thrown out of their seats,
Fled, carried off on the winds of fear.
Dashkandhar steadied himself and stood up.
His magnificent crowns lay upon the ground—
Some he picked up and set upon his heads,
Some Angad threw towards the Lord.
When they saw the crowns come flying through the air, the
    monkeys ran away, crying,
'Are stars falling during the day, dear God?
Or has Ravan in his anger released
Four thunderbolts that come with such great speed?
The Lord smiled and said, 'Do not be afraid,
These are not stars or thunderbolts, nor even Ketu or Rahu.
These are ten-headed Ravan's crowns,
Which come here sent by Baali's son.

The Wind's son leapt and caught them in his hand,
And brought and placed them before the Lord.
The bears and monkeys gazed at them in wonder,
For their brilliance was like that of the sun.   (32A)

And in his court the furious Dashanan
Cried angrily to all,
'Seize the monkey, seize and kill him!'
Hearing this, Angad smiled.   (32B)

'Kill him and then run quickly, all you great warriors,
And devour every bear and monkey wherever you find them.
Go, clear this earth of monkeys,
And capture those two ascetic brothers alive!'
Then Prince Angad angrily said,
'Are you not ashamed to brag and bluster thus?
Cut your throat and die, you shameless destroyer of your
     own clan!
Does your heart not burst upon seeing my might?
You villainous woman-stealer!
Aggregate of everything evil and impure! You lustful dimwit!
You babble vile and vicious words as though delirious—
Death has you in its grip, you vile, man-eating Rakshasa!
The fruit of this you will receive in the future,
When you feel the blows of the monkeys and bears.
Calling Ram a mortal man—
How do your tongues not fall off?
But—and of this there is no doubt—your tongues will fall off,
Along with your heads, upon the field of battle.

Is he a mere man, Dashkandhar,
He who slew Baali with a single shaft?
For all your twenty eyes you are still blind.
Cursed be your birth, you base-born fool!   (33A)

Ram's arrows are thirsty,
Longing for your blood.
I spare you only for fear of him,
You vile and bitter-tongued demon!   (33B)

I am capable of breaking your teeth,
But Raghunayak has not given me permission.
I am so furious I could break all your ten heads,
And picking up Lanka, sink it into the sea.
Your Lanka is like the fruit of the wild fig tree,
And you the unsuspecting insect that lives in its centre.
I am a monkey, I would have devoured this fruit in an instant,
But the gracious Ram did not give me the command.'
Ravan smiled to hear his clever metaphor,
'Fool, where did you learn to tell such falsehoods?
Baali never bragged or blustered thus!
Associating with the ascetics, you have become a liar!'
'I am truly a liar, twenty-armed one,
If I do not pull out your ten tongues!'
Remembering Ram's majesty, the monkey grew furious,
And determinedly planted his foot in the middle of the assembly.
'If you can move my foot, you fool,
Ram will go back, and I will give up Sita.'
'Hear that, you brave warriors all!' cried the ten-headed one.
'Grab his foot and dash the monkey to the ground!'
Indrajit and other mighty warriors
Rose up, rejoicing, wherever they sat,
And fell upon him using all their great strength,
But his foot did not move, and they sat back down with bowed heads.
Again those enemies of the gods rose up and fell upon him,
But could not move the monkey's foot in the same way
That one devoted to worldly pleasures, Uragari,[xi]
Cannot uproot the tree of delusion.

[xi] 'Devourer of snakes', i.e., Garud

Countless warriors as mighty as Meghnad
Rose up rejoicing.
Try as they might, they could not move the monkey's foot,
But sat down again, heads bowed in defeat.   (34A)

The monkey's foot would not leave the ground
In the same way that the heart of a holy man,
Despite countless obstacles, will not give up righteousness.
Seeing this, the enemy's pride was broken.   (34B)

Seeing the monkey's strength, all lost heart.
Upon being challenged by the monkey, Ravan himself rose,
And as he reached out to grasp his foot, Baali's son said,
'You won't find deliverance in grabbing my foot.
Why don't you go and clasp Ram's foot, fool?'
At this, Ravan turned away, deeply mortified.
He lost his majesty, and all his splendour left him,
As when the moon shines faintly at midday.
He sat upon his throne with bowed head,
As though he had lost all his riches.
Ram is the spirit of the universe, the lord of life—
Can one hostile to him ever find peace?
Uma, at the play of Ram's brows
The universe comes into existence and is again dissolved.
He can turn a blade of grass into a thunderbolt, and a thunderbolt
    into a blade of grass—
So how could his ambassador's challenge fail?
Then the monkey explained righteousness and right policy to him
    in many ways,
But Ravan would not listen for his death had drawn near.
Having crushed the enemy's pride and recounted the glory of
    his Lord,
King Baali's son departed with these words:
'Till I kill you on the battlefield in play,
Why do I bother to praise myself?'

Ravan was already stricken with grief, when he had heard
That the monkey had killed his son.
Now the demons, upon witnessing Angad's challenge,
Grew even more distraught.

     Having crushed the enemy's power, the mighty monkey,
     Baali's son,
     His body trembling, his eyes full of tears,
     Rejoicing, clasped Ram's lotus feet.   (35A)

     Perceiving that it was evening, Dashkandhar
     Returned sadly to his palace.
     Mandodari again reasoned
     With Ravan and said,   (35B)

'Think, dear husband, and give up this foolishness,
War with Raghupati does not become you.
Ram's younger brother drew a little line—[4]
You could not cross even that, such is your valour.
Beloved, can you conquer him in battle
Whose messenger performed such a feat?
Leaping across the ocean in sport, that monkey
Like a fearless lion entered your Lanka,
Killed your guards, laid waste your orchard,
Slew your son Aksh even as you watched,
And setting fire to the whole city, reduced it to ashes.
Where was your pride of power then?
Now husband, desist from idle boasts,
And think a little on what I have said.
Husband, do not take Raghupati to be an ordinary king,
But know him to be the master of all creation, moving and
     unmoving, and of unequalled might.
Marich, too, knew the power of his arrows,
But you did not listen even to him.
In Janak's assembly had gathered countless kings—

You too were there, with your enormous and unmatched strength.
There, he broke Shiv's bow and married Janaki—
Why did you not vanquish him in battle then?
Indra's son also felt a little of his might—
Ram caught him but let him live, only putting out his eye.
You also saw Supnakha's condition,
Yet your heart remains unabashed.

He who slew Viradh, and Khar and Dushan,
Killed Kabandh in sport,
And dispatched Baali with a single shaft—
Recognize him, Dashkandh!   (36)

He who bridged the ocean in play,
And crossed over with his army to Suvela,
That same merciful Lord, the banner of the solar line,
Out of consideration for you, sent an envoy,
Who trampled upon your might in the midst of your assembly,
Like a lion in the midst of a herd of elephants.
His servants are Angad and Hanuman,
Both distinguished heroes, unequalled in battle—
And yet, my beloved, you persist in speaking of him as a man.
In vain do you bear the burden of arrogance, ego and pride.
Ah dear husband, you have chosen strife with Ram—
You are in the clutches of your own doom, and wisdom cannot
    awaken in your mind.
Fate does not strike anyone with a stick,
But merely robs one of piety, strength, wisdom and good sense.
He whose doom draws near, my lord,
Becomes lost and confused, just as you are now.

Two of your sons have been killed, your city burnt—
Even now, beloved, make an end of this.
Worship Raghunath, the ocean of mercy,
And so win untarnished fame, my lord.'   (37)

Ravan heard out his wife's speech as sharp as an arrow,
And left for his assembly as soon as it was dawn.
He took his seat upon his throne, puffed up with pride,
All his fears and terror forgotten.
Here, on Suvela, Ram summoned Angad,
Who came and bowed his head at his lotus feet.
But the kind and compassionate Kharari seated him by his side
With great courtesy, and smiling said,
'Son of Baali, I am full of curiosity,
So answer truthfully, dear son, to what I ask you.
Ravan is the glory of the Rakshasa race,
And the unparalleled might of his arms is renowned throughout
    the world.
Yet you threw me four of his crowns.
Tell me, son, how did you get hold of them?'
'Listen, omniscient one, you who bestow bliss upon the suppliant,
They were not crowns, but the four prerogatives of a sovereign—
Conciliation, concession, coercion and dissension,
Which abide in the heart of a king. So declare the Vedas, sire.
These are the four noble pedestals upon which stand righteousness
    and duty—
Knowing this in their hearts, they came, master, of their own
    accord to you.

    Devoid of piety, hostile to the Lord's feet,
    And in the clutches of his own doom is the
        ten-headed one.
    And so those royal prerogatives abandoned him
    And came to you, O Koshal's king.'   (38A)

    Hearing his very clever reply,
    The gracious Ram began to laugh.
    Baali's son then related to him
    All the news from the fort.   (38B)

When Ram had heard his report about the enemy,
He called all his ministers to draw near.
'Lanka has four great gates—
Think by what means we may breach them.'
Then Sugriv, king of the monkeys, Jamvant, king of the bears, and
    Vibhishan
Invoked the jewel of the solar line in their hearts,
And after consulting each other decided upon a firm plan.
They divided the monkey army into four companies,
And appointed suitable commanders for each.
Then, summoning all the commanders,
And praising the Lord's might, gave them their orders,
Upon hearing which, the monkeys rushed forward, roaring
    like lions.
Rejoicing, they bowed their heads at Ram's feet,
And then, armed with mountain peaks, the heroes rushed forth.
With thunderous shouts of 'Victory to Raghubir, Koshal's king!'
The bears and monkeys taunted the enemy.
Though they knew that Lanka was the most formidable of forts,
The monkeys proceeded undaunted, secure in the strength of
    their Lord.
Massing like clouds in every direction, they surrounded Lanka on
    all four sides,
With a roar like that of war drums.

'Victory to Ram, victory to Lakshman,
Glory to the monkey king, Sugriv!'
Thus like lions they roared,
Those mighty monkeys and bears.   (39)

Confusion and turmoil broke out in Lanka.
Hearing the uproar, Ravan in his great arrogance said,
'Look how bold these monkeys are!'
And laughing, summoned his demon host.

'These monkeys have come here, impelled by Death.
All my demons were hungry,'—
So saying, the wretch laughed loudly—
'And God has sent food to their doorsteps!
Brave warriors all, set forth in every direction,
Seize those bears and monkeys, and devour them all!'
Uma, this arrogance of Ravan's
Was like the tittibh bird's, which sleeps with its legs in the air and
     thinks that they support the sky.
Receiving their orders, the demons set forth,
Armed with slings and sturdy spears,
Cudgels, clubs and fierce battle-axes,
Lances, swords, bludgeons and boulders.
Like stupid carrion-eating birds that see
A pile of red rubies and swoop down upon it,
The agony of broken beaks not having occurred to them—
So did these foolish man-eaters rush forth.

     With bows and arrows and weapons of every description,
     Millions upon millions of Rakshasa warriors,
     Valiant, strong, resolute in battle,
     Climbed up on to the walls and battlements of Lanka.   (40)

They looked upon those walls and battlements
Like dark clouds hanging on Sumeru's summit.
War drums sounded,
And, hearing their beat, the hearts of the warriors were stirred
     to battle.
Countless trumpets and bugles brayed,
And, at their sound, the hearts of cowards cracked.
The demons saw the monkey host,
The valiant bear and monkey heroes, each of enormous size.
They rushed on, considering the uneven valleys and steep mountain
     passes of no account,

Tearing down boulders and clearing a path for themselves.
Millions of warriors gnashed their teeth,
Snarling, threatening, roaring,
There calling upon Ravan, and here upon Ram.
Amidst cries of 'Victory, victory!' the battle began.
The demons rained down boulders as huge as mountain peaks,
The monkeys leapt up and caught them, and hurled them
   back again.

Seizing the massive rocks and boulders,
The monkeys and bears hurled them back at the fort.
Jumping upon the demons, they grabbed them by the leg and dashed
   them to the ground,
Then, running off, they challenged and taunted them again.
Exceedingly nimble, youthful and strong, they climbed,
Bounding and leaping, to the top of the fort,
And entering palaces and mansions,
They sang Ram's praises everywhere.

   Then, each one seizing a demon,
   The monkeys ran back,
   And dropped to the ground from the walls of the fort,
   Crushing the demons beneath them.   (41)

Made strong by Ram's great power, the monkey troops
Crushed the horde of demon warriors.
Swarming up the fort once again, the monkeys shouted,
'Victory to Raghubir, as glorious as the sun!'
The demon host fled before them,
Like dark clouds before a strong wind.
Loud lamentation filled the city,
And children, the sick and women wailed and wept.
All came together in cursing Ravan,
Who, as king, had invited ruin.

When he heard of his own army's retreat,
Lanka's king angrily sent back his warriors into battle.
'If I hear of anyone running away from the battle,
I will kill him myself with my dreadful sword!
You consumed all my bounty, enjoyed every luxury,
And now on the field of battle, your lives have become so dear
        to you!'
On hearing his wrathful words, the warriors all grew afraid.
Chastened, they worked themselves up into battle fury and set
        forth again.
'To die in battle with his face to the foe is a hero's glory!'
        they thought,
And then gave up their greed to live.

Armed with many kinds of weapons, the valiant warriors
Closed with the enemy, challenging their foes again and again.
Striking them with clubs and tridents, they
Maddened the monkeys and bears.   (42)

Overcome by terror, the monkeys began to flee,
Even though, Uma, they were victorious in the end.
Said one, 'Where are Angad and Hanuman?
Where Nal and Nil, and the mighty Dwivid?'
When Hanuman heard that his army was in disarray,
The mighty hero was at the western gate.
There, Meghnad led the defence—
The gate so far had not been breached, and Hanuman was in
        great difficulty.
The heart of the Wind's son filled with rage,
And, with a terrible roar, that warrior, invincible as death,
Sprang up upon Lanka's fort,
And seizing an enormous rock, rushed at Meghnad,
Shattered his chariot, slew his charioteer,
And kicked him in the chest.

Another charioteer, seeing Meghnad in distress,
Threw him into his own chariot, and quickly brought him home.

When Angad heard that the Wind god's son
Had gone into the fort alone,
Then he too, Baali's son, so daring and intrepid in war,
Leapt up onto the walls of the fort, as easily as
      though in play.   (43)

The two monkeys swelled with battle-fury,
And invoked Ram's majesty in their hearts.
Then, springing to the top of Ravan's palace,
They loudly proclaimed the glory of Koshal's king.
They wrecked the palace with its domes and spires,
And seeing this, the king of the demons grew afraid.
The women all beat their breasts and wailed,
'Now two of these fierce and all-destroying monkeys have come!'
Angad and Hanuman terrified them with their monkey antics,
And proclaimed to them the glory of Ramchandra.
Then, each taking a golden pillar in his hands,
They said to each other, 'Let us now start the destruction.'
Roaring, they rushed into the midst of the enemy army,
And began to thrash and pound them, laying them low with their
    great strength of arm,
With here a kick and there a blow, and crying,
'You do not worship Ram, so here's the reward for that!'

They crushed the demons, one against another,
And snapped off their heads and hurled them away
So that they fell at Ravan's feet,
And smashed like pots of curds.   (44)

All of the great commanders they encountered,
They seized by their feet and threw them to the Lord.

Vibhishan told him their names,
And Ram gave even them a place in his abode.
Those vile man-eaters and devourers of the twice-born
Thus attained the state for which ascetics yearn.
Uma, Ram is soft-hearted and a mine of compassion—
He thought, 'These demons remembered me, albeit in enmity.'
And knowing this, he bestowed upon them the supreme state.
Tell me, Bhavani, who is as merciful as this?
Hearing of such a Lord, those men who do not cast off delusion
      and worship him,
Are dull-witted and exceedingly unfortunate.
'Angad and Hanuman have entered
The fort,' cried the lord of Avadh,
'And Lanka, with the two monkeys,
Is like the sea being churned by two Mount Mandars.'

            After crushing the enemy army,
            And seeing that the day was ending,
            The two leapt down effortlessly
            And returned into the presence of their Lord.   (45)

They bowed their heads at the lotus feet of the Lord,
And Raghupati was delighted to see the noble heroes again.
Ram looked with his grace upon them both,
So that their fatigue disappeared, and they were completely
      refreshed.
Perceiving that Angad and Hanuman had left the fort,
The other bear and monkey warriors also returned.
But the demons, gaining strength from the evening twilight,
Rushed to attack, crying, 'Victory to the ten-headed one!'
Seeing the demon army, the monkeys turned again,
And with gnashing teeth, warriors closed with each other everywhere—
Two mighty armies, their heroes challenging the enemy again
      and again,

Fighting their foes, and refusing to admit defeat.
The demons were all supremely valiant and black of hue,
The monkeys were of enormous size and of different colours.
Both armies were strong and powerful, their heroes
    equally matched—
They fought furiously, and showed off their prowess as warriors.
It was as though dense monsoon clouds and gathered
    autumn clouds
Battled each other, driven by the wind.
When the army commanders, Akampan and Atikaya,
Saw their legions wavering, they resorted to illusion,
So that in an instant, it became utterly dark,
And blood, stones and ashes began to rain down.

     Seeing the dense darkness all around,
     The monkey army grew alarmed.
     They could not see each other,
     And made a great outcry.   (46)

Raghunayak understood the mystery,
And summoning Angad and Hanuman,
Explained to them what was happening.
Hearing this, the two great monkeys rushed back in fury.
Then the merciful one laughed and strung his bow,
And at once let loose a fiery arrow.
Light blazed forth, no darkness remained anywhere,
As when enlightenment dawns and doubts disappear.
The bears and monkeys now had light,
And forgetting their fatigue and fear, rushed forth rejoicing.
Hanuman and Angad thundered aloud on the battlefield,
And hearing their furious roar, the demons fled.
The bears and monkeys seized the fleeing demon warriors,
And dashed them to the ground, performing spectacular feats
    of valour,

Or grabbing them by their feet, hurled them into the sea
Where crocodiles, serpents and fish snatched them up and
    ate them.

    Some were killed, some wounded,
    And some fled back to the fort.
    The bears and monkeys roared in jubilation
    At routing the mighty enemy host.   (47)

Seeing that it was now night, the four monkey divisions
Returned to the lord of Koshal.
Ram looked upon them all with his mercy,
And instantly the monkeys became free of fatigue.
In Lanka, Dashanan summoned his ministers,
And told them all of the valiant warriors who had been killed.
'The monkeys have wiped out half of our army.
So tell me quickly, what should we do?'
Malyavant, a very aged Rakshasa,
Who was Ravan's mother's father, and an important minister,
Spoke words that were prudent and pure.
'Listen, dear son, to a little of my advice.
From the moment that you stole Sita away and brought her here,
So many ill omens have occurred that they are beyond telling.
No one has ever attained any benefit by opposing Ram,
Whose glory has been sung by the Vedas and the Puranas.

    He who slew Hiranyaksh and his brother,[xii]
    And Madhu and mighty Kaitabh,
    That same compassionate God,
    Has descended amongst us as Ram.   (48A)

_____

[xii] The Daitya Hataklochan and his brother, Kanakakasipu

He who is Time incarnate, the fire that destroys the forest
    of wickedness,
The abode of all virtue, the embodiment of wisdom,
And the one whom Shiv and Viranchi serve—
What enmity can there be towards him?   (48B)

Stop fighting, give back Vaidehi,
And worship the abode of mercy, the supremely loving Lord.'
His words pierced Ravan like arrows,
'Blacken your face and get out of here, wretch!
You have grown old, or else I would have killed you.
Now do not show yourself to me again!'
Hearing his words, Malyavant came to the conclusion
That the all-merciful Ram now wanted to kill him.
Cursing Ravan, he rose and left.
Then Meghnad in a rage declared,
'Watch the spectacle I shall put on at dawn—
Whatever I say will be too little to describe what I will do!'
Hearing his son's words, Ravan's confidence returned,
And he seated him lovingly on his lap.
Day broke while they were still thus deliberating,
And the monkeys attacked the four gates again.
As the angry monkeys surrounded the impregnable fort,
A great commotion broke out in the city within.
Armed with weapons of every description, the demons
    rushed forth,
And hurled down rocks as huge as mountain tops from the
    ramparts of the fort.

They hurled down thousands of rocks like mountain peaks,
And missiles of every kind began to fly,
Thundering down like lightning bolts,
As warriors roared like the clouds of doom.
The enormous monkey warriors closed in combat with their foe—

Though wounded, their bodies hacked and broken, they did not fall back,
But picking up those mountain tops, hurled them at the fort,
And the demons died where they stood.

When Meghnad heard that the monkeys
Had again attacked the fort,
The valiant hero stepped out of the citadel,
And with a beating of drums, set forth to confront them.   (49)

'Where are the two brothers, the lords of Koshal,
Those archers renowned in all the spheres?
Where are Nal and Nil, Dwivid and Sugriv,
And Angad and Hanuman, the most mighty of all?
Where is Vibhishan, his own brother's enemy?
I will kill him and all the rest today!'
So saying, he made ready his terrible arrows,
And in his great rage, drew the string to his ear.
He began to fire volley upon volley of arrows
Which flew like multitudes of winged serpents.
Monkeys could be seen falling everywhere,
And none dared face him at that moment.
Bears and monkeys fled away in every direction,
And forgot all their desire for battle.
Not a single monkey or bear remained on the battlefield
Whose life he had not taken.

He struck them all with ten arrows each,
And the monkey warriors dropped to the ground.
The mighty Meghnad, resolute in war,
Roared in triumph like a lion.   (50)

Seeing the army in disarray, the Wind god's son
Was enraged and rushed forth like death incarnate.
He immediately uprooted a huge mountain,

And hurled it at Meghnad in great fury.
Seeing the rock hurtling towards him, Meghnad fled up into the sky,
Leaving his chariot, charioteer and horses, all to die.
Again and again Hanuman challenged him to fight,
But he would not come closer, for he knew the monkey's
       true strength.
Meghnad then approached Raghupati,
And hurled every foul word at him.
He threw at him arrows, daggers and weapons of every kind,
But the Lord cut them down as easily as in play and destroyed them.
Seeing Ram's power, the brute was infuriated,
And began to try all kinds of trickery and delusion,
Like one trifling with Garud
By trying to frighten him with a tiny snake.

    He whose mighty maya holds sway
    Over Shiv and Viranchi, over great and small—
    It was to him that that evil-minded demon
    Tried to show off his tricks and delusions!   (51)

Flying up into the sky, he rained down fire,
And streams of water sprang forth upon the earth.
Fiends and witches of various forms
Leapt and danced, crying, 'Kill him, maim him!'
Now he would rain down dung, pus, blood, hair and bones,
Now hurl down an avalanche of rocks and stones.
Then he rained down dust and made it so dark
That one could not see one's own hand spread out.
The monkeys grew uneasy at the sight of these illusions,
'We are all doomed if this keeps up!'
But Ram smiled to see the show,
And seeing that the monkeys were all terrified,
He destroyed the delusion with a single arrow,
Like the sun destroys deep darkness.

He glanced with compassion at the monkeys and bears,
And they, empowered by his glance, grew eager once more for battle.

> Taking Ram's permission,
> And accompanied by Angad and the other monkeys,
> Lakshman wrathfully set forth,
> Bow and arrows in hand—   (52)

With bloodshot eyes, broad chest and mighty arms,
And his fair-hued form shining like the snow-clad Himalaya
    tinged with red.
Dashanan, too, sent forth his best warriors,
Who rushed forth armed with weapons of every kind.
Bearing mountains, claws and trees as weapons,
The monkeys rushed forward, calling, 'Victory to Ram!'
The two armies closed, warrior to warrior, equally matched,
Each side equally determined to win.
Raining down blows and kicks, and biting with their teeth,
The monkeys, winning, beat and threatened, crying,
'Kill them, kill them, seize, seize and kill them!
Break their heads, tear out their limbs!'
Their shouts filled all the nine regions of the world,
And headless torsos full of fury rushed here and there.
Seeing this spectacle, the company of gods in the sky
Were filled sometimes with dismay, sometimes with joy.

> Blood filled and dried in every hollow on the ground,
> And dust hung in the air
> Like smoke from burning corpses
> Above the embers of funeral pyres.   (53)

The wounded warriors shone
Like kinshuk trees in full bloom.[5]
The two warriors, Lakshman and Meghnad,

Closed furiously in combat with each other.
Neither could win over the other,
And so the Rakshasa resorted to deceit and unfair means.
Then Lakshman, Anant[xiii] incarnate, became full of wrath,
And with a single blow broke Meghnad's chariot and killed his
    charioteer.
Shesh struck him in so many ways
That the Rakshasa had barely any life left in him.
Ravan's son came to the conclusion,
'I am in trouble, he will take my life!'
And let fly his hero-destroying spear—
Shining with power, it struck Lakshman in the chest.
Hit with that force, Lakshman fell unconscious.
Then Meghnad drew near, no longer afraid.

> Innumerable warriors as mighty as Meghnad
> Attempted to lift him,
> But could Shesh, the supporter of the universe,
> Be thus lifted? They returned, mortified.   (54)

Listen, Girija—the fire of whose wrath
Consumes in an instant the fourteen spheres—
Can anyone conquer him in battle,
He, whom gods, men and all creation, moving and unmoving, serve?
He alone can understand this mystery
Upon whom rests Ram's grace.
Dusk fell, and the two armies retired,
And the commanders called their scattered troops together.
The all-pervading Supreme Spirit, the compassionate
And invincible Lord of the universe asked, 'Where is Lakshman?'
By this time, Hanuman had carried him back from the battlefield.
Upon seeing his younger brother, the Lord grew intensely sorrowful.

[xiii] 'The infinite', another name for Sheshnag

Jamvant said, 'The physician, Sushen,
Lives in Lanka. Who should be sent to fetch him here?'
At once, Hanuman assumed his tiny form, and went
And brought him, house and all.

> Sushen came and bowed his head
> At Ram's lotus feet,
> And, giving him the name of a medicinal herb and the
>   mountain upon which it grew,
> Said to Hanuman, 'Go, son of the Wind, and bring
>   it here.'   (55)

With Ram's lotus feet in his heart,
The son of the Wind set forth resolutely.
On the enemy side, a spy disclosed this secret,
And Ravan went to Kalnemi's house.
The ten-headed one told Kalnemi, and hearing it,
Kalnemi beat his head again and again and cried,
'He who burnt down your city in front of your eyes—
Who can stop his path?
Do yourself a good turn—worship Raghupati,
And cease this foolish bluster, my lord!
Hold in your heart that lovely form,
As dark as the blue lotus, and the delight of all eyes.
Give up this foolishness of "I", "you", "mine",
And awaken from your sleep in the night of deep delusion.
He who devours the serpent that is Time—
Can anyone conquer him, even in dream?'

> Hearing this, Dashkanth grew furious,
> And Kalnemi thought to himself,
> 'It will be better to die at the hands of Ram's messenger,
> Than to be killed by this scoundrel, who is steeped
>   in sin!'   (56)

So saying, he set off, and using his power of illusion, created
A lake, a temple and a beautiful garden by the wayside.
The Wind's son saw this charming retreat and thought,
'Let me ask the muni's permission and drink of the water so that
    my tiredness disappears.'
The Rakshasa was sitting there in fake hermit's attire,
Wishing to delude the messenger of the Lord of delusion himself.
The Wind's son went and bowed his head before him,
And the Rakshasa began to recite Ram's praises.
'A great war is raging between Ravan and Ram,
But Ram will win, of this there is no doubt.
I see all, my friend, while sitting here,
For my vision, untainted by ignorance or sin, is remarkably
    powerful and clear.'
Hanuman asked him for water, and he handed him his
    water-pot,
But the monkey said, 'My thirst will not be quenched by
    this little quantity of water.'
'Then go bathe in the lake and quickly return,
I will then give you a mantra, by which you will attain
    spiritual wisdom.'

As soon as the monkey stepped into the lake,
A female crocodile seized his foot in alarm.
He killed her, but she took on a celestial form,
And, mounting a chariot, rose up into the sky.   (57)

'Dear monkey, upon seeing you I have become free of all sin
And the great sage's curse has ended.
This is no muni but a dreadful demon—
Believe the truth of my words, monkey.'
The apsara left, uttering these words,
And the monkey returned to the demon.
'Muni, first take your guru's fee,

Then teach me the mantra!' he cried,
And, wrapping his tail around the demon's head, dashed him to
    the ground.
Dying, the Rakshasa revealed his true form,
And, calling 'Ram, Ram', gave up his life's breath.
Hanuman rejoiced to hear Ram's name and continued on
    his journey.
He found the mountain but could not identify the herb,
So, without another thought, he uprooted the mountain.
As he flew through the night sky holding the mountain,
The monkey passed over the city of Avadh.

    Bharat, seeing his vast form in the sky,
    Concluded that it was a demon,
    And, drawing his bow to his ear,
    Struck him with a headless shaft.   (58)

Hit by the arrow, Hanuman fell to the ground in a swoon
Calling, 'Ram! Ram! Raghunayak!' as he fell.
Hearing this dear name, Bharat rushed
At once to the monkey's side.
Seeing him hurt, he clasped the monkey to his bosom,
But though he tried in every way to revive him, he would not
    wake up.
Deeply grieved, his face full of sorrow,
And his eyes streaming with tears, he spoke.
'The same providence that alienated me from Ram
Has now given me this dreadful grief.
If in thought, word, and deed I have
True love for Ram's lotus feet,
And if Raghupati is graciously disposed to me,
May this monkey become free of all weariness and pain.'
Hearing these words, the monkey chief at once sat up,
And cried, 'Victory, victory, to Koshal's king!'

Bharat took the monkey and clasped him to his heart,
His body trembling, his eyes full of tears.
He could not contain his love within his heart
As he thought of Ram, the glory of the Raghu clan.   (59)

'Dear friend, tell me—is all well with Ram, the abode of bliss,
Our younger brother Lakshman, and mother Janaki?'
The monkey told him in brief all that had happened,
And hearing it, Bharat grew sad and began to lament,
'Ah Fate, why was I born into this world?
I have been of no help at all to the Lord!'
But realizing the unfitness of the moment, that valiant hero
Steadied himself and spoke once again to the monkey.
'Dear friend, you will be late reaching,
And your task will come to nothing once day breaks.
So climb onto my arrow with the mountain,
And I will send you straight to Ram, the abode of mercy.'
Hearing this, pride sprang up in the monkey's heart,
'How can his arrow fly with my weight?'
Then, reflecting upon Ram's power,
The monkey touched Bharat's feet, and spoke with folded hands.

'Holding your majesty in my heart, my lord,
I will travel swiftly.'
So saying, and receiving leave to depart,
Hanuman bowed at Bharat's feet and set off.   (60A)

And as he went, the Wind god's son
Praised again and again to himself,
Bharat's might of arm, his courtesy and goodness,
And his unbounded love for the Lord's feet.   (60B)

Meanwhile, Ram, gazing at Lakshman,
Spoke words befitting a mortal man,

'Half the night is gone and the monkey hasn't returned!'
Ram raised his brother, and clasped him to his heart.
'Brother, you could not bear to see me sad,
Your nature was always so tender and kind.
For my sake, you left father and mother,
And endured the forest, the cold, the heat and the wind.
Where is that love now, brother,
That you do not wake even upon hearing my grief-stricken
      words?
If I had known that I would lose my brother in the forest,
I would never have obeyed my father's command.
Sons, wealth, wives, houses and kinsfolk
Come and go again and again in this world,
But a real brother cannot be found more than once—
Reflect upon this and wake up, dear one.
Just as a bird is utterly wretched without its wings,
A cobra without its jewel, a noble elephant without its trunk,
So is my life without you, my brother.
If unfeeling fate keeps me alive,
With what face can I return to Avadh,
Having lost my dear brother for a woman's sake?
I would rather have endured disgrace in the world,
For the loss of a wife is no great loss in comparison to this.
Now both disgrace and grief for you, dear child,
My hard and cruel heart shall endure.
You were your mother's only son, dear brother,
The stay and support of her life.
She took you by the hand and entrusted you to me,
Believing that I was your greatest benefactor and would make you
      happy in every way.
What answer will I give her when I return?
Why don't you wake up, brother, and tell me what I should say?'
Thus greatly sorrowed the destroyer of sorrow,
And tears flowed from his lotus-petal eyes.

Uma, Raghurai is one and indivisible,
But ever compassionate to his devotees, he displayed the ways
    of mortals.

    Hearing the Lord's lament,
    The monkey hosts grew distraught,
    Till arrived Hanuman
    Like valour in the midst of pity.   (61)

Joyfully, Ram embraced Hanuman,
For the Lord is exceeding grateful and supremely wise.
The doctor then immediately applied the remedy,
And Lakshman cheerfully rose and sat up.
The Lord clasped his brother to his heart,
And all the bears and monkeys rejoiced.
Hanuman then took the physician back to Lanka
In the same way that he had brought him away.
Dashanan heard of this incident,
And beat his head again and again in great distress.
Deeply agitated, he went to his brother, Kumbhakaran,
And after much effort, succeeded in waking him.
The Rakshasa awoke and sat up, looking
As though death itself sat there in bodily form.
Kumbhakaran asked Ravan, 'Tell me, brother,
Why do you look so downcast?'
The arrogant Ravan told him the whole tale
Of how he had carried away Sita.
'Dear brother, the monkeys have killed all the demons,
And slain warrior after great warrior.
Durmukh, the man-devouring Narantak, and the enemy of the
    gods, Devantak,
The mighty warriors, Atikaya and Akampan,
And other champions like Mahodar,
Have all fallen upon the field of battle, all these steadfast heroes.'

Upon hearing Dashkandhar's words,
Kumbhakaran was infuriated.
'You carried off the mother of the universe,
And now, fool, you expect success!   (62)

You have not acted well, king of the demons!
Why come now to wake me?
Even now, dear brother, abandon pride
And adore Ram—and you will prosper.
Is Raghunayak a mortal man, ten-headed Ravan,
He who has servants like Hanuman?
Ah brother, you made a mistake
In not coming and telling me this before.
You have defied that Supreme Lord
Whom Shiv, Viranchi and the other gods serve.
The knowledge which Muni Narad once imparted to me,
I would have told you, but now the time has passed.
Now embrace me, brother, for the last time,
For I go to reward my eyes with the sight
Of the dark-hued Lord with the lotus eyes,
Who removes the three-fold anguish of the triple fires.'

Remembering Ram's beauty and perfection,
He was immersed in love for a moment.
Meanwhile, Ravan called for ten million pots
     of wine
And a great number of buffaloes.   (63)

After eating the buffaloes and drinking the wine,
Kumbhakaran roared like the crash of a lightning bolt,
And drunk with wine and flushed with battle frenzy,
He set forth from the fort, unaccompanied by any troops.
Seeing him, Vibhishan stepped forward,
And falling at his feet, called out his own name.

Kumbhakaran raised up his younger brother and clasped him to
　　his heart,
Pleased to learn that he was a devotee of Raghupati.
'Dear brother, Ravan kicked me
When I gave him advice that was for his own best good.
In that resentment I came to Raghupati,
And seeing me in distress, the Lord took me in his heart.'
'Listen, dear brother, Ravan is in the grip of doom
And will now not heed the best advice.
Blessed are you, blessed, Vibhishan,
You have become the ornament of the demon clan,
And made bright our whole lineage, brother,
By worshipping Ram, the ocean of beauty and bliss!

　　　Giving up deceit in thought, word and deed,
　　　Worship Ram, the resolute in battle.
　　　Now go—for in the grip of death, brother,
　　　I can no longer tell who is my own.'   (64)

At his brother's words, Vibhishan left
And went to Ram, the ornament of the three worlds.
'Lord, Kumbhakaran approaches, that warrior
Colossal as a mountain and steadfast in battle.'
The monkeys did not wait to hear more,
But rushed with cries of joy, those mighty warriors,
And uprooting trees and mountains,
Hurled them at him, gnashing their teeth in fury.
Tens of millions of mountain peaks, one after another,
Did the bears and monkeys hurl at him,
But neither did his spirit falter, nor did his body move from
　　its position—
He was like an elephant being pelted with seeds.
Then the Wind's son struck him with his fist,
So that he fell to the ground and beat his head in annoyance.

Rising again, he struck Hanumant,
Who spun round and fell to the ground.
He then hurled Nal and Nil to the ground,
And knocked down warriors on every side.
The monkey army began to flee and scatter,
So afraid and terrified that none dared face him.

> Rendering Angad and the other monkeys,
> Including Sugriv, unconscious,
> He tucked the king of the monkeys under his arm
> And went off, that culmination of unparalleled strength.   (65)

Uma, Raghupati enacts the part of a human being
In the same way that Garud might play with snakes.
He, by the mere raising of an eyebrow, can destroy Time itself—
So why then does he engage in such a war?
It is because the fame of it, when spread abroad, sanctifies the world,
And takes all men who sing of it across the ocean of this existence.
When the Wind's son recovered from his swoon, he awoke,
And began at once to search for Sugriv.
Sugriv, too, awoke from his swoon,
And slipped out from under Kumbhakaran's arm—who had
     believed him to be dead
And realized he had escaped only when he bit off his nose and ears—
And rose, roaring, into the sky.
Grabbing his foot, Kumbhakaran hurled him to the ground,
But swiftly Sugriv rose again and struck him,
And then returned to the Lord, that mighty hero,
Crying, 'Victory, victory to the most merciful God.'
Realizing that his nose and ears had been bitten off,
Kumbhakaran turned back, furious and distressed.
Seeing him thus—inherently frightening, and now without ears
     and nose—
The monkey troops were terrified.

'Victory, victory, victory to the jewel of the Raghu clan!'
Whooped the monkeys rushing forward,
And hurled at him all together
A hail of boulders and trees.   (66)

Kumbhakaran, steeped in the rage of battle,
Advanced upon them like furious death itself.
He caught and devoured millions upon millions of monkeys,
Like insects swallowed up by a mountain cave.
He caught and crushed tens of millions against his body,
And countless others he crushed between his palms and mixed with
    the dust on the ground,
While multitudes of the bears and monkeys he had swallowed
Poured out through his mouth and nose and ears and fled.
Drunk on the wine of war, the demon arrogantly
Devoured the whole world as though the Creator had offered it
    to him.
The monkey warriors all fled the battlefield and refused to return,
They could neither see with their eyes nor hear any call to rally.
When they heard that Kumbhakaran had scattered the
    monkey army,
The demon hosts rushed forth.
Ram saw his own army was in trouble,
And that enemy troops of every description had arrived.

'Listen, Sugriv, Vibhishan, Lakshman,
Rally your troops,
While I test the might of this wretch's army,'
Said the lotus-eyed one.   (67)

With his bow, Sarang, in his hand, and a quiver at his waist,
Raghunath set forth to destroy the enemy host.
First the Lord twanged his bow,
And the enemy troops were deafened by the sound.

Then the steadfast one let loose a hundred thousand arrows,
Which flew like black-winged serpents.
As the dreadful iron bolts flew everywhere,
The mighty demon warriors began to fall.
Feet, torsos, heads and limbs were severed,
And innumerable warriors were cut into a hundred pieces.
The wounded spun round and round and fell to the ground,
But, valiant warriors, they rose and joined the fight again.
Struck by the arrows, they roared like storm clouds,
And many ran away merely at the sight of those cruel shafts.
Torsos without heads rushed furiously around,
To cries of 'Seize! Seize! Kill! Kill!'

> In an instant, the Lord's arrows
> Cut down the fearsome demons.
> Then into Raghubir's quiver,
> All his arrows returned.   (68)

When Kumbhakaran saw for himself
That Ram had wiped out the demon army in an instant,
That mighty warrior grew exceedingly wrathful,
And let out a roar as deep and loud as a lion's.
Furious, he tore out mountains by their roots,
And hurled them at the mighty monkey warriors.
The Lord, seeing the enormous rocks coming,
Shattered them with his arrows to dust.
Raghunayak, wrathful, drew his bow again,
And let fly a great number of his fierce arrows.
They went through Kumbhakaran's body,
Like lightning through dense clouds.
The blood flowing from his black form shone like
Rivulets of ochre issuing forth from a black mountain.
Seeming him in distress, the bears and monkeys rushed forward—
But he laughed when they drew near.

With a tremendous roar
He caught millions upon millions of the monkeys
And, like an enormous elephant, dashed them to the ground,
Whilst invoking ten-headed Ravan. (69)

Crowds of bears and monkeys fled
Like herds of sheep at the sight of a wolf.
And as the monkeys and bears, Bhavani, fled
Distraught with fear, they cried out in their distress.
'This Rakshasa is like a famine
That wants to lay waste the land that is the monkey host!
O Ram! Kharari! Rain-bearing cloud of compassion!
Save us, protect us, you who relieve the sorrow of the suppliant!'
The instant he heard these piteous words, the divine Lord
Set forth, armed with his bow and arrows.
Pushing his army behind him,
The most mighty Ram marched forth full of anger.
Drawing his bow he fitted a hundred arrows to the string—
The shafts, loosed, disappeared into the demon's body.
Struck by the arrows, he rushed forward, full of rage—
The mountains swayed and the earth shook as he ran.
He pulled up a mountain by the root—
The glory of the Raghu clan cut off that arm of his.
He rushed forward with the enormous rock in his left hand—
But the Lord cut off that arm too, and it fell to the ground.
With his arms cut off, the Rakshasa looked
Like Mount Mandar without its wings.
Fiercely he glared at the Lord,
As though ready to devour the three worlds.

Giving a most dreadful yell,
He rushed forward with his mouth wide open,
So that the Siddhas and gods in the sky
Cried out piteously in terror. (70)

The abode of mercy, realizing that the gods were terrified,
Drew the string of his bow to his ear,
And filled the demon's mouth with arrows.
Even then, that mighty Rakshasa did not fall to the ground,
But, with his mouth full of arrows, rushed forward
Like Death's quiver endowed with life.
Then the Lord, full of anger, took a sharp arrow,
And separated his head from his body.
That head fell in front of the ten-headed one,
Who became as distraught as a cobra that has lost its jewel.
The earth sank beneath the weight of the terrible torso that still
        rushed about,
Till the Lord cut it in two.
The pieces fell upon the ground like two mountains from the sky,
Crushing beneath them monkeys, bears and demons.
His spirit entered the Lord's mouth,
Which gods, munis and all regarded a marvel.
The gods beat their drums, rejoicing,
And singing the Lord's praises, rained down flowers.
After paying him homage, the gods all departed,
And at that very moment, the divine rishi, Narad, arrived.
From high in the sky, he sang of Hari's perfections,
And his bright song of valour delighted the Lord's heart.
'Now quickly destroy that scoundrel,' said the muni and departed,
As Ram stood shining upon the field of battle.

Upon the battlefield shone Raghupati,
Of unequalled strength, the king of Koshal,
With beads of toil upon his face, his lotus eyes
Reddened, and body flecked with blood.
With both hands he toyed with his bow and arrows,
The bears and monkeys crowding all around him.
Even Shesh, who has countless tongues, cannot describe
His beauty—so says Tulsidas, his servant.

To that vile demon, accumulation of every impurity,
Did Ram give a place in his own abode.
Girija, dull-witted indeed are those men
Who do not worship the beautiful and gracious Ram.   (71)

At the end of the day the two armies turned back.
The day's battle had deeply wearied the warriors,
But by Ram's grace the strength of the monkey host was renewed
As a fire blazes up when fed with straw.
The demon numbers dwindled night and day,
Like the merit of one's good deeds diminishes when related by
    one's own lips.
Dashkandhar greatly lamented his brother's death,
Clasping his head again and again to his heart.
Women wept and beat their breasts with their hands,
Praising his immense majesty and might.
At that moment, Meghnad came,
And consoled his father with many tales.
'Watch my gallantry tomorrow—
How can I praise it just now?
I have received from Shiv, my chosen god, magical powers and
    a chariot,
Which, dear father, I have not yet shown you.'
While they bragged and blustered in this way, day broke,
And hordes of monkeys attacked the four gates.
On one side were the monkeys and bears, resolute as death,
On the other, the night-wandering demons, utterly steadfast in war.
The mighty heroes fought for victory, each for his own side—
The battle, O king of the birds, defies description.

    Meghnad mounted his magic chariot
    And rose up into the sky
    With a thunderous laugh
    That terrified the monkey host.   (72)

Spears, javelins, swords, knives,
Scimitars, battle-axes, hatchets, clubs, boulders—
He let fly weapons and missiles of every kind,
And then began to rain down arrows countless in number.
The sky was dark with arrows falling in every direction,
As though monsoon clouds in the month of Magh had brought
    incessant rain.
Cries of 'Seize, seize, kill!' filled every ear,
But no one could tell who it was that struck them!
Grabbing trees and mountains, the monkeys rushed up into the sky,
But they could not see him and fell back disappointed,
And Meghnad, with his magic powers, filled
Every crooked valley, path and mountain cave with arrows.
'Where do we run?' cried the monkeys in a panic,
All as helpless as Mount Mandar imprisoned by Indra.
Hanuman, Angad, Nil, Nal, and every mighty warrior,
Meghnad made uneasy with fear and dismay.
At Lakshman, Sugriv and Vibhishan,
He shot his arrows, piercing their bodies full of holes.
He then engaged with Raghupati himself,
And the arrows he loosed turned to snakes as they struck,
And he, the destroyer of Khar, eternal and immutable, and subject
    only to his own will,
Was overpowered by the serpents' coils.
Like a conjuror, he performs many delusive acts,
He, the One, the Absolute, the ever self-willed God.
It was to enhance the battle's glory that the Lord allowed himself
    to be bound
By the serpent snares, but the gods grew afraid.

    By repeating whose name, Girija,
    Munis sever the bonds of rebirth,
    Can he ever be brought into bondage,
    He, the all-pervading God, in whom dwells the Universe? (73)

The deeds of the incarnate Ram, Bhavani,
Cannot be understood by strength of intellect or discussion.
Thus reflecting, those ascetics who perceive his true nature
Adore him completely, without argument or analysis.
Meghnad threw the monkey army into confusion,
And then revealed himself, hurling imprecations.
Jamvant cried, 'Stay, you scoundrel!'
Hearing this, his fury increased.
'Knowing you to be old, fool, I let you be,
And now, vile wretch, you dare challenge me?'
So saying, he let fly a glittering trident.
Jamvant caught it in his hand, and, rushing forward,
Struck Meghnad with it on the chest
So that killer of gods reeled and fell to the ground.
Then, in his fury, he took him by the foot, and, swinging him around,
Dashed him to the ground, showing him his strength.
But as a result of the boon granted him, he did not die—[6]
So Jamvant seized him by the foot and tossed him into Lanka.
At this point, the divine rishi Narad sent Garud,
Who rushed at once to Ram's side.

> The lord of the birds caught and devoured
> The swarm of false serpents created by Meghnad's maya.
> Freed of delusion, the monkey troops
> All rejoiced.   (74A)

> Armed with mountains, trees, rocks and claws,
> The furious monkeys rushed forth.
> The demons retreated in utter confusion,
> And fled into the fort.   (74B)

Meanwhile, Meghnad awoke from his swoon,
And seeing his father there, felt deeply ashamed.
He went at once to a deep mountain cave,

Resolving to perform a sacred sacrifice for victory.
Meanwhile, Vibhishan, reflecting, gave Ram counsel,
'Hear me, O incomparably mighty and generous king.
Meghnad, that deceitful scoundrel and tormentor of the gods,
Is performing an unholy sacrifice.
If, Lord, he successfully completes it,
Sire, he will not be easy to overcome.'
Raghupati was greatly pleased to receive this information,
And summoning Angad and various other monkeys, he said,
'Go with Lakshman, all of you,
Destroy Meghnad's sacrifice.
And you, Lakshman, you must slay him in battle,
For it grieves me deeply to see the gods so terrified.
Kill him by means of your strength or your wit,
But make sure, brother, that the demon is destroyed.
Jamvant, Sugriv, Vibhishan,
Remain by his side, all three, with your troops.'
When Raghubir had completed his orders,
Lakshman, resolute in war, fastened his quiver at his waist and
    strung his bow,
And, holding the majesty of the Lord in his heart,
Spoke in a voice as deep as rumbling rainclouds.
'If I return today without slaying him,
May I be no longer called Raghupati's servant.
Even if a hundred Shankars help him,
I will kill him in Raghubir's name.'

Bowing his head at Raghupati's feet,
Anant set forth at once.
With him were Angad, Nil, Mayand, Nal
And the mighty warrior, Hanumant.   (75)

When the monkeys arrived, they saw him sitting there,
Making an offering of blood and buffaloes.

The monkeys destroyed the sacrificial ceremony,
But when he did not rise, they began to taunt him.
When he still did not stand up, they went up to him, and, grabbing
    him by the hair,
Kicked him again and again and ran away.
At this, he seized his trident and rushed at them, and the
    monkeys fled,
Leading him to where stood Ram's brother, Lakshman.
Driven by immense rage, he came on,
With deep and terrible roars.
Hanuman and Angad rushed at him in fury,
But he struck them on the breast with his trident, and threw them
    to the ground.
He let fly his terrible trident at the Lord,[7]
But Anant shot it with his arrow and broke it in two.
The Wind's son and the monkey prince rose up again,
And struck him again in fury, but their blows could do him
    no injury.
Despite their every effort, the enemy refused to die, and as the
    monkey warriors fell back,
Meghnad rushed at them with a dreadful shout.
Seeing him come, like Death enraged,
Lakshman let loose his fierce shafts.
At the sight of the arrows approaching like bolts of lightning,
The scoundrel at once became invisible.
He fought assuming diverse forms,
Sometimes revealing himself, sometimes disappearing.
Seeing their enemy undefeated, the monkeys were afraid.
Then Lakshman, the serpent king incarnate, grew exceedingly
    wrathful,
And firmly made up his mind,
'I have played with this sinner enough!'
Recalling the majesty of Koshal's king,
He haughtily fitted an arrow to his bow,

And let it fly—the arrow struck Meghnad in the centre of
    his breast,
And in the moment of his death, the Rakshasa gave up all deceit.

> Calling 'Where is Lakshman? Where is Ram?'
> He gave up his life's breath.
> 'Blessed, blessed is your mother!'
> Cried Angad and Hanuman.   (76)

Effortlessly, Hanuman picked him up,
And laying him down at Lanka's gate, returned.
When the gods and Gandharvas all heard of his death,
They mounted their chariots and gathered in the sky.
They rained down flowers and beat their drums,
And sang of Raghunath's unblemished fame.
'Victory to Anant, victory to the support of the universe!
Lord, you have delivered all the gods!' they cried.
After singing their songs of praise, the gods and Siddhas departed,
And Lakshman presented himself before the ocean of mercy.
When Dashanan heard of the slaying of his son,
He fainted and fell to the ground that instant.
Mandodari wept and wailed aloud,
Beating her breast and lamenting unceasingly.
The people of the city were distraught with grief,
And all declared Ravan a despicable wretch.

> Then the ten-headed one tried to console
> All his wives in every way he could.
> 'The whole universe is transitory—
> Consider, and realize this in your hearts.'   (77)

Ravan gave them wise counsel—
Though a wretch himself, his words were good and pure.
There are many who are good at giving advice to others,

But those who act in accordance with their own advice—such men
    are not many.
The night ended and day broke,
And the bears and monkeys again attacked the four gates.
Dashanan summoned his warriors and said,
'If there is anyone whose heart flinches at facing battle,
It is best that he runs away now,
For there is no virtue in turning and fleeing in the midst of
    the fight.
It is relying on the strength of my own arm that I have continued
    this war,
And I will take care of any enemy who attacks us.'
So saying he made ready his chariot, swift as the wind,
And all the musical instruments of war began to play.
The heroes, all of unequalled might, set forth
Like a raging storm of blackness.
Innumerable ill omens occurred at that time,
But he took no account of them, so great was his pride in the
    strength of his arm.

So great is his pride he does not heed the omens, good and bad.
Weapons slip from his hands,
Warriors fall from their chariots, and elephants
And horses break free and run away screaming.
Jackals, vultures, crows and donkeys call
And great packs of dogs loudly bark,
While owls, as though messengers of death,
Give their most terrifying cries.

Can one intent upon the destruction of created beings, in the
    grip of delusion,
Hostile to Ram, and devoted to the pleasures of the senses,
Expect prosperity, or omens of good fortune,
Or peace of mind, even in dream?   (78)

The vast demon force set forth,
A fourfold army, complete in all its divisions.
There were chariots and vehicles of every kind,
With banners and flags in many colours,
Innumerable battalions of furious elephants marching forward,
Like dark clouds driven by the wind in the rainy season,
And legion after legion of warriors, clad in uniforms of
    various colours,
Valiant in battle and well-versed in delusive tricks.
The magnificent demon host shone resplendent
As though heroic Spring had mustered his army.
As it marched forth, the elephants of the eight quarters
    stumbled,
The ocean seethed and mountains swayed,
Dust rose so that the sun was hidden,
The wind stopped, and the earth grew weary.
War drums beat with a dreadful sound,
Like the thundering of storm clouds on the final day.
Kettledrums, trumpets and clarinets played
Warlike music that pleased the warriors.
The heroes roared like lions all,
And each proclaimed his might and valour.
Said Dashanan, 'Hear me, noble warriors,
Pulverize the bear and monkey hordes,
And I myself will slay the princes, the two brothers!'
So saying, he ordered his army forward.
When the monkeys heard that his army was advancing,
They rushed forth to meet it in Raghubir's name.

Huge and terrifying as death
The monkeys and bears rush forth
Like hosts of winged mountains flying,
Of diverse shades and hues.
With claws, teeth, huge rocks and enormous trees

For weapons, they are strong and powerful and know no fear,
And proclaim the glory of Ram, the lion
To the mad elephant that is Ravan.

> With shouts of 'Victory! Victory' from both directions,
> The warriors each chose their match
> And closed in combat,
> One side praising Ram, the other side Ravan.   (79)

Seeing Ravan in a chariot and Raghubir on foot,
Vibhishan grew apprehensive.
Great love filled his heart with doubt,
And bowing at the Lord's feet, he lovingly said,
'Lord, you have no chariot, no armour to protect your body,
    and no shoes for your feet—
How will you conquer that powerful warrior?'
'Listen, dear friend,' replied the abode of mercy,
'The chariot that leads to victory is a different one.
Valour and fortitude are the wheels of that chariot,
Truth and goodness its unwavering banners and flags,
Strength, discernment, self-restraint and altruism its horses,
With forgiveness, compassion and equanimity their harness.
The worship of Shiv is its skilful charioteer,
With dispassion his shield, contentment his sword,
Charity his battle-axe, intellect his fierce javelin,
And supreme wisdom his unyielding bow.
A clear and steady mind is his quiver,
Equability, abstinence and religious observance his various
    arrows,
And homage to Brahmans and to his guru his impenetrable
    armour.
There are no other means to victory equal to these.
Dear friend, he who has such a chariot of righteousness
Has no enemy to conquer anywhere.

Listen to me, my grave and steadfast friend—
The warrior
Who has such a powerful chariot,
Can conquer even the great and unconquerable enemy
　　　　that is this existence.'　　　　　　　　　(80A)

Upon hearing the Lord's words, Vibhishan
Joyfully clasped his lotus feet.
'You have taken this opportunity to give me a lesson
　　　in wisdom,
O Ram, accumulation of mercy and bliss!'　　　(80B)

From one side Ravan defiantly called and taunted,
From the other, Angad and Hanuman.
The demons against the bears and monkeys, each side
Fought the other invoking its own lord.　　　　(80C)

Brahma and the other gods, and numerous Siddhas and munis,
Mounted upon their chariots, watched the battle from the sky.
I, too, was with them, Uma,
Watching Ram's exploits upon the field of battle.
The warriors on both sides were drunk on war—
The monkeys were winning for they had Ram's might
　　　with them.
With shouts of defiance, each closed in single combat,
Crushing his adversary and grinding him into the ground.
They beat, they bite, they seize, they throw,
They tear off heads and hurl those heads as missiles.
They rend stomachs, rip out limbs,
Grab feet and dash warriors to the ground.
The bears buried the demon warriors in the earth,
And over them piled great heaps of sand.
The valiant monkeys battling the enemy
Looked like innumerable forms of furious Death incarnate.

The monkeys shone like furious Death incarnate,
Their bodies streaming with blood.
They crushed the mighty warriors of the demon army
And roared like storm-cloud thunder.
They threatened them and beat them,
Tore at them with their teeth, and crushed them underfoot.
Yelling and shouting, the bears and monkeys used strength
And every stratagem to diminish the demon host.

They tore out their cheeks, ripped open their bellies
And hung their entrails around their own necks
As though Prahlad's Lord[xiv] had assumed multiple bodies
And was amusing himself on the battlefield.
Dreadful cries of 'Seize! Kill! Bite! Throw!'
Filled the earth and sky.
Glory to Ram, who can in truth turn a blade of grass into a thunderbolt,
And a thunderbolt into a blade of grass!

> When he saw his own army in disarray,
> Ten-headed Ravan mounted his chariot,
> And, armed with ten bows in his twenty arms,
> Set forth proudly to rally them, urging them to
>   return to the fray.   (81)

In greatest fury, Dashkandhar rushed forth,
And the monkeys, with warlike whoops, advanced to meet him.
Taking in their hands trees, rocks and boulders,
They flung them, all together, at him.
The massive boulders struck his adamant-hard body,
And shattered at once into tiny pieces.
He did not flinch, but stopping his chariot, stood as firm as
   a mountain,

[xiv] Vishnu, in his Narsingh avatar of half-man, half-lion

The war-drunk Ravan, terrible in his anger.
This side and that he assailed and attacked the monkey warriors,
Crushing and killing them, and growing ever more furious.
The numerous bears and monkeys fled
Crying, 'Save us, save us, Angad, Hanuman!
Protect us, save us, Lord Raghubir!
This Rakshasa is devouring us like Death!'
When Ravan saw all the monkeys in flight,
He fitted an arrow to each of his ten bows.

Fitting the arrows to his bows, he let loose a fusillade—
They flew and struck like snakes.
The arrows filled the earth and sky in each and every direction—
Where could the monkeys run?
A terrible uproar arose amongst the panic-stricken monkeys and bears,
Who called out in frantic despair,
'O Raghubir, ocean of mercy! O friend of the distressed!
O Hari, protector of your devotees!'

> Seeing his own army distraught,
> Lakshman tightened his quiver at his waist, took his
>   bow in his hand,
> And, after bowing his head at Ram's feet,
> Set forth in great wrath.   (82)

'Vile wretch! You kill monkeys and bears, do you?
But now look at me, I am your doom!'
'I have been searching for you, you killer of my son!
Today I will soothe my heart by killing you.'
So saying, Ravan let loose his terrible arrows.
Lakshman shattered them all into a hundred pieces.
Countless missiles did Ravan hurl at him,
But Lakshman warded them off by reducing them to the size of
     sesame seeds.

He then assailed him with his own arrows,
Broke his chariot and killed his charioteer.
He shot a hundred arrows at each of his ten heads—
They lodged there like serpents boring into mountain peaks.
Then with a hundred arrows more he struck him in the breast—
Ravan fell to the ground, insensible.
Reviving, the mighty Rakshasa rose
And let fly the spear given him by Brahma.

That terrible spear, Brahma's gift,
Struck Anant full in the breast.
The hero, wounded, fell to the ground. Dashmukh tried
To pick him up, but failed—so much for the glory of his
        matchless strength!
He upon whose head rests the entire universe
As lightly as a grain of sand—
It was him that that fool Ravan tried to carry off!
He did not recognize the king of the three worlds.

Seeing Lakshman lying upon the ground, the Wind's son
        rushed forward,
Hurling harsh words at Ravan.
But as the monkey came near,
He struck him a dreadful blow with his fist.   (83)

The monkey fell to his knees, but did not fall to the ground.
Recovering, he stood up again, full of rage,
And struck Ravan such a blow with his fist,
That he fell like a mountain struck by a thunderbolt.
When he woke up from the swoon,
He began to praise the monkey's great strength.
'Fie on my strength, fie on me,
That you still live, you enemy of the gods!'
Thus exclaiming, the monkey carried Lakshman away—

To the astonished wonder of the ten-headed one.
Said Raghubir, 'Dear brother, know in your heart,
You are the devourer of death and the protector of the gods.'
Upon hearing these words, the gracious one sat up at once,
And that terrible spear vanished into the sky.
Picking up his bow and arrows again, Lakshman rushed forth,
Eager and impatient to confront the enemy.

Once again, with great despatch, he broke Ravan's chariot,
Killed his charioteer, and threw him into confusion.
He pierced his heart with a hundred arrows, and wounded,
The ten-headed one fell to the ground.
Another charioteer threw him into his chariot
And immediately carried him away to Lanka,
While Raghubir's brother, accumulation of splendour,
Once again bowed at the Lord's feet.

> In Lanka, Dashanan recovered,
> And began to perform a sacrifice.
> Obstinate and exceedingly foolish,
> The wretch sought victory even while opposing Ram!   (84)

Vibhishan heard all the news,
And hurrying to Raghupati, said to him,
'My lord, Ravan is performing a fire sacrifice.
If he completes it, the unfortunate wretch will never die.
So send at once your monkey warriors, my lord,
That they may destroy his sacrifice, and Dashkandhar return to
        the fight.'
As soon as it was morning, the Lord sent out his brave warriors—
Hanuman, Angad and others, all set forth.
Leaping as though in play, the monkeys climbed up into Lanka,
And fearlessly entered Ravan's palace.
When they saw him engaged in his sacrifice,

The monkeys all grew furious.
'Shameless wretch! You run away from battle and come home,
And sitting here, you pretend to be engaged in divine
    contemplation!'
So saying, Angad kicked him,
But the wretch, completely absorbed in gaining his own end,
    did not even look at him.

When he did not even look at them, the monkeys
Grew even angrier and began to bite and kick him.
They seized his women by their hair and dragged them
Outside—the women cried out piteously in their distress.
Then Ravan rose, like Death enraged,
And grabbing them by their feet, began hurling the monkeys away.
In the midst of all this, the monkeys ruined his sacrifice—
When he saw this, he lost heart and gave way to despair.

> Having ruined his sacrifice, the monkeys
> Safely returned to Raghupati.
> The Rakshasa set out in fury,
> Having abandoned all hope of life. (85)

As he set forth, dreadful ill omens occurred,
And vultures flew and alighted on his heads.
In the grip of death, he heeded no omen,
But 'Sound the drums of war!' he ordered.
The endless demon army set forth,
With its innumerable elephants, chariots, foot soldiers
    and horsemen.
The wretches rushed to confront the Lord,
Like a multitude of moths into the flame.
Meanwhile, the gods invoked the Lord,
'He has inflicted terrible misfortunes upon us.
Now play with him no more, Ram,

For Vaidehi is suffering greatly.'
Hearing the gods' words, Raghubir smiled,
And rising, made ready his arrows.
His matted hair is twisted firmly upon his head,
Adorned with the flowers caught in it here and there.
With his bright eyes and body dark as a rain cloud,
He delights the eyes of all the worlds.
He fastened his quiver with his sash around his waist,
And took in his hand his unbending bow, Sarang.

He took Sarang in his hand, and fastened about his waist
His beautiful quiver that never emptied of arrows.
His arms were mighty, and his broad and handsome chest
Was adorned with the mark of the Brahman's foot.[8]
When the Lord, says his servant Tulsi, began
To twirl his bow and arrows in his hands,
The universe, the elephants of the eight quarters, the celestial tortoise,
The divine serpent, the earth, the ocean and the mountains all trembled.

    Seeing his beauty, the gods rejoiced,
    And rained down flowers endlessly,
      Crying, 'Victory, victory, victory to the compassionate Lord,
      Abode of all beauty, strength, and virtue!'   (86)

Meanwhile, the vast demon army
Arrived, jostling and shoving.
Upon seeing it, the monkey warriors set forth,
Like massing clouds at the end of the world.
Countless swords and daggers glittered,
Like gleams of lightning in every direction.
Elephants, chariots and horses made a dreadful clamour,
Like storm clouds rumbling, frightening and terrible.
The monkeys' huge tails spread across the heavens,
As though brilliant rainbows had appeared in the sky.

The dust rose up in clouds,
And an unceasing rain of arrows fell.
Both sides hurled huge boulders at each other,
Which fell like thunderbolts again and again.
Raghupati, in battle fury, let fly a storm of arrows—
The demon hordes were wounded.
As the arrows struck, the warriors screamed,
And, reeling, fell to the ground.
Rivers of blood flowed like great mountain-torrents
Terrifying the cowardly.

A river of blood, terrifying to cowards,
And most impure, began to flow.
Between the two warring sides that were its banks—with the war
chariots sand
And their wheels its whirlpools—that terrible river flowed.
The war elephants, foot soldiers, horses, mules,
And the many diverse vehicles beyond count were the water creatures
upon that stream.
Arrows, spears and lances were the water snakes, bows the waves,
And shields the numerous turtles in that flood.

Warriors fall like falling trees on the river's banks,
And the flowing marrow of their bones becomes the foam
upon its surface.
Cowards are terrified at the sight,
The valiant pleased at heart.   (87)

Ghouls, ghosts and goblins bath in that river,
And Shiv's fiendish attendants,[9] and frightful imps with matted hair.
Crows and kites fly off with severed arms,
Which they snatch from each other and eat.
Says one, 'There is such abundance,
You rogue, but still your wretched neediness does not abate!'

Wounded warriors lie groaning on the banks of that river
    everywhere,
Half in, half out, as though left on the side of a sacred stream to die.[10]
Vultures upon the banks pull out entrails from that river,
Like fishermen plying their rods with full attention.
Many dead soldiers float down that stream with birds perched
    upon them
As though boating for pleasure on a river.
Joginis fill skulls with blood,
While the wives of ghouls and goblins dance in the air.
Chamundas clash warriors' skulls like cymbals
And sing in diverse strains.[11]
Packs of jackals gnash their teeth and tear at the corpses,
Snarling, quarrelling, devouring till glutted.
Countless bodies without heads reel and totter about,
While the heads, lying on the ground, call 'Victory, victory!'

Severed heads call 'Victory, victory!'
While terrifying torsos without heads rush about.
Birds quarrel and squabble amongst the skulls,
As warriors bring down warriors.
The monkeys, made arrogant by Ram's might,
Crush the demon hordes.
The heroes struck by Ram's arrows lie
In eternal sleep on the field of battle.

    Ravan thought to himself,
    'The demons are destroyed,
    I am alone, the bears and monkeys many—
    Let me put forth my unbounded maya.'   (88)

When the gods saw the Lord was fighting on foot,
Great anguish arose in their hearts.
The king of the gods sent his own chariot at once,

Which his charioteer, Matali, joyfully brought there.
Upon that celestial chariot, unparalleled in splendour,
The king of Koshalpur mounted, rejoicing.
Harnessed to it were four spirited, handsome horses,
Ever youthful, deathless, and as swift as thought.
Seeing Raghunath mounted upon the chariot,
The monkeys rushed forth with renewed strength.
The monkeys' attack was impossible to withstand,
So Ravan then used his powers of illusion.
Raghubir recognized his illusions for what they were,
But Lakshman and the monkeys thought they were real.
The monkeys saw amongst the demon army,
Many kings of Koshal with his brother.

Seeing these numerous illusory Rams and Lakshmans,
The bears and monkeys grew terrified.
Together with Lakshman, they stood staring, transfixed wherever
    they were,
As still as figures in a picture.
Seeing his own army so bewildered, the king of Koshal
Smiled and fitted an arrow to his bow.
In an instant did Hari destroy Ravan's maya,
And the entire monkey army rejoiced.

Then Ram looked at everyone,
And gravely said,
'My brave warriors, you are all very tired—
So now watch my duel with Ravan.'   (89)

So saying, Raghunath urged forward his chariot
After bowing his head at the Brahmans' lotus feet.
Then great fury arose in the king of Lanka's breast,
And, challenging Ram in a thunderous roar, he rushed to meet him.
'The warriors whom you have vanquished in battle,

Listen, ascetic, I am not like them!
My name is Ravan, whose fame the whole world knows,
And in whose dungeons lie imprisoned the guardians of the
　　　eight quarters!
You have slain Khar and Dushan and Viradh,
And killed poor Baali like a huntsman his prey.
You have destroyed hosts of demon heroes,
And killed Kumbhakaran and Meghnad.
Today I will have my revenge,
Provided, king, you do not flee the field of battle.
Today, wretch, I will hand you over to Death,
For now you have to deal with remorseless Ravan!'
Hearing Ravan's angry words and knowing him to be in the
　　　clutches of his own doom,
The abode of mercy laughed and said,
'It's true, all true, all your power and majesty,
But now brag no more and show me your strength.

Do not destroy your glorious fame by boasting,
But pardon me if I relate to you a basic truth.
There are three kinds of men on this earth,
Resembling the patala, the mango and the jak fruit trees.
One bears flowers, the second flowers and fruit,
And the third bears only fruit.
The first kind of man only talks, the second talks and acts,
And the third kind acts but says not a word.'

Upon hearing Ram's words, Ravan laughed and said,
　　　'So you would teach me wisdom?
You were not afraid to wage war on me then,
But now you hold your life dear!'　　　　　　　　(90)

With these insulting words, the furious Dashkandhar
Began to let loose his arrows harsh as thunderbolts.

Arrows of diverse forms and shapes flew
And filled sky and earth in every direction.
Raghubir let fly his arrow of fire,
And in an instant the demon's arrows were reduced to ashes.
Enraged, he hurled his sharp spear,
But the Lord turned it back with an arrow.
Millions of discs and tridents he threw,
But the Lord without effort turned them aside.
Ravan's arrows were as fruitless
As are the desires of the wicked.
He then struck Matali with a hundred arrows,
Who fell to the ground crying, 'Victory to Ram!'
Ram in his mercy lifted up his charioteer,
But a terrible fury now possessed the Lord.

Raghupati grew enraged in battle against his foe,
And the arrows in his quiver grew restless.
Hearing the wrathful twang of his bow,
The man-eating demons were terrified,
Mandodari's heart trembled, the celestial tortoise,
The earth, and the mountains grew afraid,
And the elephants guarding the eight quarters trumpeted, scoring the
*   earth with their tusks.*
The gods laughed to see this spectacle.

Drawing his bow to his ear,
Ram let loose his terrible arrows,
Which flew, brightly flashing,
Like serpents.   (91)

Ram's arrows sped forth like winged serpents.
First they killed Ravan's charioteer and horses,
Then shattered his chariot, and tore down his flags
    and banners.

Though inwardly weary, Ravan gave a terrible roar,
And mounted another chariot at once. Full of rage,
He let fly weapons and missiles of every description.
But all his efforts were as fruitless
As those of a mind bent only upon harming others.
Then Ravan hurled ten spears at once,
Which struck Ram's four horses and threw them to the ground.
Raghunayak raised the horses, and full of wrath,
Drew his bow, and let fly his arrows.
At the cluster of lotuses that was Ravan's heads,
Like a string of bees flew Raghubir's shafts.
Each of the ten heads he struck with ten arrows—
Great spouts of blood began to flow.
Though streaming with blood, the mighty Ravan came rushing,
And the Lord once again fitted arrows to his bow.
Thirty shafts did Raghubir let fly,
And Ravan's twenty arms and ten heads all fell, severed,
    to the ground.
But as soon as they were cut off, they grew anew—
Ram once again struck off his arms and heads.
The Lord cut off his arms and heads many times,
But each time, the instant they were struck off, they
    grew again.
Again and again did the Lord cut off his arms and heads,
For Koshal's king is very fond of play.
The sky was covered with heads and arms,
Like countless Rahus and Ketus.

It seemed as though innumerable Rahus and Ketus,
Streaming with blood, were rushing through the sky,
For struck by Raghubir's terrible arrows,
They could not fall to the ground.
The arrows, as they flew through the air,
Each stringing together a set of heads, shone

Like the rays of an angry sun,
Beaded here and there with Rahus.

As quickly as the Lord struck off Ravan's heads,
They grew again without end,
Like sensual desires when indulged
Grow daily more and more.   (92)

When Dashmukh saw his heads thus multiply,
He forgot about his own death and was seized by a deep rage,
And, roaring, the arrogant fool
Rushed forward with all his ten bows drawn.
Ravan, raging upon the field of battle,
Let loose a rain of arrows such that it hid Raghupati's chariot
     from sight.
For a full half hour, the chariot could not be seen—
It was as though the sun had been obscured by mist.
When the gods cried out in dismay,
The Lord, full of wrath, picked up his bow,
And turning Ravan's arrows, cut off his heads,
Which covered sky and earth in every direction.
The severed heads flew through the air,
Producing terror with their shouts of victory
And cries of 'Where is Lakshman, where Sugriv, the monkey-king,
And where the Raghu hero, Koshal's sovereign?'

Calling 'Where is Ram?' the crowd of heads
Rushed about. Seeing them, the monkeys began to flee.
Making ready his bow, the jewel of the Raghu clan
Smiled, and with his arrows pierced the heads right through.
With garlands of skulls in their hands,
Horde upon horde of Kalikas[12] gathered
And bathed in the river of blood
As though setting off to worship the banyan tree that was war.

Then the ten-headed one, enraged,
Threw his terrible spear.
It flew straight towards Vibhishan
Like the staff of death itself.   (93)

When he saw that dreadful spear coming,
Ram thought, 'It is my sacred vow to destroy the distress of the suppliant!'
He at once put Vibhishan behind him,
And, stepping forward, endured that spear himself.
When the spear struck him, he fell insensible for a while.
At this sport of the Lord's, the gods grew distraught,
And Vibhishan, seeing that the Lord had been hurt,
Grabbed his club and rushed at Ravan, enraged.
'You miserable wretch! You vile and perverse fool,
Against gods, men, munis, Nagas, all!
You with reverence offered your heads to Shiv,
And for each one you gave, you received ten million back.
That is the only reason, wretch, that you are still alive,
But now death is dancing upon your heads.
Fool, you oppose Ram and still expect victory?'
Thus saying, he struck Ravan on the chest with his club.

The instant he received on his chest that terrible blow
From Vibhishan's dreadful club, Ravan fell to the ground,
And blood streamed from all his ten mouths.
But picking himself up again, he rushed forward, full of fury.
The two mighty warriors slammed into each other,
And began to wrestle ferociously. Each was bent on killing the other.
Vibhishan, inspired by Raghubir's strength,
Deemed Ravan to be of no account.

Uma, had Vibhishan ever dared
Look Ravan in the eye?
But now that he had Raghubir's might,
He fought with him like death itself.   (94)

Seeing that Vibhishan was utterly exhausted,
Hanuman rushed forward with a huge rock in his hand.
Destroying Ravan's chariot, horses and charioteer,
He kicked him full in the chest.
Ravan remained standing, but trembled violently all over,
While Vibhishan withdrew into the presence of the protector of
    the faithful.
Then Ravan taunted and struck the monkey,
Who stretched out his tail, and flew into the sky.
Ravan grabbed his tail, and was borne by the monkey into the air.
Turning, the strong and mighty Hanuman then closed with him,
And there in the sky they fought, two warriors equally matched,
Full of fury, and each determined to kill the other.
Using strength and every stratagem they battled, like
A black mountain and Sumeru fighting each other in the sky.
Unable to beat the demon through wit or strength,
The son of the Wind invoked the Lord.

Invoking the Lord, the steadfast Hanuman
Shouted defiantly and struck Ravan a blow.
They fell to the ground, then, rising, continued to fight
So that the gods called out 'Victory, victory!' to both.
Seeing Hanuman in trouble, the monkeys
And bears rushed forth in rage,
But Ravan, drunk on battle, crushed
All the warriors with the tremendous might of his arms.

Then, rallied by Raghubir,
The furious monkeys rushed forth again.
Seeing the monkeys' strength prevailing,
Ravan used his power of illusion.   (95)

The wretch became invisible for a moment,
And then made himself visible again in innumerable forms.
On every side there appeared as many ten-headed Ravans

As there were bears and monkeys in Raghupati's army.
At the sight of these countless ten-headed Ravans,
The bears and monkeys fled in every direction.
Losing their courage, the monkey army ran,
Calling, 'Save us, Lakshman! Protect us, Raghubir!'
Millions of Ravans rushed after them in the ten directions,
With dreadful, harsh and frightening roars.
The gods were all terrified, and fled, crying,
'Give up all hope of victory now, brother!
One Dashkandhar had singly vanquished all the gods,
And now there are so many! Let's make for the mountain caves!'
Only Viranchi, Shambhu and the wisest munis remained,
Who had some understanding of the Lord's power.

Those who understood his glory stood fast, unafraid,
But the monkeys believed the enemy to be real.
The monkeys and bears all fled, distraught,
And, in their fear, cried out, 'Protect us, merciful Lord!'
The strong and valiant Hanumant,
Angad, Nil and Nal fought on,
Crushing the million upon millions of ten-headed warriors
That had sprouted like shoots from the earth of deceit.

Seeing the gods and monkeys so frantic,
The king of Koshal laughed,
And fitting a single arrow to his bow, Sarang,
He killed all the false Ravans.   (96)

The Lord dispelled all the maya in an instant,
Just like the rising of the sun dispels the dark.
Seeing only one Ravan, the gods rejoiced,
And returning, rained down flowers upon the Lord.
Raising his arms, the Lord turned back the monkeys,
Who returned, calling to each other to come back.

Drawing strength from the Lord's might, the bears and monkeys
    came rushing,
And leaping nimbly, returned quickly to the field of battle.
Seeing the gods singing the praises of the Lord,
Ravan thought, 'In their calculations, I am only one!'
He called out, 'Fools, you have ever been my victims!'
And rushed, full of rage, up into the sky.
The gods ran, crying out in fear.
'Wretches, where do you run from me?' called Ravan.
Seeing the gods distraught, Angad came rushing.
Leaping, he seized Ravan by his foot, and hurled him to the ground.

He seized him and hurled him to the ground, kicked him and beat him,
And then Baali's son returned to the Lord.
Dashkanth, recovering, stood up again,
And gave a deep and dreadful roar.
Haughtily, he strung his ten bows,
And, fitting a shaft to each, shot forth a rain of arrows.
He wounded all the enemy warriors, and, seeing them
Distraught with fear, rejoiced at his own might.

    Then Raghupati cut off Ravan's
    Heads and arms, broke his bows and arrows,
    But each time they grew again and multiplied,
    Like sins committed at a pilgrimage place.   (97)

Seeing their enemy's heads and arms multiply,
The bears and monkeys grew enraged.
'The wretch does not die though his arms and heads be cut off!'
Cried the bear and monkey warriors, and rushed at him,
    full of fury.
Baali's son, with Nal, Nil and the son of the Wind,
And Sugriv, king of the monkeys, and the mighty Dwivid,
Hurled trees and mountains at him,

But he caught those very trees and mountains and hurled them
    back at the monkeys.
Some tore at his body with their nails,
Some kicked him and ran away.
Then Nal and Nil climbed up on to his heads,
And began to tear at his foreheads with their nails.
When Ravan saw blood, he became deeply disconcerted,
And stretched up his arms to seize them.
But they were not to be caught and hovered above his hands,
Like two bees over a cluster of lotuses.
At last, he gave an angry leap and grabbed them,
But as he hurled them to the ground, they twisted his arms and
    ran away.
Then, full of rage, he took all his ten bows in his hands,
And smiting them with his arrows, wounded the monkeys.
Having rendered Hanuman and the other monkeys senseless,
And seeing that it was now dusk, Ravan rejoiced.
Seeing all the monkey warriors lying unconscious,
Jamvant, resolute in war, came rushing.
The bears with him were armed with boulders and trees,
Which they hurled at Ravan with taunts and shouts of defiance.
The mighty Ravan became enraged—
Seizing several warriors by the foot, he dashed them to the ground.
When the king of the bears saw his own troops hurt,
He grew furious, and kicked Ravan full in the chest.

At this violent kick upon his breast,
Ravan fell, reeling, to the ground.
In each of his twenty hands he held a bear—
Like bees nestled in lotus flowers at night.
Seeing Ravan lying insensible, the king of the bears
Kicked him again, and then returned to the Lord.
Seeing that it was night, Ravan's charioteer
Laid him in his chariot and tried to revive him.

Recovering from their swoon, the bears and monkeys
All returned to the Lord,
While the demons all surrounded Ravan
In greatest fear and alarm.   (98)

That same night, Trijata went to Sita,
And told her all that had happened.
When she heard how Ravan's heads and arms had multiplied,
Great dread arose in Sita's heart.
Then, with downcast face and worry springing up in her heart,
Sita said to Trijata,
'Why do you not tell me, Mother, what is to happen?
How will this tormentor of the world die?
He does not die even though Raghupati's arrows have cut off his heads.
Fate is making all things contrary.
It is my misfortune that keeps him alive,
The same misfortune that took me away from Hari's lotus feet.
The fate that made that false golden deer of deceit
Is displeased with me even today.
That providence which made me suffer unendurable grief,
And utter those sharp and cruel words to Lakshman,
And which pierces me again and again
With the terrible poisoned arrows of separation from Raghupati,
Keeping me alive even in such anguish—
It is that providence and no other that keeps Ravan living!'
In many such ways did Janaki weep and lament,
Calling to mind the abode of mercy again and again.
Said Trijata, 'Listen, princess,
The enemy of the gods will die the instant an arrow pierces his heart.
But the Lord does not aim his arrow at his breast,
For he knows that Vaidehi dwells in his heart.'

'In his heart does Janaki dwell,
In Janaki's heart is my abode,

And within me are many worlds—
The instant an arrow pierces Ravan's heart, they will all be destroyed.'
Hearing these words, great joy and sorrow arose in Sita's heart.
Trijata, seeing this, spoke again and said,
'Now this is the way your enemy will die—
So listen, beautiful one, and no longer be anxious and afraid.

> Having his heads cut off again and again will so
>   disconcert Ravan
> That his contemplation of you will break,
> And that is when the all-knowing Ram
> Will send his arrow into his heart.'   (99)

With these and many such words, Trijata comforted Sita,
And then returned to her own home.
Remembering Ram's gentle disposition, Vaidehi
Was overcome with the anguish of separation.
She reproached the night and the moon in many ways,
'The night is as long as an aeon, it does not end!'
Janaki, made sorrowful by separation from Ram,
Weeps and laments within her heart.
When the agony of separation was at its greatest,
Her left eye and arm began to tremble.
Considering this to be a good omen, she took courage,
'Now I will be with the all-merciful Raghubir again!'
Meanwhile, at midnight, Ravan awoke from his swoon,
And began to berate his own charioteer.
'Fool, you have brought me away from the battlefield!
Curse you, you dim-witted wretch!'
The charioteer clasped his feet and tried to reason with him in
       many ways.
As soon as it was dawn, Ravan mounted his chariot and set
       forth again.
Hearing that Dashanan approached,

A great commotion arose in the monkey army.
Tearing up mountains and trees on every side,
The terrible warriors rushed forth, gnashing their teeth.

They rushed forth, those fearsome monkeys
And menacing bears, holding mountains in their hands,
Which they hurled in fury at the demon host—
The demons fled at the onslaught.
Thus scattering his army, the mighty monkeys
Then surrounded Ravan.
Pounding and slapping him from every side,
Clawing and tearing at his body, they drove him to distraction.

> Seeing the monkeys' great strength,
> Ravan considered.
> Then, becoming invisible, he unleashed
> In an instant, his power of illusion.   (100)

As he unleashed his illusions,
Dreadful beings appeared—
Goblins, ghosts and evil spirits,
With bows and iron arrows in their hands.

Joginis clutching swords,
In one hand a human skull
From which they drink fresh blood,
Wildly dance and sing
With dreadful cries of 'Seize them! Kill them!'
That fill every direction all around.
Mouths wide open, they rush to devour them—
That's when the monkeys turn to run.

Wherever the monkeys fled,
They saw fires blazing.

The monkeys and bears grew distraught—
And then began showers of sand.

Having thus exhausted the monkeys,
The ten-headed one roared again,
And all the heroes fell unconscious,
Including Lakshman and the monkey king.

'Ah Ram! Ah Raghunath!'
The valiant warriors wrung their hands.
Having thus broken the might of all,
Ravan put forth another delusion.

He made a host of Hanumans appear,
Who rushed forth holding rocks,
And running, surrounded Ram
In dense crowds all around.

'Kill him! Seize him! Don't let him go!'
They cried, with gnashing teeth and waving tails.
Their tails rose on every side,
And in their midst shone Koshal's king.

In their midst the king of Koshal shone
With his dark and lovely form,
Like a tall tamal tree encircled
By a fence of gleaming rainbows.

At the sight of the Lord, joy and sorrow arose
In the hearts of the gods, and they hailed him with cries of victory.
Wrathful, Raghubir, with a single arrow,
Now dispelled the delusion in an instant.

With the phantasms gone, the bears and monkeys rejoiced,
And all returned, bearing trees and giant rocks.

Ram let loose a flight of arrows,
And Ravan's heads and arms fell once again to the ground.

Even if a hundred Sheshnags and Sharada,
And the Vedas and countless poets, were to sing of his deeds for aeons,
The would not be able to explain all the mystery
Of Lord Ram's battle with Ravan.

Of that battle some wondrous episodes,
The dull-witted Tulsidas has related,
Like a fly that flies up into the sky
Only as high as its strength allows.   (101A)

His heads and arms are cut off many times,
But the heroic king of Lanka does not die.
The Lord is at play, but the gods, Siddhas and munis
Are bewildered by the fight.   (101B)

The instant they were cut off, his multitude of heads
    would multiply,
Just as greed increases with every gain.
Despite all Ram's great exertions, his enemy did not die.
He then looked at Vibhishan.
Uma, he by whose wish death itself dies,
That same Lord thus tested his devotee's love.
'O all-wise master of creation moving and unmoving,
Protector of the humble, delight of the gods and sages—listen!
In Ravan's navel is a pool of nectar—
It is on the strength of that, sire, that Ravan lives.'
Hearing Vibhishan's words, the merciful Lord rejoiced
And took in his hand his dreadful arrows.
All kinds of ill-omens then began to appear.
Donkeys, jackals and dogs began to howl,
Birds screeched to announce the world's distress,
And comets appeared everywhere in the sky.

Great fires broke out in all ten directions,
And the sun was eclipsed without a new moon.
Mandodari's heart beat violently,
And statues streamed tears from their eyes.

Statues wept, lightning flashed and thunder crashed,
Fierce winds began to blow, the earth shook,
And clouds rained downed blood, hair, and dust.
There were so many ill-omens—who can describe them all?
Seeing this unbounded confusion, the gods in the sky
Grew alarmed and began calling for victory.
Realizing that the gods were afraid, the merciful
Raghupati fitted arrows to his bow.

> He pulled the bow to his ear,
> And let fly thirty-one shafts.
> Raghunayak's arrows shot forth
> Like venomous serpents of doom.   (102)

One arrow dried up the pool of nectar in Ravan's navel,
The others struck off his arms and heads with great force.
The iron shafts carried away his heads and arms with them,
While his headless, armless torso danced upon the battlefield.
The trunk rushed furiously on, so that the earth sank beneath it—
Then the Lord struck it with an arrow and split it in two.
As he died, Ravan roared in a voice of thunder,
'Where is Ram? I will challenge and kill him in battle!'
The earth swayed as Dashkandhar fell,
And the ocean, the rivers, the elephants of the quarters, and the
     mountains all trembled.
He fell to the ground, his two halves growing,
Crushing multitudes of bears and monkeys beneath them.
Depositing Ravan's arms and heads in front of Mandodari,
His arrows returned to the Lord of the universe,

And dropped into his quiver.
Seeing this, the gods beat their drums.
Ravan's energy entered the Lord's mouth.
Seeing this, Shambhu and four-faced Brahma rejoiced.
The whole universe resounded with cries of triumph,
'Victory to Raghubir, mighty of arm!'
Crowds of gods and munis rained down flowers,
'Glory to the All-merciful! Glory to Mukund, the giver of liberation!'

'Mukund, giver of liberation, source of all mercy and dispeller of opposites,
Bestower of joy upon those who take refuge in you,
Destroyer of the wicked, the prime cause of all causes,
Ever compassionate, all-pervasive—victory to you, O Lord.'
The gods, full of joy, rained down flowers,
And drums and kettle-drums sounded loudly.
Upon the battlefield, Ram's limbs took on
The radiance of innumerable gods of Love.

Flowers of heart-enchanting beauty, caught
In the crown of matted hair upon his head, shine
Like lightning glittering upon the star-lit peak
Of a dark mountain.
He twirls his bow and arrows between his arms,
And drops of blood adorn his body
Like a flock of red Raimuni birds
Joyously perched upon a tamal tree.

    With a shower of gracious glances,
    The Lord reassured the gathered gods.
    The bears and monkeys all rejoiced,
    Crying 'Glory to Mukund, the abode of bliss!'   (103)

The instant Mandodari saw her husband's heads,
She fainted with grief and fell to the ground.

Weeping, the royal women ran and raised her up,
And carried her to where lay Ravan's body.
Seeing their lord's condition, they broke into loud lamentation.
Their hair fell loose, and they lost all control of their bodies.
Wildly, they beat their breasts,
And, weeping, recounted his glory.
'Before your strength, my lord, the earth ever trembled,
And fire, moon and sun dimmed in splendour before you.
Neither Shesh nor the divine tortoise could bear your
      body's weight—
That same body now lies on the ground covered in dust.
Varun, Kuber, Indra, the Wind,
Never had the courage to face you on the battlefield.
By the might of your arm, my lord, you conquered fate and death,
Yet today you lie there like one destitute.
Your great power is famed throughout the world,
And the might of your sons and kinsfolk defies description.
It is because you turned against Ram that you are in this
      state today,
That no one from your line remains to mourn you.
In your power was all of God's creation,
And the terrified guardians of the quarters ever bowed their heads
      to you.
Now jackals devour your heads and arms,
A fate not undeserved for one hostile to Ram.
In death's grip, my husband, you did not listen,
And took the master of all creation to be an ordinary man.

You took as an ordinary man Hari himself,
That fire to destroy the forest of demons.
He whom Shiv and Brahma and the other gods revere—
You worshipped him not, that compassionate Lord, my beloved.
From birth this body of yours has been bent on hurting others,
And been imbued with every sin.

Yet Ram has given you his own abode—
I bow to him, the immutable brahm.

Ah my lord, there is no one else
As compassionate as Raghunath,
The divine Lord who has bestowed upon you a state
Difficult even for holy men to attain.'   (104)

Gods, munis and Siddhas were all pleased
To hear Mandodari's words.
Brahma, Mahesh, Narad, Sanak and his brothers,
And those great sages who knew and taught the highest truth,
Gazed upon Raghupati, filling their eyes with his form,
And thus immersed in love, grew full of joy.
Seeing all the royal women weep,
Vibhishan went up to them, his heart heavy with grief,
And lamented to see his brother's condition.
The Lord commanded his younger brother,
And Lakshman did all he could to comfort him.
Then Vibhishan came back to the Lord.
The Lord looked at him with compassion and said,
'Perform the funeral rites, abandoning all grief.'
Obeying the Lord's command, Vibhishan performed Ravan's last rites
As prescribed, and keeping in mind the place and time.

Mandodari and the others
Made the ritual offering of sesame seeds,
And returned to the palace,
Praising Ragupati's virtues in their hearts.   (105)

Vibhishan returned and once more bowed his head.
Raghunath, ocean of mercy then summoned his brother, Lakshman,
And said, 'All you righteous ones—you, and Sugriv, king of
    the monkeys,

And Angad, Nal, Nil, Jamvant and Maruti—[xv]
Go with Vibhishan
And consecrate him king.
In obedience to my father's command, I will not enter the city,
But send instead the monkeys and my younger brother, who are
       the same as me.'
Upon hearing the Lord's words, the monkeys set forth at once,
And, entering Lanka, made ready for Vibhishan's coronation.
Seating him with reverence upon the throne,
They placed the tilak of kingship on his forehead and sang his glory,
And, folding their hands, bowed their heads to him.
Then, with Vibhishan, they all returned to the Lord.
Raghubir then called the monkeys together
And spoke sweet words that made them glad.

He made them glad with these words sweet as nectar,
'By your might, the enemy has been killed,
And Vibhishan made king. Your fame
Will remain ever fresh in all the three spheres.
Those who, with perfect love,
Sing of your renown and mine,
Shall without effort cross the boundless ocean
Of the cycle of birth and rebirth.'

> The assembled monkeys do not tire
> Of listening to the Lord's words.
> Again and again they bow their heads,
> And embrace his lotus feet.   (106)

Ram summoned Hanuman.
'Go to Lanka,' said the divine Lord,
'Tell Janaki all that has happened,

[xv]   Hanuman

And come back with news of her well-being.'
Hanumant then entered the city of Lanka.
Hearing of his coming, Rakshasa and Rakshasi all ran to welcome him.
They honoured him in every possible way,
And showed him where Janak's daughter was.
The monkey made obeisance from a distance.
Janaki recognized Raghupati's messenger, and said,
'Tell me, son, is my lord, the abode of mercy,
Well, with his brother and the monkey host?'
'The king of Koshal is well in every way.
He has vanquished the ten-headed one in battle,
And Vibhishan is undisputed king of Lanka.'
Hearing the monkey's words, Sita's heart filled with joy.

Her heart flooded with happiness, and, with her body trembling
And eyes full of tears, Ramaa asked again and again,
'What shall I give you, monkey? There is nothing
In the three spheres to equal these words of yours!'
'Mother, I have without a doubt obtained
The whole universe as my kingdom today,
When I beheld the noble Ram and his brother,
Triumphant in war over the enemy.'

'May every virtue, Hanumant,
Dwell in your heart, my son.
And may Koshal's lord with his brother, Anant,
Remain ever gracious to you.   (107)

But now, dear son, arrange it so
That I may with my own eyes see his dark and tender form.'
Then Hanuman returned to Ram,
And told him of Sita's well-being.
On hearing news of Sita, the jewel of the solar dynasty,
Summoned Prince Angad and Vibhishan, and said,

'Go with the Wind's son,
And with every reverence, bring back Janak's daughter.'
They went at once to where Sita was,
Humbly waited upon by the Rakshasa women.
Vibhishan quickly explained the circumstances,
And they helped her bathe and dress herself,
And adorned her with jewels of every description.
Then they made ready and brought a lovely palanquin,
Into which Vaidehi climbed with joy,
Thinking of Ram, her beloved, the abode of bliss.
On all four sides were guards with staffs in their hands.
They set forth, their hearts full of delight.
The bears and monkeys all ran to watch,
But the guards rushed angrily to keep them away.
Said Raghubir, 'Listen to what I say—
Bring Sita on foot, my friend,
So that the monkeys may gaze upon her as their mother.'
Thus said the Lord Raghunath with a smile.
Hearing the Lord's words, the bears and monkeys rejoiced,
And the gods rained flowers from the sky.
Ram had earlier placed Sita in fire,
And now he, who is witness to all secrets, sought to reveal her.

It was for that reason that the abode of compassion
Spoke some harsh words,
Upon hearing which the Rakshasa women
All began to grieve.   (108)

Sita, pure in thought, word and deed,
Deferred to the Lord's words, and said,
'Lakshman, be the officiating priest at this test of my virtue,
And quickly light the fire.'
Upon hearing Sita's words steeped in her pain of separation,
And imbued with discernment, piety and wisdom,

Lakshman's eyes filled with tears, and he stood with folded hands.
He could not speak a word to the Lord.
Then, seeing Ram's expression, Lakshman ran
And fetched wood to light the fire.
Vaidehi rejoiced to see the blazing flames—
There was no fear in her heart.
'If in my heart, in thought, word, or deed,
There has never been anyone other than Raghubir,
Then may Fire, which knows the ways of all,
Become as cool as sandal-paste for me.'

Into the flames as cool as sandal-paste
Entered Maithili[xvi] *meditating on the Lord—*
'Glory to Koshal's king, whose feet
Mahesh reveres and I cherish with purest devotion.'
Sita's shadow image and the blemish of worldly disgrace
Were consumed by the fierce flames.
Gods, Siddhas and munis stood watching in the sky,
But no one understood this action of the Lord's.

Then Fire, assuming bodily form took the hand
Of the true Shri, famed in the Vedas and the world,
And, leading her forth, gave her to Ram
In the same way that the Ocean of Milk had given Indira to Vishnu.
Her great beauty radiant,
The true Sita now stood shining on Ram's left side,
Like a golden lily bud
Beside a fresh-blooming blue lotus.

The gods rejoiced and rained down flowers,
While drums beat in the sky.
Kinnaras sang and apsaras danced
Upon celestial chariots.　　　　　　　　　　　(109A)

[xvi]　Sita

Gazing upon the infinite beauty
Of Ram reunited with Janak's daughter,
The bears and monkeys rejoiced,
Crying, 'Glory to Raghupati, essence of joy!'   (109B)

Then, receiving Raghupati's permission,
Matali bowed his head at his feet and left.
Then the gods, ever selfish, came
And spoke as though concerned with the welfare of the universe.
'O friend of the lowly, compassionate Raghurai,
You have shown great mercy to the gods, divine Lord.
This lustful wretch, hostile to the whole world,
Ever walking the path of evil, has perished because of his own wickedness.
You are brahm, unchanging, indestructible,
Ever equable, inherently detached,
Indivisible, without attributes, uncreated, sinless, immutable,
Invincible, of unfailing power, full of compassion,
Who assumed the form of a fish, a tortoise, a boar,
Narhari, the dwarf and Parashuram.
Whenever, Lord, the gods have been in distress,
It is you who have put an end to their troubles by taking on these
     various forms.
This vile wretch, ever the enemy of the gods,
Immersed in lust and greed, arrogant and exceedingly wrathful,
This most contemptible wretch attained your supreme state—
This surprises and puzzles us.
We gods are supremely deserving,
But, immersed in our own self-interest, we forgot to worship you,
And so we are ever caught in the stream of birth and rebirth.
But now, Lord, we have come to you, so grant us refuge!'

Having thus beseeched the Lord,
The gods and Siddhas stood there with folded hands.
Then, his body trembling with devotion,
Vidhi broke into a song of praise.   (110)

Glory to Ram, ever the abode of bliss, the remover of all affliction,
Chief of the Raghus, with his bow and arrows!
Lord, you are the lion that tears into pieces the elephant that is
*   this existence,*
The ocean of all virtue, the all-wise, all-pervading master.

In your form is the incomparable beauty of countless Kamdevs,
Siddhas, munis and poets sing your virtues,
And unblemished is your fame. Like Garud,
You seized in wrath the great serpent that was Ravan.

You give joy to your devotees, destroy sorrow and fear,
And are ever without anger—Lord, you are pure intelligence.
Beneficent are your descents upon earth, and of unbounded virtue;
Aggregations of wisdom, they relieve the earth of its burdens.

Uncreated, all-pervading, ever one, without beginning,
I joyously bow to you, Ram, the most compassionate.
O ornament of the Raghu clan, slayer of Dushan, and remover of all faults,
You made Vibhishan king of Lanka, lowly though he was.

Abode of virtue and wisdom, without pride, unborn,
I ever adore you, Ram, the omnipresent and immutable.
Terrible is the power and strength of your arms,
Which are adept in the destruction of the wicked.

Merciful and kind to the needy without cause,
I salute you, the abode of beauty, with Ramaa.
Deliverer from the cycle of rebirth, you are beyond cause and effect,
And destroy the terrible faults born of the mind.

You bear a heart-enchanting bow and arrows and quiver,
And have eyes as bright as the red lotus. In you resides bliss.
You are the most illustrious of kings, Shri's handsome beloved,
And the destroyer of pride, lust and false attachment.

You are indivisible, free of all faults and cannot be known through the senses.
You are ever manifest in all forms, yet never were those forms,
Like the sun and sunlight, which are separate and not separate—
This is not an idle statement, for the Vedas have so declared.

Blessed are all these monkeys, all-pervading Lord,
Who gaze with reverence upon your countenance.
Cursed are our lives and our celestial bodies, Hari—
Without devotion to you, we wander lost in worldly concerns.

Now, O you who are merciful to the lowly, show me your compassion,
And take away that disposition of my mind that makes the world appear
      separate from you
Because of which I do what I should not,
And wander cheerfully, mistaking affliction for happiness.

Destroyer of the wicked, and lovely ornament of the earth,
Your lotus feet are adored by Shambhu and Uma.
King of kings, grant me the boon
Of loving devotion to your lotus feet, the source of everlasting well-being.'

    Thus did four-faced Brahma beseech the Lord,
    His body trembling with love.
    His eyes, gazing upon the ocean of beauty,
    Refused to be satisfied.   (111)

At that very moment, Dasharath arrived there,
And upon beholding his son, his eyes filled with tears.
The Lord with his brother touched his feet in homage.
Their father then gave them his blessings.
'Father, this is all the result of your virtuous deeds,
That I have conquered the invincible king of the demons.'
Upon hearing his son's words, his love increased even more,
So that his body trembled and his eyes overflowed with tears.

Raghupati considered his father's earlier love for him,
And merely by looking at him, gave to him unwavering knowledge
   of his own form.
Dasharath had set his heart on separation and devotion,[13]
That is why, Uma, he did not receive the gift of liberation.
Those who adore the incarnate form, do not accept salvation,
So to them Ram gives devotion to himself.
Bowing again and again to the Lord,
Dasharath returned, rejoicing, to his abode with the gods.

    Beholding the beauty of Koshal's noble king
    Together with his brother and Janaki,
    The king of the gods rejoiced in his heart,
    And broke into a song of praise.   (112)

'Glory to Ram, the abode of beauty,
The giver of rest to the obeisant,
Who holds a quiver, a great bow, and arrows,
And whose arms are mighty and powerful.

Glory to the slayer of Dushan and Khar,
The destroyer of the Rakshasa horde.
When you killed that rascal, master,
The gods found a protector again.

Glory to the reliever of earth's burden,
Whose greatness is generous and unbounded.
Glory to Ravan's compassionate foe,
Who reduced the demons to helplessness.

The king of Lanka was proud of his great strength,
He had brought the gods and Gandharvas under his sway.
Munis, Siddhas, men, birds and serpents—
He had relentlessly persecuted them all.

Bent on harming others, vicious and cruel,
He received his reward, that wicked sinner.
Listen now, O friend of the humble,
With the large lotus eyes—

My arrogance was excessive,
There was no one equal to me.
But now that I have seen your lotus feet, Lord,
That pride, which gave so much sorrow, has gone.

Some contemplate the unembodied brahm,
Whom the Vedas praise as imperceptible.
But I hold dear your embodied form
As Ram, the king of Koshal.

Abide in my heart
With Vaidehi and your brother,
And acknowledging me as your servant,
O Ramaa's beloved, grant me devotion.

Grant me devotion, O Ramaa's beloved,
Dispeller of fear, and bestower of bliss upon those who seek refuge
    in you.
I adore you, O Ram, abode of peace,
Prince of the Raghu line, with the beauty of countless Kamdevs.
Delight of the gods, dispeller of opposites,
Embodied as a man of unparalleled strength,
And worshipped by Brahma, Shankar and the other gods—
I salute you, Ram, the compassionate, the benign.

Now look graciously upon me, merciful Lord
And command me what to do.'
Upon hearing Indra's loving request,
The cherisher of the lowly replied,   (113)

'Listen, king of the gods, our monkeys and bears,
Those killed by the demons, lie on the ground.
They gave up their lives for my sake.
Bring them back to life, all-wise king of the gods!'
O king of the birds, this request of the Lord's
Is so unfathomable that only the wisest munis can understand it.
The Lord can himself destroy and restore to life the three spheres,
Here he only wished to give Sakr importance.
Causing a shower of amrit, Indra restored to life the monkeys
    and bears,
Who rose up rejoicing and returned to the Lord.
The shower of nectar had fallen upon the dead of both armies,
But only the monkey and bears came back to life, not the demons.
The demons' spirits, at the point of death, had taken on
    Ram's form,[14]
And so they had been freed from the bonds of rebirth and
    attained salvation.
But the monkeys and bears were all partial incarnations of
    the gods,
And so they all came back to life by the will of Raghupati.
Who is as benevolent to the afflicted as Ram,
Who freed from rebirth the multitude of demons?
Even that abode of sin, that wicked Ravan, steeped in lust,
Attained to that state which the greatest of munis cannot reach.

    Raining down flowers, all the gods departed,
    Each in his own shining chariot.
    Then, seeing it to be an opportune moment,
    Wise Shambhu came to the Lord.   (114A)

    With supreme love, he folded his two hands.
    Then, his lotus eyes full of tears,
    His body trembling and his voice choking with emotion,
    Tripurari entreated him thus: (114B)

'Protect me, chief of the Raghu clan,
You who hold a noble bow and bright arrows in your hand.
You are the fierce wind that blows away the dense cloud canopy of delusion,
The fire that destroys the forest of doubt, and the bestower of joy upon
     the gods.

You are with attributes and without, you are beautiful,
     the abode of virtue,
And the bright and blazing sun that dispels the darkness of ignorance,
You are the lion that destroys the elephants of lust and anger and pride.
Abide for ever in the forest of this devotee's heart.

You are the severe frost to blight the lotuses of worldly desire.
You are generous, transcend mind and intellect,
And are a Mount Mandar to churn the ocean of this existence.
Dispel my greatest fear and take me across this unnavigable ocean of rebirth.

O Ram, with the dark form and lotus eyes,
Friend of the needy, and dispeller of the sorrow of suppliants,
Dwell for ever in my heart, O king,
With your brother and Janaki.

You bestow joy upon the sages, you are the jewel adorning this
     earthly sphere,
The destroyer of every fear, and Tulsidas's own Lord.

When your coronation, my master,
Takes place in Koshal's city,
Then, O ocean of mercy,
I will come to witness your great act.'   (115)

When Shambhu had made his plea and departed,
Vibhishan approached the Lord.
Bowing his head at Ram's feet, he spoke soft and humble words.

'Hear my prayer, Lord, you who hold the great bow Sarang in
   your hand.
You have slain Ravan with his kin, his clan and his army,
And spread your unblemished glory in all the three spheres.
Upon me—lowly, impure, lacking both sense and noble lineage—
You have showered your grace in innumerable ways.
Now, Lord, make pure your devotee's home,
Bathe there and recover from the fatigue of battle.
Inspect my treasury, my palace and my wealth,
And gladly give, gracious Lord, whatever you wish to the monkeys.
Master, acknowledge me as your own in every way,
And then, when you go to Avadh, take me with you.'
When the compassionate Lord heard these mild and gentle words,
His large eyes filled with tears.

'Listen, brother, what you say is true—
Your treasury, your home and all you have are as my own.
But when I think of Bharat's condition,
A moment passes as slowly as an aeon for me.   (116A)

In ascetic garb, with emaciated body,
He unceasingly repeats my name.
Therefore, dear friend, make every effort
Such that I may see him soon.   (116B)

If I go at the end of my period of exile,
I may not find my brother still alive.'
Thinking of his brother's love,
The Lord's body trembled again and again.   (116C)

'But may you rule for a full kalpa,
Remembering me always in your heart.
And then may you attain to my abode,
Where all good men go.'   (116D)

Upon hearing Ram's words, Vibhishan
Joyfully embraced the feet of the abode of mercy.
The monkeys and bears all rejoiced,
And clasping the Lord's feet, began to recount his immaculate
    perfections.
Then Vibhishan departed for his palace.
There, he loaded the Pushpak with jewels and fine raiment,
And then returned with the flying chariot and set it before
    the Lord.
The ocean of mercy laughed and said,
'Dear friend, Vibhishan, climb into this flying chariot,
And ascending into the sky, throw down these clothes and jewels.'
Vibhishan flew up into the sky at once,
And rained down all the jewels and clothes.
The monkeys picked up whatever pleased their hearts,
Cramming the jewels into their mouths and spitting them
    out again.
Ram and Sita and Lakshman laughed at the sight,
For supremely playful is the abode of mercy.

He whom sages cannot attain even by contemplation,
And whom the Vedas describe as 'Not this, not this!'
That same compassionate Lord
Is playing joyfully with the monkeys.   (117A)

Uma, ascetic practices and prayer, charity and diverse
    austerities,
The performance of fire sacrifices and the observance of fasts
    and vows
Do not evoke Ram's compassion
As does complete and absolute love.   (117B)

The bears and monkeys found the clothes and jewels,
And dressing up in them, they came, each one, to Raghupati.

Seeing all the monkeys in assorted attire,
Koshal's king laughed again and again.
Looking at them, Raghurai felt great affection
And speaking kind and gentle words, he said,
'It is with your support that I killed Ravan
And then made Vibhishan king.
Now return to your own homes, each one.
Remember me and fear no one.'
Upon hearing his words, the monkeys were overwhelmed with love,
And folding their hands, all reverently replied,
'Whatever you say, Lord, comes well from you,
But we are confused by your words.
Knowing us to be but lowly creatures
You gave us your protection.
You are the ruler of the three worlds, Raghunath,
And hearing your words, Lord, we die of shame—
Can mosquitos help the mighty king of the birds?'
Seeing Ram so gracious towards them, the monkeys and bears
Were lost in love. They had no desire to return home.

> But, upon the Lord's command, the monkeys and bears,
> Holding his image in their hearts,
> And with many prayers and entreaties,
> Left for their homes with mingled joy and sorrow.   (118A)

> Sugriv, Nil, Jamvant,
> Angad, Nal, Hanuman,
> Vibhishan and the other
> Valiant monkey commanders,   (118B)

> Were overcome with love and could not speak a word.
> Their eyes full of tears,
> They stood gazing at Ram,
> Forgetting even to blink.   (118C)

Raghurai, seeing their extreme love,
Took them all up into the flying chariot.
Then, mentally bowing his head at the Brahmans' feet,
He turned the chariot towards the north.
As the chariot took off, a great tumult arose,
With everyone shouting 'Glory to Raghubir!'
Upon a high and lovely throne
Sat the Lord with Shri.
There, Ram and his beloved glittered,
Like dark cloud and lightning upon Mount Meru's peak.
The shining chariot flew swiftly on—
The gods, rejoicing, rained flowers upon it.
Supremely pleasing, cool, soft and fragrant breezes blew,
And oceans, lakes and rivers shone clean and pure.
There were good omens all around,
All hearts were happy, and the whole sky clear and bright.
Said Raghubir, 'Look, Sita, the field of battle.
Here Lakshman killed Indrajit,
And here, upon the battleground, lie
The huge demons slain by Hanuman and Angad.
And the two brothers, Kumbhakaran and Ravan,
Were killed here, those tormentors of gods and saints.

> Here I had a bridge built,
> And set up a shrine to Shiv.'
> The all-merciful Ram and Sita,
> Bowed in homage to Shambhu.   (119A)

> All the places in the forest where
> The compassionate Lord had stayed or rested,
> He pointed out to Janaki,
> And told her what they were called.   (119B)

Swiftly the chariot reached
The beautiful Dandak forest.

Ram visited the hermitages
Of Kumbhaj and of the other great munis who lived there.
After receiving the blessings of all the sages,
The Lord of the universe came to Chitrakut,
And filled with delight all the munis there.
The chariot flew swiftly on.
Ram then showed Janaki the lovely Jamuna,
That washes away the sins of this age of Kali.
Then, seeing the pure and sacred Ganga,
Ram said, 'Do it homage, Sita.
Now see also Prayag, the chief of all holy places,
The mere sight of which drives away the sins of countless births.
See also the supremely sanctifying triveni,
The dispeller of sorrow, and ladder to Hari's abode.
And now behold the most sacred city of Avadh,
That destroys the anguish of the triple fires and heals the disease
    of rebirth.'

    The merciful Lord and Sita
    Did homage to Avadh.
    Ram's eyes filled with tears, his body trembled,
    And he was overwhelmed with happiness and joy.   (120A)

    Then the Lord stopped at the triveni
    And joyfully bathed in the confluence.
    Together with the monkeys,
    He gave the Brahmans many gifts.   (120B)

The Lord then instructed Hanuman,
'Assume the form of a young Brahman and go to Avadh.
Tell Bharat that I am well,
And then return with news of him.'
The Wind's son left at once.
Then the Lord went to Bharadvaj.
The muni paid homage to him in many ways,

And singing a hymn of praise, gave him his blessing.
The Lord in reverence touched the muni's feet, and then, folding
    his hands,
Ascended his flying chariot and continued on his way.
The Nishad chief, Guha, heard of the Lord's approach,
And crying, 'A boat, bring a boat!' called all his people to him.
Meanwhile, the flying chariot crossed the sacred Ganga,
And, at the Lord's command, landed upon its bank.
Sita then paid homage to the divine river,
And threw herself at the river goddess's feet.
Rejoicing, Ganga gave Sita her blessing,
'May your state of wedded bliss never cease, beautiful princess.'
On hearing that the Lord had come, Guha rushed
To him, brimming with love and joy.
Seeing Vaidehi with the Lord,
He fell to the ground, overcome.
Raghurai, upon seeing his great devotion,
Raised him and clasped him joyfully to his heart.

Ramaa's beloved, the abode of mercy and wisest of the wise,
Took and clasped him to his heart.
He seated him by his side, and asked of his well-being.
Guha humbly replied,
'Now all is well, for I have seen your lotus feet
That Shankar and Viranchi adore.
O Ram, abode of bliss, you who are free from all desire,
I bow to you in homage!'

Hari embraced that base-born Nishad
As though he were Bharat himself.
Dull of mind, says Tulsidas, is he
Who, in folly's grip, forgets such a Lord.
This story of Ravan's enemy ever sanctifies.
It inspires perpetual love for Ram's feet,

Destroys lust and other passions, engenders true wisdom,
And gods, Siddhas and sages sing it with delight.

> To those wise men who listen to the story
> Of Raghubir's triumph in battle,
> The divine Lord ever grants
> Success, wisdom and wealth.   (121A)

> This age of Kali is the dwelling place of sin—
> Think on it and see for yourself, O mind.
> Except for the name of Ram,
> There is no other succour.   (121B)

Thus ends the sixth descent into the Manas lake of Ram's acts, that destroy all the impurities of the Kali age.

Book VII

UTTARKAND
(EPILOGUE)

Mangalcharan

Dark-complexioned like the dark-blue lustre of a peacock's neck,
The greatest of the gods, adorned with the imprint of the Brahman's
*   lotus foot,*
Full of beauty, clad in yellow, lotus-eyed,
Ever gracious and kind,
With a bow and iron arrows in his hand, accompanied by a
*   host of monkeys,*
Served by his brother, Lakshman,
Worthy of worship, Janaki's lord, the jewel of the Raghu clan,
Mounted upon the Pushpak—Ram, I adore him.   (1)

The lotus feet of Kosala's king are beautiful and soft,
Worshipped by Brahma and Mahesh, caressed by Janaki's
*   lotus hands,*
And ever attended upon by the bees
That are the hearts of those who meditate upon them.   (2)

Bright and lovely as the jasmine, the moon and the conch shell,
Ambika's lord, lotus-eyed, ever compassionate,
Who fulfils the most cherished desires—
Shankar, the annihilator of Anang, I worship him.   (3)

Only one day remained of Ram's exile,
And the citizens of Avadh were restless.
Everywhere, men and women fretted and worried,
Their bodies worn out with the grief of separation
     from Ram.   (0A)

Then auspicious omens of every kind occurred,
And the hearts of all became glad.
The city itself grew beautiful all around,
As though announcing the Lord's arrival.   (0B)

Kaushalya and the other queen mothers
Were as full of joy as though
Expecting to hear any instant
That the Lord, with Shri and his brother, had arrived.   (0C)

Bharat's right eye and arm
Twitched again and again.
Knowing this to be a good sign,
He rejoiced deeply, but began to worry.   (0D)

The end of Ram's exile had been the hope and support of his life.
    Now only a day remained,
And his heart filled with immeasurable grief as he wondered,
'Why has the Lord not returned yet?
Has he forgotten me, thinking I am dishonest?
Ah, blessed is Lakshman, and so fortunate,
True lover of Ram's lotus feet!
The Lord knew me to be deceitful and untrue,
Which is why he did not take me with him.
Were the Lord to consider my actions,
There would be no salvation for me even after countless kalpas.
But the Lord does not consider the faults of his devotees,
For he is the friend of the wretched, and most sweet-natured.

I firmly believe in my heart
That Ram will come, for the omens are favourable.
But should my life's breath still remain at the end of his exile,
Who in this world would be as contemptible as me?

    While Bharat's heart was thus drowning
    In the ocean of the grief of separation from Ram,
    The Wind's son in the form of a Brahman
    Arrived like a boat to rescue him.   (1A)

    Hanuman saw him seated upon a mat of kush grass,
    With his wasted frame and crown of matted hair,
    Repeating 'Ram, Ram, Raghupati',
    His lotus eyes streaming with tears.   (1B)

Seeing him, Hanuman was overcome with happiness,
So that his body trembled, and his eyes rained tears of joy.
His heart full of bliss,
He spoke words that were like nectar to the ear.
'He whose absence you mourn day and night,
Unceasingly repeating his list of virtues,
That ornament of the Raghu clan, the bestower of joy upon
    his devotees,
The protector of gods and munis—he has safely returned.
After vanquishing his enemy in battle, and with the gods singing
    his glory,
The Lord is on his way with Sita and Lakshman.'
Hearing these words, Bharat forgot all his grief,
Like a thirsty man finding nectar.
'Who are you, friend, and from where have you come,
You who have spoken such dear words to me?'
'I am the son of the Wind, a monkey,
And my name is Hanuman, O merciful one.
I am a servant of the benevolent Raghupati.'

Hearing this, Bharat rose at once to meet him reverently.
As he embraced him, he could not contain his love within his heart—
His body trembled and his eyes overflowed with tears.
'Monkey, upon seeing you, all my sorrows have disappeared,
For today I have met my beloved Ram in you.'
Again and again he asked of Ram's well-being and said,
'What shall I give you, dear brother, in return?
I have thought and I find there is nothing
In the world to equal this news you have brought.
So, dear friend, I can never be free of my debt to you.
Now tell me of the Lord's doings.'
Then Hanumant bowed his head at Bharat's feet,
And related to him the whole tale of Raghupati's deeds.
'Tell me, monkey,' said Bharat, 'does the merciful Lord
Ever remember me as his servant?

Does the jewel of the Raghu clan
Ever remember me as his own servant?'
Hearing Bharat's meek and gentle words, the monkey
Quivered with joy and fell at his feet.
How can he be other than modest, supremely pure
And an ocean of every virtue, he whose virtues
Raghubir, the lord of all creation, moving and unmoving,
Recites with his own lips?

    'You are dear as life to Ram, my lord.
    I speak the truth, dear master.'
    Bharat embraced him again and again,
    His joy more than his heart could contain.   (2A)

    Then, bowing his head at Bharat's feet,
    The monkey returned at once to Ram,
    And told him that all was well.
    The Lord then mounted his chariot and joyfully
       set forth.   (2B)

Rejoicing, Bharat came to Koshal's city,
And told his guru, Vasishtha, all the news.
He then had it known in the palace
That Raghurai was returning safe and well to the city.
Upon hearing this, the queen mothers all started up in haste,
But Bharat reassured them by telling them that the Lord was well.
When the residents of Ayodhya heard the news,
Men and women all rushed forth in joy.
Women set forth with graceful gait,
Singing as they went, and bearing golden salvers
Laden with curd, darbh grass, gorochan, fruits, flowers
And fresh, new sprigs of tulsi, the source of all well-being.
All rushed out, just as they were,
Without stopping to bring children or the old with them.
They asked each other, 'Brother,
Have you seen the gracious Raghurai?'
Knowing that the Lord was coming, the city of Avadh
Became a treasure house of beauty.
Pleasing breezes, cool, soft and fragrant, blew,
And the water of the Sarju flowed clear and pure.

Joyously, with a heart full of love,
And accompanied by his guru, his kinsfolk
His brother, and a crowd of Brahmans,
Bharat went forth to meet the abode of mercy.   (3A)

Many of the women climbed up on to the rooftops
To look for the chariot in the sky,
And seeing it they began to joyfully sing
Songs of celebration in sweet voices.   (3B)

The ocean that is the city of Avadh is swelling with joy
At the sight of the full moon that is Raghupati,
Rising to meet him with a great uproar,
The women its tumultuous waves.   (3C)

Meanwhile, Ram, the sun to the lotuses of the Raghu clan,
Was showing the heart-enchanting city to the monkeys.
'Listen, O monkey-king, king of Lanka and Angad,
This city is holy and this land beautiful.
Though all men praise Vaikunth—
Which is renowned in the Vedas and known to the
    whole world—
It is not as dear to me as the city of Avadh.
Only a few are aware of this.
This lovely city is my birthplace.
To its north flows the sanctifying Sarju river,
By bathing in which men, without effort,
Find a home near me.[1]
Those who live here are very dear to me.
This city, the abode of bliss, bestows upon them a place in
    my heaven.'
The monkeys all rejoiced to hear the Lord's words,
'Blessed is Avadh to be praised by Ram!'

When the divine Lord, ocean of compassion,
Saw all the people coming to meet him,
He directed the chariot to land near the city.
Pushpak then came down on the ground.   (4A)

Alighting, the Lord said to Pushpak,
'Return now to Kuber.'
Ordered by Ram, it went away,
Filled with joy and sorrow both.   (4B)

With Bharat came all the people,
Their bodies thin and wasted with the grief of separation
    from Raghubir.
When the Lord saw Vamdev, Vasishtha and the other great munis,
He threw down his bow and arrows upon the ground,

And ran, he and his brother Lakshman,
To clasp their guru's lotus feet, their bodies trembling with joy.
Vasishtha, chief of the sages, embraced them and asked after
    their well-being.
'By your grace,' they replied, 'we are all well.'
Ram, chief of the Raghu dynasty, and upholder of righteousness,
Greeted all the Brahmans, bowing his head before them.
Then Bharat clasped the Lord's lotus feet,
Worshipped by gods, munis, Shankar and Brahma.
He lay prostrate upon the ground and refused to get up,
Till Ram, the ocean of mercy, raised him by force and clasped him
    to his heart.
His dark form trembled with emotion,
And his eyes, like new-blooming lotuses, filled with tears.

His lotus eyes streamed with tears,
And his lovely form trembled with emotion.
Ram, lord of the three worlds,
Clasped his brother to his heart with deep affection.
I have no simile or metaphor to describe
The beauty of the Lord's meeting with his brother.
It was as though Love and Desire had assumed bodily form
And met in an embrace of supreme loveliness.

When the compassionate Lord asked of his welfare,
Bharat could reply only with difficulty.
Listen, Shivaa, Bharat's joy at that moment was beyond speech
    or mind,
It can only be understood by those who experience it.
'Now all is well with me, O king of Koshal,
For, knowing your servant to be in distress, you have revealed
    yourself.
You took me by the hand, O abode of mercy,
Just as I was drowning in the sea of separation from you.'

Then the Lord joyfully
Embraced Shatrughna and held him to his heart,
And the two brothers, Lakshman and Bharat,
Embraced each other with supreme love.   (5)

Finally, Shatrughna and Lakshman embraced each other.
Thus ended that intolerable anguish born of separation.
Then Bharat and his brother Shatrughna bowed their heads
At Sita's feet and knew supreme delight.
The residents of the city rejoiced at the sight of the Lord,
And all the grief and sorrow arising from his absence came to
    an end.
Seeing the people impatient with love,
The all-merciful Ram, slayer of the demon Khar, created
    an illusion:
The gracious Lord appeared at once in countless forms
And in this way met everyone in the appropriate manner.
Raghubir looked upon them with compassion,
And freed all the men and women of sorrow.
In an instant the divine Lord embraced everyone,
But Uma, no one understood this mystery.
In this way, Ram, the abode of courtesy and goodness,
Made everyone happy and proceeded on his way.
Kaushalya and the other royal mothers all ran to meet him,
Like cows that have just given birth rush to meet their calves.

They rushed to meet him like cows that, driven by force to graze in
    the forest,
Have left their new-born calves at home,
And so hurry back to their village at the end of the day,
Lowing, with flowing teats.
The Lord embraced all the royal mothers with deep affection,
And spoke many sweet words to them.
Thus their great anguish at separation from him disappeared,
And in its place, they found immeasurable joy and bliss.

Sumitra hugged her son,
Knowing his devotion to Ram's feet.
Kaikeyi embraced Ram,
But felt deeply abashed. (6A)

Lakshman hugged all the royal mothers,
And rejoiced to receive their blessings.
Though he embraced Kaikeyi again and again,
His anger towards her would not leave him. (6B)

Vaidehi met all her mothers-in-law,
And pleased them greatly by touching their feet.
They asked about her well-being and blessed her,
'May your state of wedded joy last forever!'
All the royal mothers gazed at Raghupati's lotus face,
But knowing it to be a happy occasion, they checked the tears that
    rose in their eyes.
They performed arti with golden salvers,
And gazed again and again at the Lord's divine person.
They showered him with offerings of many kinds,
Their hearts filled with supreme joy.
Kaushalya gazed again and again at Raghubir,
That ocean of mercy, so steadfast in battle,
And thought to herself each time,
'How did he kill the king of Lanka?
My two boys are so tender and delicate,
And the demon warriors strong and mighty!'

Their mother gazed at the Lord
With Lakshman and Sita—
Her heart filled with supreme joy,
And her body trembled with love. (7)

Vibhishan, king of Lanka, Sugriv, king of the monkeys, Nal, Nil,
Jamvant, the courteous and handsome Angad,

And Hanuman and all the other brave monkeys,
Took on beautiful human forms.
With great love and reverence, they praised
Bharat's love, his courtesy, his penance and vow.
Seeing the way of life of Ayodhya's people,
They praised them for their devotion to the Lord's feet.
Then Raghupati called all his friends and allies to him,
And instructed them to touch the muni's feet.
'My guru Vasishtha,' he said, 'is revered by my whole clan,
It is by his grace that the demons were slain in battle.'
He turned to his guru and said, 'These are all my friends, O muni.
They were the rafts that took me across the ocean of war.
They staked their lives for my sake,
And are dearer to me than even Bharat.'
Hearing the Lord's words, all became lost in love and wonder.
Every moment gave birth to some new joy.

They then bowed their heads
At Kaushalya's feet,
Who, delighted, gave them her blessing, saying,
'You are as dear to me as Raghunath.'   (8A)

A rain of flowers fell from the sky
As Ram, the source of all bliss, made his way to the palace.
Crowds of men and women climbed on to the city's
        rooftops
To look at him.   (8B)

They decorated golden pitchers of many kinds
And placed them at their doors.
They hung out bunting and banners,
And festooned their doorways with festive wreaths of leaves
        and flowers.
All the lanes and alleys were washed with fragrant water,

And many sacred ornamental squares were drawn, all filled in with
    elephant pearls.
Every kind of preparation to bring in good fortune was made,
And drums and kettledrums sounded joyously throughout
    the city.
Everywhere, women scattered offerings for good fortune in
    his path,
Calling blessings upon him with hearts full of joy.
Young women with golden arti salvers
Sang auspicious songs.
Performing arti, they welcomed him—the remover of all distress,
And the sun to the cluster of lotuses that is the Raghu clan.
The Vedas, Shesh and Sharada have praised
The city's splendour, its wealth and magnificence.
But even they were overwhelmed at the spectacle.
So how can any mortal, Uma, describe its glory?

    The city of Avadh was the lake, the women the water-lilies,
    Drooping in the sun that was their grief at separation from
        Raghupati.
    But now that sun had set, and the lilies bloomed again
    At the sight of the full moon that was Ram.   (9A)

    Auspicious omens of every kind occurred
    And drums of celebration sounded in the sky
    As the divine Lord moved towards the palace,
    Giving again a king to the men and women of the city.   (9B)

The Lord knew that Kaikeyi was ashamed,
So he went first to her palace, Bhavani.
There Hari reassured and comforted her,
And then proceeded to his own abode.
When the ocean of mercy entered his palace,
All the men and women of the city grew glad.

Guru Vasishtha summoned all the Brahmans, and said,
'The day, the hour and all else is auspicious today,
So, all you Brahmans rejoice and give instruction
That Ramchandra takes his seat upon the throne.'
Upon hearing Muni Vasishtha's pleasing words,
All the gathered Brahmans were delighted.
Many Brahmans spoke sweet words and said,
'Ram's investiture will please and gladden the world,
So great muni, delay no further,
And put the royal tilak upon the king's forehead.'

    Then the muni instructed Sumantra,
    Who proceeded with joy to make ready numerous
    Chariots, horses and elephants
    As soon as he heard the order.　　　　　　　(10A)

    He sent out messengers in every direction
    To fetch auspicious items,
    Then joyfully returned to Vasishtha
    And bowed his head at his feet.　　　　　　(10B)

The city of Avadh was beautifully decorated,
And the gods rained down flowers unceasingly.
Then Ram summoned his attendants and said,
'Go, first help my friends with their baths.'
Upon hearing his command, his attendants immediately ran
To help Sugriv and the others with their baths.
Then Ram, abode of mercy, called Bharat to him,
And, with his own hands, unknotted his coil of matted hair.
Then the Lord, the merciful Raghurai, cherisher of devotees,
Helped his three brothers to bathe.
Not even a thousand million Sheshnags would be able to relate
Bharat's blessedness and the Lord's sweet tenderness.
Then Ram undid his own matted hair,

And with his guru's permission, bathed.
After bathing, the Lord adorned himself with jewels,
And the beauty of his form put to shame a hundred gods of Love.

>Her mothers-in-law with reverence
>Helped Janaki to bathe.
>They dressed her in bright raiment
>And adorned every part of her body with
>>precious jewels.   (11A)

>Upon Ram's left side shone
>Ramaa, full of beauty and goodness.
>Gazing upon her, the royal mothers all rejoiced,
>And considered their births rewarded.   (11B)

>Listen, O king of the birds, at that moment,
>Brahma, Shiv, the munis and all the gods
>Arrived in their chariots
>To look upon Ram, the source of all bliss.   (11C)

Gazing at the Lord, Muni Vasishtha's heart filled with love.
He sent at once for a magnificent throne,
As bright as the sun. Its splendour defies description.
Bowing his head to the Brahmans, Ram took his seat upon it.
Looking upon Raghurai with Janak's daughter at his side,
The assembled munis were filled with joy.
The Brahmans then recited mantras from the Vedas,
While the gods and munis in the sky cheered in celebration.
First, Muni Vasishtha put the sacred tilak upon Ram's forehead,
And then instructed all the other Brahmans to do the same.
Seeing their son upon the throne, the royal mothers rejoiced
And performed arti again and again.
They gave many and diverse gifts to the Brahmans,
And gave every beggar so much that he begged no more.

Seeing the master of the three worlds upon Ayodhya's throne,
The gods beat their drums in jubilation.

Drums resounded in the sky,
Gandharvas and Kinnaras sang,
And crowds of apsaras danced
To the supreme delight of gods and munis.
Bharat, and his brothers Lakshman and Shatrughna,
Vibhishan, Angad, Hanuman and the rest
Held the royal insignia—umbrella, whisk, fan, bow, sword, shield and spear—
And stood in splendour beside the Lord.

With Shri by his side, the jewel of the solar dynasty
Shone with the beauty of many gods of love.
His noble form, dark as a raincloud, clad in yellow,
Captivated the hearts of the gods.
His crown, his armbands and other lovely ornaments
Adorned every part his body.
Blessed indeed are those who beheld him,
With his lotus eyes, broad chest, and mighty arms.

I cannot relate the beauty of the occasion, Khagesh,
And the joy and the magnificence of that gathering.
Sharada, Shesh and the Vedas describe them,
But Mahesh alone knows their true essence.   (12A)

Each praising the Lord, the gods
Returned to their own abodes.
Then arrived the Vedas in the form of minstrels
Into the presence of Lord Ram.   (12B)

The omniscient and compassionate Lord
Received them with reverence—
Though no one else understood this secret.
The Vedas then began to sing of his perfections.   (12C)

*Glory to you, visible manifestation of the Absolute, who transcends all
    attributes of maya!*
Incomparable is your beauty, you, the best and greatest of kings,
Who, by the strength of your arm, slew ten-headed Ravan
And other fierce and powerful demons,
And who, becoming incarnate as a man, destroyed the burdens of this world
And put an end to its terrible suffering.
Glory to you, protector of the suppliant, compassionate Lord!
We worship you, O omnipotent God, and Sita, your Shakti, by your side.

O Hari, overcome by your impenetrable maya,
And subject to time, karma and the gunas,
Gods and Asurs, Nagas, men, and all creation, moving and unmoving,
Wander for numberless nights and days along the paths of birth and rebirth.
Lord, those upon whom you have looked at with compassion,
They have been released from the triple afflictions.
Protect us, O Ram!
*You who are so quick to destroy the sorrows of this existence—we
    worship you.*

They who, drunk on the pride of learning,
Do not respect devotion to you— which takes away the fear of rebirth—
May reach the state that even gods find difficult to attain;
Yet we see them fall from it again, O Hari.
They who give up reliance on all others, and, reposing their trust in you alone,
Continue to remain your servants,
Cross without effort the ocean of this existence
By merely repeating your name. This is the Lord we invoke.

The feet that Shiv and Brahma adore,
By touching the dust of which the muni's wife was saved,
From beneath the nails of which flows the celestial stream of the Ganga,
Revered by munis, and sanctifier of the three spheres,
*The feet, the soles of which bear the marks of the flag, the thunderbolt,
    the elephant-goad and the lotus,*

And which took on the scars of thorns during your wanderings in
    the forest—
Those lotus feet, O Mukund, O Ram, O Ramaa's beloved,
We forever worship.

The tree whose root is the imperceptible brahm, which is without
    beginning and uncreated,
Whose bark is fourfold, as the Vedas and Shastras declare,
Which has six trunks, five and twenty branches,
Innumerable leaves and countless flowers,
Which bears fruits of two kinds, bitter and sweet,
Which has a single creeper clinging to it, and which remains protected by it,
Which constantly bears fresh new leaves and flowers—
As that tree of the Universe, we adore you.[2]

Let those who meditate upon you as the Absolute, the unborn, the one
    without a second,
Perceptible only by inference, and beyond the mind,
Preach and believe that. But we, O Lord,
Ever sing of the glory of your manifest form.
O abode of compassion, O mine of all virtue, O divine Lord,
We ask this boon of you—
That in thought, word and deed, without change or alteration,
We remain devoted to your feet.

In the sight of all,
The Vedas sang this noble prayer.
They then became invisible,
And returned to Brahma's abode.   (13A)

O Vainateya, king of the birds,
Then Shambhu came to Raghubir,
And made entreaty, his voice choking
And his body trembling with emotion.   (13B)

'Glory to you, O Ram, Ramaa's beloved, destroyer of the world's afflictions!
Protect this devotee, who is overcome by the fear of rebirth.
O glorious one, king of Avadh, chief of the gods, and Ramaa's lord,
Have mercy on me who has come to you for refuge.

O destroyer of Ravan, with his ten heads and twenty arms,
You have rid the earth of great and numerous afflictions.
The demon hosts, like swarms of moths,
Perished in the fierce flames of your purifying arrows.

Holding a noble bow, arrow and quiver, you are
The most beautiful ornament of this earthly orb.
You are the radiant rays of the sun that dispel the dense darkness
Of the night that is pride, ignorance and attachment.

Mind-born Love, like a savage hunter,
Killed the deer that is men with the arrow of lust.
O Hari, slay this hunter and save these foolish and helpless creatures
Who have lost their way in the forest of sensual desire.

The many ills and sorrows that afflict people,
Are the fruit of their disregard for your feet.
Those men who do not love your lotus feet,
Forever drift upon the bottomless ocean of birth and rebirth.

Those who cherish no love for your lotus feet,
Remain eternally wretched, miserable and sad,
But those for whom your story, master, is their support,
Forever hold dear the saints and you, the eternal Lord.

They are free from anger, greed, arrogance and pride,
So that, for them, prosperity and adversity are the same.
And for this reason, munis abandon faith in asceticism forever,
And joyfully become your servants.

Making a solemn vow, and with a pure heart,
They everlastingly love and serve your lotus feet.
All such holy men, whether they receive reverence or scorn,
Regard both the same, and happily wander the world.

You who are the honey bee to the lotuses that are the hearts of holy men,
O Raghubir, invincible and steadfast in battle—I worship you.
Your name I repeat unceasingly and bow to you, O Hari,
You who are the enemy of pride, and the remedy for the disease of rebirth.

O supreme abode of virtue, goodness and compassion,
Shri's beloved—I worship you without ceasing.
O Raghunandan, put an end to all dualities,
And, O protector of this earth, look upon your humble servant.

Again and again, I ask this boon of you—
Be pleased to grant it, gracious Vishnu—
Of unceasing devotion to your lotus feet,
And constant association with your devotees.'   (14A)

After thus relating Ram's virtues,
Uma's lord returned joyously to Kailash.
Then the Lord had assigned to the monkeys,
Residences comfortable and pleasing in every way.   (14B)

O king of the birds, this tale is all-purifying.
It removes the afflictions of the triple fires and destroys the fear
    of rebirth.
Upon hearing this story of great King Ram's royal investiture,
Men acquire detachment and discernment.
Those who listen to it or sing it with intent,
Obtain every kind of happiness and prosperity,
And, after enjoying in this world bliss that is difficult even for gods
    to attain,

They go, at the end, to Raghupati's divine abode.
If those freed from all future existence, the detached from the
    world, and the worldly hear it,
They acquire faith, union with the Absolute, and ever-increasing
    prosperity.
O king of the birds, Ram's story, which I have narrated according
    to my understanding,
Takes away fear and sorrow.
It reinforces dispassion, discernment and devotion,
And is a beautiful boat in which to cross the river of delusion.
Each day there was some new celebration in Koshal's city,
And the people all continued to rejoice.
All felt an ever-increasing love for Ram's lotus feet,
Which Shiv, the munis and Brahma adore.
Mendicants were given clothes in great abundance,
While Brahmans received gifts of many kinds.

> The monkeys were immersed in divine bliss,
> All devoted to the Lord's feet.
> They did not notice the passing of the days,
> And six months went by.   (15)

They forgot their homes, and did not remember them even
    in dream,
Just as holy men never even think of harming others.
Then Raghupati summoned all his friends and allies,
Who came and reverently bowed their heads to him.
With supreme love, he seated them beside him,
And spoke sweet words to gladden their devoted hearts.
'You have done me great service,
But how can I praise you to your face?
You gave up your homes and your comforts for my sake,
And for that, I hold you most dear.
I love my brothers, my kingdom, my wealth,

Vaidehi, my life, my home and my family.
They are all dear to me, but none as dear as you.
These are true, these words of mine.
As a rule, all love their followers,
But I have special love for those who serve me.

> Now, my friends, return home, all of you,
> And there worship me most steadfastly.
> Knowing me ever to be all-pervading and beneficent to all,
> Love me most dearly.'   (16)

Listening to the Lord, all grew so engrossed
That they forgot their own bodies and who or where they were.
They stood with folded hands, gazing at him unblinkingly.
Overwhelmed with love, they could not utter a word.
The Lord saw their great love,
And discoursed at length to them on wisdom and true
     understanding.
They were unable to speak in the presence of the Lord,
But turned their gaze again and again to his lotus feet.
Then the Lord called for jewels and rich garments
Of many colours and incomparable splendour.
First Bharat with his own hands prepared a set
And conferred it upon Sugriv.
By the Lord's command, Lakshman next bestowed the robes
     of honour
Upon Vibhishan, king of Lanka. This pleased Raghupati greatly.
But Angad remained seated and did not move,
And the Lord, seeing his love, did not call him.

> Raghunath himself bestowed the jewels and garments
> Upon Jamvant, Nil and the others,
> And holding Ram's image in their hearts,
> They all bowed their heads at his feet and left.   (17A)

Then Angad rose and bowed his head,
And, with eyes full of tears and folded hands,
He spoke with deep humility,
Words that were steeped in love.   (17B)

'O all-knowing Lord, ocean of compassion and bliss,
Merciful to the lowly, and friend of the distressed,
In his moment of death, Lord, my father Baali
Placed me in your charge.
Uphold your especial attribute of being the refuge of the helpless,
And do not abandon me, O benefactor of the faithful.
You are my guru, my father and my mother, Lord.
Where shall I go, leaving your lotus feet?
Think on it yourself and tell me, O king of men,
Separated from you, what use is my home to me?
Lord, keep me with you. A child without wisdom, intellect, or strength,
And your humble devotee,
I will do all the lowliest tasks in the palace,
And gazing upon your lotus feet, I will cross the ocean of this existence.'
So saying, he fell at the Lord's feet and said,
'Now, my master, do not ask me to go home.'

Upon hearing Angad's meek and humble words,
Lord Raghupati, pinnacle of compassion,
Raised him and clasped him to his heart,
His lotus eyes full of tears.   (18A)

Giving Baali's son his own necklace,
And clothing him in his own robes and jewels,
The divine Lord sent him away
With many words of comfort.   (18B)

Recalling the devoted Angad's great deeds, Bharat,
With his brothers Shatrughna and Saumitri, proceeded to see him off.

But Angad's heart was so full of love,
That he turned again and again to look at Ram.
Again and again he prostrated himself, wishing,
'If only Ram would ask me to stay!'
Sadly, treasuring up in his mind Ram's way of looking,
Speaking, walking and of meeting people with a smile,
But understanding the Lord's wish, he departed,
With many words of homage and the Lord's lotus-feet in
    his heart.
After seeing off all the monkeys with great respect,
Bharat and his brothers returned.
Then Hanuman clasped Sugriv's feet,
And earnestly entreated him,
'After another ten days in Raghupati's service,
I will return to serve at your feet, my lord.'
'You are the aggregation of virtue, O son of the Wind!
Go serve the abode of mercy!' said Sugriv
So saying, all the monkeys at once departed.
Angad hung back and said, 'Listen, Hanuman,

> With folded hands I beseech you,
> Pay homage to the Lord on my behalf,
> And from time to time
> Remind Raghunayak of me.'   (19A)

> Thus saying, Baali's son departed,
> And Hanumant came back to Ram.
> When he told him of Angad's devotion,
> The divine Lord was overcome with love.   (19B)

> Harder than adamant
> And softer than a flower,
> Is Ram's heart, Khagesh.
> Tell me, who can understand it?   (19C)

Then the merciful Lord summoned the Nishad,
And bestowed upon him jewels, clothes and gifts.
'Return home, but remember me,
And, in thought, deed and word, follow the dictates of dharma.
You are my friend and as much my brother as Bharat,
So continue to visit this city often.'
Guha was overcome with joy at these words
And fell at his feet, his eyes full of tears.
Holding Ram's lotus feet in his heart, he returned home,
And there told all his kinsfolk of the Lord's generous nature.
Seeing the actions of Raghupati, the residents of Ayodhya
Said again and again, 'Blessed is he, the storehouse of bliss!'
Upon Ram's assuming the throne of Ayodhya,
The three spheres rejoiced and all sorrow disappeared.
No one held enmity towards another,
And all differences vanished under Ram's influence.

Intent on dharma, the people walked in the path of the Vedas,
Each according to his station and stage of life,
In perfect happiness,
And free of fear, sorrow and disease.   (20)

Under Ram's rule, no one anywhere suffered from any affliction,
Whether of the body, caused by gods or fate, or other beings.
All men loved one another, followed the course of conduct
Appropriate to their own caste, and lived according to the rules
    prescribed in the Vedas
The four precepts of dharma[xvii] became established throughout
    the world,
And no wickedness remained even in dream.
Men and women were absorbed in devotion to Ram,
And all were deserving of freedom from rebirth.

—————————

[xvii] These are truth, purity, compassion and charity

No one died an early death, nor was anyone in pain,
But everyone was pleasing to look at, with bodies free
    from sickness.
No one was poor, or sad, or in distress,
No one was ignorant or lacking good fortune.
All, men and women, were without deceit, pious and virtuous,
Clever and accomplished.
All appreciated the virtues of others, and all were learned
    and wise.
All were grateful for help given, and no one was cunning or sly.

> Under Ram's rule, O Garud,
> No being in all the world, whether moving or unmoving,
> Suffered any sorrow or distress that arises
> From time or past action, disposition or personal
>   attributes.   (21)

The earth, encircled by the seven seas,
Had only one king, Raghupati of Koshal.
Such sovereignty was no great matter for him,
Every hair on whose body holds countless universes.
To those who understand the Lord's infinite greatness,
This description will seem utterly disparaging.
But, Khagesh, those who understand his divine glory
Are the very ones who become enamoured of his story—
For the reward of understanding his divine majesty is knowledge of
    these acts of the Lord.
So say the greatest munis and ascetics.
Not even Sharada or Shesh could describe
The joy and prosperity of Ram's reign.
All were generous, all helpful to others,
And all, men and women alike, revered the Brahmans.
All men had one wife, and were devoted to her,
And she was, in thought, word and deed, devoted to her husband.

A rod was found only in the hands of ascetics,
Discord only in the music of dancers,
And the only conquests were of the self—
Such was Ramchandra's rule.   (22)

The trees of the forest were always in flower and laden with fruit,
The elephant and the lion lived in peace together,
And the birds and animals forgot their natural enmity
And lived in friendship with each other.
Birds called and herds of deer
Roamed fearlessly in the forest in delight.
Soft, cool and fragrant breezes blew,
And bees laden with honey hummed.
Vines and trees yielded their nectar merely upon being asked,
The cows gave as much milk as was desired,
The earth was ever replete with crops,
And every aspect of the golden Krityug[xviii] became repeated in
    the Tretayug.
Knowing the king of the world to be the Supreme Spirit of
    the Universe,
The mountains revealed mines of jewels of every kind.
The rivers all flowed with abundant water,
Cool, clear and pleasing to the taste.
The seas remained within their bounds,
And deposited jewels upon their shores, which men gathered.
Every lake and pond was full of lotuses,
And all the quarters of the world were happy.

The moon filled the earth with its radiance,
The sun's heat was only as much as was needed,
And the clouds gave rain whenever asked
In Ramchandra's reign.   (23)

_____

[xviii] The first of the four ages of the world

The Lord performed countless Ashvamedha sacrifices,[3]
And gave innumerable gifts to the Brahmans.
He was the guardian of the Vedas, the upholder of
    righteousness,
And transcended the three gunas. In the luxury and
    splendour of his court, he was another Indra.
Sita, of incomparable beauty, good-natured and gentle,
Remained ever obedient to her husband.
She understood the greatness of the all-merciful Lord,
And served his lotus feet with all her heart.
Though there were many attendants in the palace,
All skilled in their work,
She looked after the housework herself
In accordance with Ramchandra's wishes.
Shri did whatever gave delight to the ocean of mercy,
For she knew how best to serve him.
Without pride or arrogance, she attended upon Kaushalya
And all her other mothers-in-law in the palace.
O Uma, Ramaa is revered by Brahma and the other gods,
She is the mother of the universe and ever irreproachable.

> She, whose gracious look the gods crave,
> But who never even glances at them,
> Remains devoted to Ram's lotus feet,
> Forgetting her own inherent greatness.   (24)

All his brothers served Ram with great devotion,
For their love for him was boundless.
They gazed unceasingly at the Lord's lotus face,
In the hope that the merciful one might ask something of them.
Ram, too, loved all his brothers,
And instructed them on morality and statesmanship.
The residents of the city were blissful and happy,
And enjoyed comforts difficult even for the gods to attain.

Day and night they prayed to the Creator,
Asking for devotion to Lord Raghubir's feet.
Sita gave birth to two beautiful sons,
Lav and Kush, of whom the Vedas and Puranas have sung.
Both were outstanding in battle, modest and accomplished,
And so handsome that they seemed the very image of Hari.
Ram's other brothers, too, each had two sons,
All exceedingly beautiful, gifted and good-natured.

> The Supreme Spirit who transcends knowledge, speech
>   and the senses,
> Who is unbegotten, unaffected by maya, the mind and the
>   properties of material things,
> It was that same all-pervading brahm, imbued with truth,
>   knowledge and bliss,
> Who thus exhibited and exalted the actions of an
>   ordinary man.   (25)

After bathing in the Sarju every morning,
Ram sits in assembly with Brahmans and holy men,
Vasishtha recites the Vedas and Puranas,
And Ram listens attentively, though he already knows
    everything.
He takes his meals with his brothers,
All their mothers looking on with great joy.
Then Bharat and Shatrughna, the two brothers,
Go with the Wind's son to some garden or grove.
There, they sit down and ask him about Ram's acts,
And Hanuman recounts them, his mind immersed in
    his virtues.
The two brothers feel so joyful, hearing of Ram's unblemished
    perfections,
That they beg him to repeat his tale again and again.
In every house, the Puranas were recited

And the sacred story of Ram's deeds narrated.
Men and women sang of Ram's virtues,
And did not notice the passing of the days and nights.

> A thousand Sheshnags cannot describe
> The happiness and prosperity
> Of the people of Avadh,
> Where Ram reigned as king.   (26)

Narad, Sanak and his brothers, and other great munis
Come to Ayodhya every day
For a sight of the king of Koshal—
Gazing upon the city, they forget all their detachment from
    the world.
There were gilded balconies encrusted with jewels,
Their multi-coloured floors inlaid with precious stones.
Enclosing the city on all sides was a magnificent boundary wall
With battlements painted in different colours,
As though the nine planets had mustered an army
And surrounded Amaravati.
The ground was paved in diverse hues,
Seeing which the minds of even the greatest munis would
    be distracted.
Glistening white palaces kissed the sky,
Their glittering spires putting to shame the brightness of the sun
    and the moon.
Latticed windows gleamed with jewels,
And jewelled lamps shone bright in every house.

In the light of jewelled lamps, the mansions gleamed
With their thresholds of glittering coral,
Their pillars of precious stones, and walls of gold, inlaid
    with emeralds,
As though fashioned by Viranchi himself.

The palaces were enchantingly beautiful,
With charming courtyards made of crystal,
And every doorway hung with golden doors
Inlaid with innumerable diamonds.

> In every house there was a beautiful picture gallery,
> Decorated with paintings
> Of Ram's deeds so splendid
> That they stole the hearts of the sages who looked
>   upon them.   (27)

Everyone planted flower gardens
With great care in diverse designs,
In which graceful creepers of many kinds
Were ever in flower as though in spring.
Honeybees hummed unceasingly with a pleasant sound,
And gentle breezes, cool, soft and fragrant, blew.
Birds of all kinds, looked after by the children,
Called sweetly, and were beautiful in flight.
Peacocks, swans, cranes and pigeons
Were a lovely sight upon the tops of houses,
As, seeing their own reflections everywhere,
They cooed and danced and bobbed in many ways.
Children taught parrots and mynahs
To say 'Ram', 'Raghupati', 'protector of the people'.
The palace gates were magnificent,
And the lanes, squares and marketplaces most charming.

The marketplaces were beautiful, and impossible to describe,
And things could be had without price.
How can one describe the wealth of the city
Where Ramaa's beloved is king?
The cloth-merchants, moneylenders and traders sat at their shops
Like numerous gods of wealth.

Men and women, young and old,
All were happy, good and beautiful.

> To the north of the city flowed the Sarju,
> Its waters clear and deep.
> Handsome ghats lined its shores,
> With not even a trace of mud on its banks.   (28)

Apart and at some distance was the pleasant ghat
Where the herds of horses and elephants went to drink.
There were many charming ghats for drinking water,
Where no one was allowed to bathe.
The most beautiful and well-constructed was the royal ghat,
Where men of all the four castes went to bathe.
All along the banks stood temples to the gods
Surrounded by lovely groves.
Here and there upon the river's banks, munis
And ascetics lived, indifferent to the world and intent on
    spiritual wisdom.
All along the shores grew sacred tulsi plants
In great profusion, planted by the munis.
The beauty of the city was impossible to describe,
Its outskirts were also most lovely.
Every sin is effaced at the sight of the city
With its woods, groves, wells and lakes.

Its matchless tanks and lakes,
And large and beautiful wells
With their elegant flights of steps and clear, pure water,
Were so lovely that even gods and munis were captivated by the sight.
The lakes were covered with lotuses of many colours,
Birds called and honeybees hummed,
And delightful gardens, through the cries of cuckoos and other birds,
Seemed to be calling to travellers to halt.

Can the city where Ramaa's lord is king,
Ever be described?
Anima and the other Siddhis
Had spread joy and prosperity throughout Avadh.   (29)

Everywhere men sang the praises of Raghupati,
And said to each other,
'Worship Ram, the protector of those who seek refuge in him,
In whom reside beauty, goodness, grace and virtue;
The lotus-eyed and dark-complexioned one,
Who protects his followers as the eyelids protect the eyes;
The one steadfast in battle, who holds a shining bow and arrows
    and quiver,
And is the sun to the lotuses that are holy men.
Worship Ram, a Garud to devour the terrible serpent of death;
Who destroys covetousness in those who worship him selflessly,
Who is a huntsman to kill the herd of deer that is greed and delusion,
A lion to slay the elephant that is lust, and who bestows bliss upon
    those who adore him;
Worship Ram, a sun to dispel the deep darkness of sorrow and doubt,
And a fire to consume the dense forest of demons;
O how can you not worship Raghubir, who, ever accompanied by
    Janak's daughter,
Destroys the fear of rebirth,
Who is the frost that kills the mosquito swarm of multitudinous
    desires,
Who is ever unchanging, unborn and indestructible,
Who gives joy to the munis, relieves the earth of its burdens,
And is Tulsidas's own gracious Lord?'

Thus did the men and women of Ayodhya
Sing of Ram's perfections,
And Ram, abode of mercy,
Remained ever gracious to them all.   (30)

O king of the birds, ever since
The blazing sun of Ram's glory rose,
The three spheres have been filled with light.
Many were happy, but many were sad as well.
First, let me list those who were sad—
The night of ignorance came to an end,
So that the owls of sin hid themselves where they could,
And the water-lilies of lust and anger closed up.
Diverse rituals, the three gunas, time, individual dispositions—
These chakors found no joy in the sunshine of the Lord's majesty.
Envy, pride, delusion and arrogance were thieves
Unable now to use their skill in any quarter.
But upon the lakes of righteousness,
The varied lotuses of wisdom and knowledge bloomed,
And the many koks of bliss, contentment, dispassion
     and discernment
Became free of sorrow.

> When this sun of glory
> Lights up any man's heart,
> The latter qualities grow and increase,
> While those named first disappear.   (31)

One day, Ram, with his brothers
And his especially beloved Hanuman,
Went to visit a beautiful grove
Where all the trees were bright with flowers and new leaves.
Seeing their chance, Sanak and his three brothers, the mind-born
     sons of Brahma, also came,
Glowing with spiritual power, beautiful in their virtue
     and goodness,
Ever absorbed in the rapture of union with the divine,
And youthful in appearance despite being aeons old.
It was as though the four Vedas had assumed bodily form.

The sages, with only the sky for raiment, looked impartially
    upon all.
They had but one addiction—
To listen to the exploits of Raghupati wherever they were
    being recited.
Sanak and his brothers, Bhavani, had stayed
With the learned sage, Agastya.
The great muni had told them all of Ram's story,
Which is the source of true wisdom, just as the fire-stick is of fire.

> When Ram saw the munis approaching,
> He joyfully prostrated himself before them.
> After welcoming them and asking after their well-being,
> The Lord spread his own yellow robes for them to
>   sit upon. (32)

His three brothers, together with the Wind's son,
Also prostrated themselves before the sages, and everyone felt
    great joy.
The munis, seeing Raghupati's incomparable beauty,
Became absorbed in its contemplation. They could not
    look away
Or close their eyes for an instant, but remained gazing
Upon the dark-hued form and lotus eyes of the Lord,
Shrine of beauty and destroyer of the cycle of rebirth.
Ram stood before them with folded hands and bowed head.
Seeing their state, Raghubir's
Eyes, too, filled with tears and his body trembled.
Taking them by the hand, the Lord made the great munis sit,
And spoke to them most gracious words.
'O great munis, today I am truly blessed,
For upon beholding you, all sins are destroyed.
It is only by the greatest good fortune that one attains the company
    of saints;

It is only through such communion that the cycle of rebirth is,
      without effort, broken.

> The company of saints is the path to salvation,
> While to consort with those given to worldly pleasures leads to
>   endless rebirth—
> So say the saints themselves, the poets, the learned,
> The Vedas, the Puranas and all the holy books.'   (33)

The four munis rejoiced to hear the Lord's words,
And, with quivering limbs, they began to sing a song of praise.
'Hail to the Supreme God, the infinite, the immutable, the sinless,
Existing in every form, the one, the all-compassionate!
Glory to the unembodied! Glory, glory to the ocean of virtue,
The abode of bliss, the beautiful, the accomplished!
Glory to Indira's beloved, glory to the supporter of the earth,
The incomparable, the uncreated, the one without beginning, and
      in whom resides beauty,
Treasure-house of wisdom, without pride, the bestower of honour
      upon others,
Whose purifying glory is sung in the Puranas and the Vedas,
The destroyer of ignorance, who knows the truth of all things, and
      is grateful to his devotees,
The one who transcends maya, whose names are many, and yet
      is nameless,
Who is manifest as all, pervades all and resides
Forever in every heart! Protect us,
And break the bonds of duality, adversity and rebirth that bind us!
Dwell in our hearts, O Ram, and destroy our lust and pride!

> O Supreme Bliss embodied, O abode of mercy,
> You who fulfil the heart's every desire,
> O divine Ram, grant us
> Unceasing and loving devotion to your feet.   (34)

Grant us that all-sanctifying bhakti, O Raghupati,
That destroys the threefold afflictions and the power of
    transmigration.
Lord, you who fulfil the desires of the suppliant like the celestial
    Kamdhenu and Kalpataru,
Show us your favour and grant us this boon.
You are a veritable Rishi Kumbhaj to the ocean that is this
    existence, Raghunayak.[4]
Easily attainable to those who worship you, you bestow every joy
    upon them.
Destroy the intense suffering born of the mind, O friend of
    the humble,
And increase equanimity in us.
You prevent the longing for worldly pleasures, keep away fear
    and envy,
And intensify humility, discernment and detachment.
O jewel amongst earthly kings and the ornament of this earth,
Grant us devotion to you, the only boat in which to cross the ocean
    of this existence.
You are the swan that dwells eternally upon the Manas lake that is
    the minds of sages,
And Brahma and Shankar adore your lotus feet.
Banner of the Raghu clan, custodian of the Vedas,
Devourer of time, destiny, individual dispositions and the
    three gunas,
You are both the boatman and the boat to ferry your worshippers
    across the ocean of this existence.
Destroyer of all defects, jewel of the three worlds, you are
    Tulsidas's own Lord.'

After thus praising the Lord again and again,
And lovingly bowing their heads,
Sanak and his brothers returned to Brahma's abode
With the boon they had so deeply desired.   (35)

After Sanak and his brothers had left for Vidhi's abode,
Ram's brothers all bowed their heads at his feet,
But hesitant to ask the Lord their question,
They all looked at Hanuman,
Wishing to hear from the Lord's own lips
Words that would remove all their misapprehensions.
The Lord, who pervades the inner hearts of all, understood this,
And asked, 'Tell me, Hanuman, what is the matter?'
Folding his hands, Hanuman replied,
'Listen, O all-merciful God—
Bharat, master, wishes to ask you something,
But is hesitant to put the question to you.'
'You know how I feel, Hanuman.
There are no secrets between Bharat and me.'
Hearing the Lord's words, Bharat clasped his feet, and said,
'Hear me, my master, you who take away the suffering of those
        who seek refuge in you.

    I have no doubts of any kind, sire,
    Nor anxiety or any confusion even in my dreams—
    And this is the result of your grace alone,
    O Lord, sum of compassion and bliss.   (36)

But, abode of mercy, I dare presume to ask of you a question,
For I am your servant and you the benefactor of your devotees.
The Vedas and Puranas have sung in many ways
The greatness of the saints, Raghurai.
You, too, have praised them with your own gracious mouth,
And hold great affection for them, Lord.
I would like to know, my master, of their special qualities.
O ocean of mercy, you are clear-sighted and recognize virtue
        and wisdom.
So, protector of the suppliant, explain to me
The attributes that separate the good from the evil.'

'Listen, brother, to the attributes of the good,
Innumerable and celebrated in the Vedas and Puranas.
The doings of the good and the wicked
Are like the behaviour of the axe and the sandalwood tree,
For, brother, the axe cuts down the sandalwood tree,
But the tree imparts its own virtue to the axe by infusing it
    with fragrance.

    That is why sandalwood marks the forehead of the gods,
    And is beloved of the world,
    While the axe, for its punishment,
    Is heated in fire and beaten into shape.   (37)

Indifferent to worldly pleasures, good-natured and virtuous,
Sorrowful in the sorrow of others, joyful to see their joy,
Equable, without enemies, free of pride and desire,
Having relinquished greed, anger, joy and fear,
Tender-hearted, compassionate to the afflicted,
Sincerely devoted to me in thought, word and deed,
Paying honour to others, but taking none for themselves—
Bharat, such beings are as dear to me as life.
Free of all desire, and wholly devoted to my name,
They are happy abodes of tranquillity, restraint and humility.
Gentleness, simplicity, goodwill towards all,
Devotion to Brahmans, the source of all dharma—
He in whose heart all these qualities abide,
Always know him for a true saint, dear brother.
Their calm, self-restraint, piety and moral principles never waver,
And never do they speak harsh or unkind words.

    They who regard criticism and praise both alike,
    And are attached only to my lotus feet—
    Such good men, in whom reside virtue and bliss,
    Are as dear to me as life.   (38)

Listen now to the attributes of the wicked,
With whom no one should associate even by mistake.
Association with them always brings suffering,
Like a troublesome cow that ruins a kapila cow with her company.
The heart of the wicked is filled with terrible agony,
For it is ever consumed with envy at the sight of another's prosperity.
Wherever they hear another reviled,
They are as delighted as though they have found a treasure lying in
    the road.
Completely possessed by lust, anger, pride and greed,
They are cruel, deceitful, crooked and impure.
They bear ill-will towards all without any reason,
And hurt even those who are good to them.
They are false in their giving, false in their taking,
False in every matter, great or small.
They speak sweet words but have hard hearts,
Like the peacock that eats venomous snakes.

> They are hostile to their neighbours, covet the wives
> And wealth of others and speak ill of everyone.
> Such vile and sinful men
> Are man-eating demons incarnate.   (39)

Greed is the sum total of their existence,
They are lecherous and gluttonous, but have no fear of hell.
If they ever hear anyone being praised,
They sigh as though they have caught a fever,
And when they see someone in trouble,
They are as happy as though they have been made kings of
    the world.
Steeped in self-interest, against their own families,
They are dissolute, avaricious and bad-tempered.
They respect neither their mother nor father, and have no regard
    for their guru or Brahmans.

Themselves ruined, they ruin others too.
Deluded and foolish, they are hostile to others,
And take no pleasure in the company of the good or in discourses
    about Hari.
Oceans of vice, dull-witted, degenerate,
They mock the Vedas, lay claim to the wealth of others,
And are especially hostile to Brahmans.
They pretend to be good, but hold trickery and deceit in
    their hearts.

Such vile and wicked men
Are not to be found in the Krityug or the Treta.
There will be some in the Dwapar age,
But hordes will appear in the Kaliyug.   (40)

There is no virtue like the good of others, brother,
And no wickedness like inflicting pain on others.
This is the conclusion of all the Puranas and Vedas,
Dear brother, which I have told you and which all the
    learned know.
Those who, attaining a human body, inflict pain on others,
Must endure the terrible torments of birth and rebirth.
Overcome by delusion and intent on their own selfish interests,
Men commit many sins and so ruin their prospects in the
    next world.
I am dreadful doom for them, dear brother,
And assign them the fruit of their deeds, good and evil.
Those who are truly clever realize this,
And knowing this existence to be a burden, worship only me.
They renounce action, giver of rewards good and bad,
And worship me, the king of gods, men and munis.
I have thus told you the attributes of the good and the wicked.
They who understand them will not be caught in the cycle of birth
    and rebirth.

Listen, dear brother, there are many
Virtues and faults, all the result of maya.
The greatest merit is to see neither,
To notice them is lack of understanding.'   (41)

The brothers all rejoiced to hear these words from the Lord's
     gracious lips.
They could scarcely contain their love within their hearts,
As they reverently bowed before him again and again.
Hanuman's heart, too, was filled with boundless love.
Then Raghupati returned to his own palace.
In this manner, he enacted some new deed every day.
Muni Narad visited Ayodhya time after time,
And sang of Ram's pure acts.
Each time the muni would witness some new exploit,
And, returning to Brahma's realm, recite the whole
     incident there.
Viranchi, delighted to hear of Ram's acts, would say,
'Sing of his virtues again and again, dear son.'
Sanak and his brothers praised Narad too.
Though the sages were immersed in their contemplation of
     the Absolute,
They would forget their samadhi upon hearing his song of praise,
And, supremely qualified to do so, listen to it with reverence.

Though free from this existence and absorbed in contemplation
     of the Absolute,
They interrupted their meditations to listen to the story of
     Ram's deeds.
Those who take no joy in Hari's story,
Must indeed have hearts of stone.   (42)

One day, upon being summoned by Raghunath,
Vasishtha, the Brahmans and the people of the city came together.

When his guru, the munis, the Brahmans and the nobles had taken
    their seats,
Ram, who ends the cycle of rebirth for his devotees, spoke
    these words.
'Listen to my words, people of Ayodhya.
I do not speak out of attachment or any self-interest in my heart,
I do not ask you to do anything wrong, nor do I seek to assert
    my authority.
Hear what I say, and then do what pleases you.
He is my servant and most beloved to me
Who accepts my commands.
If I say anything wrong or unjust, brothers,
Stop me without fear.
It is by great good fortune that you have been born with a
    human body,
Which, as all the scriptures declare, is difficult even for gods
    to attain.
It provides the means to spiritual endeavours and the doorway
    to salvation.
He who receives this body and still cannot prepare for the next
    world by good deeds,

    Receives only suffering in the next world,
    And beats his head again and again in regret,
    Wrongly blaming
    Time and fate and God.   (43)

The reward of this body, brothers, is not the enjoyment of
    worldly pleasures,
For even the pleasures of heaven are brief and lead to suffering.
Those who, upon receiving a human body, become intent on
    sensual enjoyment,
Are fools who exchange amrit for poison.
No one can ever speak well of him

Who throws away the philosopher's stone and picks up a worthless
    gunj seed instead.
This immortal soul wanders forever
Between the four modes of birth and the eighty-four lakh forms of
    living beings.
Impelled by maya, and imprisoned
By time, fate, individual disposition and the three gunas, it drifts
    eternally.
At some time or another, the Supreme God, who loves without
    self-interest,
Takes pity on it and grants it a human body.
This human body is a boat to cross the ocean of existence.
My grace is the favourable wind to speed it on its way,
And a true guru the helmsman of this sturdy boat.
In this way, means that are otherwise difficult to obtain are made
    easily available to the soul.

    The man who fails to cross the ocean of existence
    Even upon receiving such means,
    Is dull-witted and ungrateful, scorning what has been done
        for him,
    And achieves self-destruction.   (44)

If you want happiness here and in the next world,
Listen to my words and hold them firmly in your heart.
The path of devotion to me, my brothers, is pleasant and
    easily accessed,
And has been praised by the Vedas and Puranas.
True knowledge is difficult to attain, and there are many obstacles
    in the way.
The means to it are hard, and there is nothing to fix the
    mind upon.
After much struggle, some do attain it,
But being bereft of bhakti, they do not win my love.

Bhakti is independent and the source of all bliss,
But beings cannot attain it without communion with the saints.
Without an accumulation of merit, saints are inaccessible,
And it is only their company that ends the cycle of birth and rebirth.
There is but one meritorious act in this world—
To worship Brahmans in thought, word and deed.
Munis and gods remain ever favourable to him
Who serves the twice-born without guile or deceit.

> There is one more secret tenet
> That I with folded hands impress upon you all—
> Without the worship of Shankar,
> No man can attain devotion to me.   (45)

Tell me, what effort is required to follow the path of devotion?
Neither abstract contemplation is needed, nor fire-sacrifices,
    prayer, penance, or fasting,
Only a simple and honest disposition, a heart without crookedness,
And complete contentment with whatever comes your way.
If one who calls himself my servant, yet looks to other men
    for support,
Tell me, what faith does he have in me?
But why draw out my discourse any further?
This is the behaviour, brothers, by which I am won:
To have neither enmity nor strife, neither longings nor fear—
Every direction is full of joy for such a man.
He who undertakes nothing for gain, and is without attachment
    or pride,
Free from anger and sin, who is clever and wise,
Ever devoted to the company of the good,
And regards all pleasures, even those of heaven and ultimate
    liberation, as worthless as a blade of grass,
Who is staunch in his support of bhakti, free of wickedness,
And has pushed away all false doctrine,

Who is devoted to singing my virtues, is intent upon my name,
And free of selfishness, arrogance and delusion—
The joy that such a man experiences is known
Only to one who has become one with God, the embodiment
    of supreme bliss.'   (46)

Upon hearing Ram's words as sweet as nectar,
All clasped the feet of the all-merciful Lord, and cried,
'You are our mother, our father, our guru, our brother,
O abode of compassion, you are dearer to us than life!
You are our selves, our wealth, our home, Ram.
O remover of the distress of the suppliant, you are our benefactor
    in every way!
No one but you can give us such instruction,
For even mothers and fathers are devoted to their own interests.
In this world, there are only two disinterested benefactors—
You yourself, and your servants, O slayer of demons.
Everyone else in this world is selfish and self-serving,
And is not interested in the greater good even in dream.'
Hearing their words steeped in love,
Raghunath rejoiced in his heart,
And on receiving his permission, they returned, each to his
    own home,
Discussing the Lord's pleasing discourse as they went.

Uma, the residents of Avadh, both men and women,
Were the very picture of fulfilment,
For Raghunayak, the Absolute embodied, sum of truth,
    knowledge and bliss,
Ruled there as king.   (47)

One day, Muni Vasishtha came
To visit Ram, the abode of bliss.
Raghunayak received him with great reverence,

And washed his feet and drank of the water.
'Ram, listen to me,' said the muni with folded hands,
'I have a request, O ocean of mercy.
After seeing your deeds,
My heart is bewildered.
Even the Vedas cannot comprehend your immeasurable greatness,
So how can I describe it, divine Lord?
The profession of a family priest is very humble,
The Vedas, Puranas and the scriptures regard it with scorn.
When I would not accept the position, my father, Brahma, said to me,
"You will benefit from this in the future, son.
Brahm, the Supreme Spirit, will take on the form of a man,
And appear as a king, the ornament of the Raghu clan."

> Then I thought to myself, if, through this office,
> I find him who is the object
> Of all contemplation, fire-sacrifices, penance and charity,
> No other work can equal this.   (48)

Prayer, penance, religious observances, meditation, the
    performance of one's own duties,
The various virtuous acts prescribed by the Vedas,
The pursuit of true knowledge, compassion, self-restraint, bathing
    in holy places,
The pious practices recommended by the Vedas and holy men
The recitation and hearing of the scriptures and numerous
    Puranas—
All these are means to accomplish
But one glorious end:
Unceasing love for your lotus feet.
Can dirt be removed by washing with dirt?
Can ghee be obtained by churning water?
Without the water of loving devotion, Raghurai,
The inner dirt can never be removed.

He alone is all-wise, learned, knows the true essence of all things,
Is the abode of virtue, endowed with complete understanding,
Wise, and possessed of all auspicious attributes,
Who is devoted to your lotus feet.

> My lord, I ask of you one boon.
> Grant it, Ram, in your grace—
> In each and every future birth of mine, O Lord,
> May my love for your lotus feet never diminish.'   (49)

With these words, Muni Vasishtha returned home,
Leaving Ram, the ocean of mercy, greatly pleased in his heart.
Then he, who is ever gracious to his servants,
Took with him Hanuman, Bharat and his other brothers
And went out of the city. There, the merciful one
Called for elephants, chariots and horses.
After inspecting them, he graciously praised them all,
And distributed them amongst the people, giving each one what he
      deserved and desired.
The Lord who removes all weariness himself grew weary,
And retired to a cool mango grove,
Where Bharat spread his own robe for him.
There the Lord took his seat, with all his brothers attending upon him.
The Wind's son then began to fan him,
His body trembling with devotion, his eyes filling with tears.
There is no one as fortunate
Or as devoted to Ram's feet as Hanuman,
Whose love and devotion, Girija,
The Lord has praised again and again with his own mouth.

> At that moment, Muni Narad arrived
> With his vina in his hand,
> And began to sing Ram's sweet renown
> That remains ever fresh and new.   (50)

'Look upon me, O lotus-eyed Lord,
You who remove all sorrow by your gracious glance alone.
O Hari, dark as the blue lotus, you are the honeybee
That sips on the nectar of the lotus that is the heart of Shiv,
    Kam's enemy.
Breaker of the might of the Rakshasa hordes,
You bring joy to munis and holy men, annihilate sin,
And are as beneficent to Brahmans as a raincloud to new crops.
You are the refuge of the helpless, and the protector of the humble.
By the might of your arms, you destroyed earth's great burden,
And killed the demons Khar, Dushan and Viradh.
Hail, O slayer of Ravan, embodiment of bliss, greatest of kings,
You who are the moon to the lilies that are Dasharath's clan.
Your glory is renowned in the Puranas, the Vedas and the Shastras,
And sung by gods, munis and saints.
Kind and compassionate, the destroyer of false pride,
Infinitely noble, you are Koshal's ornament.
Your name destroys the impurities of the Kali age, and puts an end
    to worldly attachment.
O Lord of Tulsidas, protect your humble devotee!'

    Muni Narad thus lovingly
    Sang Ram's praises.
    Then, with the ocean of beauty held in his heart,
    He returned to Brahma's realm.   (51)

'Girija, pure and holy is this tale,
All of which I have now told you to the best of my understanding.
Ram's acts are without number and unbounded,
And even the Vedas and Sharada cannot relate them all.
Ram is infinite, and infinite are his virtues,
Infinite are his incarnations, his deeds and his names.
You may count the drops of water in a shower of rain, or the grains
    of dust upon the earth,

But Raghupati's doings are beyond enumeration.
This sacred tale gives entry to Hari's own abode,
And whoever hears it acquires unceasing devotion to him.
Uma, I have related to you the same pleasing tale
That Kak Bhushundi told Garud, king of the birds,
And through it, I have recounted a few of Ram's virtues.
Now, Bhavani, what shall I tell you next?'
Uma rejoiced to hear the auspicious tale,
And said in sweet and modest tones,
'Blessed I am, and most fortunate, Purari,
To have heard the virtues of Ram, which remove the fear of rebirth.

By your grace, O most gracious Lord,
I have attained my desire and am free of delusion.
I now know the glory of Lord Ram,
The sum of knowledge and bliss.   (52A)

My husband, from the moon of your mouth
Flows the nectar that is Raghubir's story.
My heart drinks it in with the cups of my ears,
But refuses to be satisfied, my steadfast lord!   (52B)

They who can be satisfied with listening to Ram's acts,
Have not understood their special and unique essence.
Even the great munis free from worldly bonds
Listen forever to Hari's virtues.
Those who wish to cross the ocean of this existence,
Find in Ram's story a sturdy ship.
Even the worldly find Hari's praises
Delightful to the ear and pleasing to the mind.
Is there anyone in this world with ears
Who finds no joy in Raghupati's story?
Those who do not like his tale must be
Dull of mind, destroyers of their own souls!

While you recited Hari's tale, the Manas lake of his exploits,
I listened, my lord, with boundless joy.
But this that you just told me—that this beautiful story
Was sung by Kak Bhushundi to Garud—

> This raises grave doubts in my mind.
> Bhushundi is free from worldly attachment, steadfast in
>   wisdom and knowledge
> And has great love for Ram's feet—
> But how can anyone in the form of a crow have attained to
>   Ram's bhakti?   (53)

Amongst a thousand men, Tripurari,
There may be one who is steadfast in his vows of piety,
And amongst ten million pious men,
There may be one averse to worldly pleasures and devoted to asceticism.
Amongst ten million ascetics, so the Vedas say,
There may be one who attains to perfect knowledge,
And amongst ten million such enlightened ones,
There may be one freed of worldly bonds whilst still in this world.
Amongst a thousand such, it is difficult to find that abode of bliss
Who has perceived his unity with the Absolute and become one
      with it.
But even more than the pious, the dispassionate, the wise,
The emancipated, and the ones who have merged with the Absolute,
The one most difficult to find, O king of gods,
Is the one devoted to Ram's worship, free of pride and illusion.
So, O master of the universe, help me understand,
How did a crow attain to Ram's bhakti?

> Explain this too, O husband—
> If he were devoted to Ram, intent upon wisdom,
> Endowed with all the virtues, and resolute of mind,
> Why did he receive the body of a crow?   (54)

And tell me, gracious Lord, where did the crow
Learn this sacred and delightful story of the Lord's doings?
And, O vanquisher of Madan, how did you hear this tale?
Tell me, for I am very curious to know.
And again, Garud is very wise and highly accomplished.
He is also Hari's worshipper and very close to him.
So why did he go to a crow to hear this story,
Instead of the multitude of sages?
Also tell me, what was the conversation between
These two devotees of Hari, the crow and the devourer of snakes?'
Pleased by Gauri's simple and gentle speech,
Shiv replied respectfully,
'Blessed are you, Sati, pure is your mind,
And great indeed your devotion to Raghupati's feet.
Listen now to that most sacred history,
Which, when heard, destroys all delusion,
For from it springs faith in Ram's feet,
And man crosses the ocean of this existence without effort.

> The king of the birds, too,
> Asked the crow such questions.
> I will reverently explain it all to you—
> So listen, Uma, with attention.   (55)

My beautiful and bright-eyed one,
Hear how I heard the story that frees one from rebirth.
You first took birth in the house of Daksh,
"Sati" was your name then.
At Daksh's fire-sacrifice you were insulted,
And in great anger, you gave up your life.
My servants then wrecked the sacrifice—
But all this you know already.
After that, my heart filled with grief,
And I was left lamenting for you, my beloved.

I wandered through lovely forests, mountains, lakes and ponds
Indifferent to their beauty.
Far away, to the north of Mount Sumeru,
There rises a majestic blue mountain.
It has four glittering golden peaks,
So lovely that I was captivated.
Upon each of those peaks grows a huge tree,
A banyan, a pipal, a fig and a mango.
On top of the mountain is a beautiful lake,
With jewelled steps enchanting to behold.

    Its water is cool, clear and sweet,
    And upon it grow lotuses of many colours.
    Flocks of swans call in melodious tones,
    And bees buzz pleasantly.   (56)

Upon that lovely mountain lives the bird, Kak Bhushundi,
Who outlives even the end of the world.
The numerous virtues and vices created by maya,
And delusion, love and other errors of judgement
Permeate the entire world,
But never go near that mountain.
Now listen, Uma, with affection,
How that crow, living there, worships Hari.
Beneath the pipal tree he practises meditation,
Under the fig tree he prays and performs fire-sacrifices,
And, having no other occupation except the worship of Hari,
In the shade of the mango tree he offers spiritual worship to
    the Lord,
And under the banyan tree he recites the story of Hari.
Countless birds come to hear him
As, with love and reverence, in many wondrous ways,
He sings of the marvellous acts of Ram.
All the swans of pure minds,

Which dwell forever upon that lake, listen to that tale.
When I went there and saw this sight,
Extraordinary joy arose in my heart.

> Then, assuming the form of a swan,
> I lived there for a time,
> And after reverently listening to Raghupati's virtues,
> I came back to Kailash.   (57)

Girija, I have thus told you the whole story
Of when I went to visit the bird Bhushundi.
Now listen to the story of why
Garud, king of the birds, went to the crow.
When Raghunath performed that act in battle,
Letting himself be bound by Indrajit,
(The thought of which fills me with shame)
The Muni Narad sent Garud to him.
After Garud had cut his bonds and left,
Great sorrow arose in his heart.
Recalling how the Lord had been tied up,
The enemy of serpents reflected to himself,
"It is the all-pervading and passionless brahm, the lord of speech,
The Supreme God transcending all maya and delusion,
Who has, I hear, taken birth in this world.
But I did not see his glory or power.

> That same Ram, by the repetition of whose name
> Men are freed from the bonds of this world,
> Was bound by a wretched demon
> In a serpent snare!"   (58)

Garud tried to reassure himself in many ways,
But could not understand and grew even more bewildered.
Weary with grief, his mind full of conjectures and suppositions,

He fell into delusion's grip just like you.
Confused and troubled he went to the divine rishi Narad,
And told him the doubt in his mind.
Hearing his words, Narad was overcome by compassion and said,
"Listen, O bird, exceedingly powerful is Ram's maya.
It robs even the wise of sense,
And taking over their minds, bewilders and confuses them.
The same delusive power that has often led me a pretty dance
Has now affected you, O king of the birds.
A great delusion has arisen in your heart, bird,
And it will not easily disappear by any words of mine.
Go to four-faced Brahma, O lord of the birds,
And do whatever he commands."

> With these words the divine rishi left,
> Singing of Ram's virtues as he went.
> The most wise sage praised again and again
> The power of Hari's maya. (59)

Then the king of the birds went to Viranchi,
And told him his doubt.
Upon hearing what he had to say, Viranchi bowed his head
    to Ram,
And, understanding his great power, was overcome with love.
The Creator thought to himself,
"Poets, scholars and wise men are all under the sway of delusion.
Unbounded is the power of Hari's maya.
It has teased and troubled me many times,
Though this whole world, moving and unmoving, is of
    my creation.
No wonder then that it has confused the king of the birds."
Then said Vidhi in gentle tones,
"The great god Shiv understands Ram's power.
Vainateya, go to Shankar,

Ask no question of anyone else, my son.
All your doubts will be resolved there."
Taking Vidhi's advice, the bird flew on his way.

> In impatient haste, the king of the birds
> Then came to me.
> I was on my way to Kuber's palace at that time,
> Uma, and you had stayed back here on Kailash.   (60)

He reverently bowed his head at my feet,
And then told me his doubts.
On hearing his plea and his gentle tones,
Bhavani, I lovingly said to him,
"You have approached me, Garud, on the road—
How do I instruct you here?
Doubts are fully resolved only
When one spends a long time in the company of the good
Listening to the delightful story of Hari's doings,
That has been sung by the munis in diverse ways,
And in which—at its beginning, middle and end—
The great god Ram is discussed.
So I will send you to a place where Hari's story
Is daily told without ceasing. Go there and listen to it, brother.
As you listen to it, all your doubts will disappear,
And you will find great love for Ram's feet.

> Hari's tale is not heard except in the company of the good,
> Without listening to it, delusion is not dispelled,
> And without delusion being dispelled,
> One cannot find unwavering love for Ram's feet.   (61)

Without love, Raghupati cannot be found,
Though you practise meditation, perform penance, pursue
     knowledge, or seek dispassion.

In the north lies a beautiful blue mountain,
Where lives the good-natured crow, Bhushundi.
He is supremely familiar with the path to Ram's bhakti,
As well as wise, full of good qualities and very old.
He recites Ram's story unceasingly,
And birds of every kind listen to it with reverence.
Go there and listen to the tale of Hari's virtues—
Your distress born of delusion will then disappear."
After I had explained all this to him,
He bowed his head at my feet and went on his way, rejoicing.
The reason, Uma, that I did not instruct him myself,
Was because, by Ram's grace, I had come to know his secret:
The all-compassionate Ram wished to rid him of pride,
Which he must have, on some occasion, shown.
There was also another reason I did not keep him with me—
A bird understands only another bird's speech.
The Lord's maya is powerful, Bhavani—
Who is so wise as not to be captivated by it?

> Even Garud, the jewel of devotees and the wise,
> And the vehicle of the lord of the three worlds,
> Was ensnared by Hari's maya.
> And yet mere mortals are vain enough to think
>   themselves immune! (62A)

> When even Shiv and Viranchi are taken in by it,
> Of what account is any other poor creature?
> The munis know this in their hearts
> When they worship Maya's Lord. (62B)

Garud went to the abode of Bhushundi,
That bird of unfettered intellect wholly devoted to Hari.
When he saw the mountain, his heart rejoiced
And delusion, confusion and worry all disappeared.

He bathed in the lake and drank of its water,
And then went to the banyan tree, his heart full of joy.
Ancient birds of all kinds had gathered there
To listen to the beautiful story of Ram's exploits.
Kak Bhushundi was just about to begin the tale
When Garud arrived.
Seeing the king of the birds approach,
The crow and all the gathering of birds were delighted.
Bhushundi received the king of the birds with great reverence,
And, after welcoming him and asking after his well-being, led him
    to a seat of honour.
Then, paying him loving homage,
The crow spoke these sweet words—

"Now I am content, O king of the birds
Now that I have seen you, my lord!
Command me, and I am ready to do as you will.
What is the reason for your visit, my king?"   (63A)

"You have ever been the image of contentment,"
Replied the king of the birds in gracious tones,
"For the great god Shiv, with his own mouth,
Has reverently sung your praises.   (63B)

The purpose for which I came, dear father,
Has already been accomplished, and I have also had the privilege of
    seeing you.
The moment I saw your most holy hermitage,
All my confusion, doubts and misconceptions fled.
Now, sire, narrate to me with all reverence
The most sanctifying story of Ram,
Which is ever pleasing and destroys all sorrow—
This, my lord, is what I earnestly request of you."
Upon hearing Garud's gentle request,

Sincere, affectionate, gracious and pious,
Bhushundi's heart filled with great joy,
And he began to recite the story of Raghupati's perfections.
First, Bhavani, he explained with great devotion
The aim and intention of Ram's acts.
Then he recounted the tale of Narad's unbounded infatuation,
And of Ravan's descent to earth as a demon.
Then he sang of the Lord's incarnation,
And, with great affection, his childhood exploits.

> He related the exploits of the Lord as a child
> With great delight in his heart,
> And then told of the rishi's coming,
> And of Raghubir's wedding.   (64)

Next, he narrated the circumstances of Ram's investiture as heir,
Told of the king's promise, the abrupt end to the coronation
    celebrations,
The grief of Ayodhya's citizens at separation from Ram,
And repeated the conversation between Ram and Lakshman.
He told of their leaving for the forest, of the boatman's devotion,
Their crossing of the divine Ganga, and their halt at Prayag.
He described at length the meeting of Valmiki and Ram,
And the manner in which the Lord then lived in Chitrakut.
He spoke of the minister Sumantra's return to the city,
    the king's death,
Bharat's return and his great love for Ram,
And how, after performing the king's last rites, Bharat
And the people went to join the Lord, abode of bliss,
And how, after Raghupati had said all he could to console him,
Bharat took his sandals back with him to the city of Avadh.
He then described Bharat's way of life, the mischievous behaviour
    of Indra's son,
And the meeting between the Lord and Atri.

He told of the slaying of Viradh,
And of how Sarabhang gave up his body.
He described Sutikshna's devotion,
And then the Lord's meeting with Agastya.   (65)

He described the purification of the Dandak forest,
And the Lord's friendship with the vulture, Jatayu.
He then spoke of how the Lord took up his abode in Panchvati,
And put an end to the fears of all the munis.
Next he spoke of the Lord's wonderful discourse to Lakshman,
And of how Supnakha was disfigured.
He then described at length the slaying of Khar and Dushan,
And how Ravan came to know all that had happened.
The conversation between Dashkandhar and Marichi,
He then repeated as it had taken place.
Next, he described the abduction of the shadow Sita,
And a little of Lord Raghubir's sorrow.
He then told how the Lord performed the vulture's last rites,
Killed Kabandh and bestowed salvation upon Shabari.
Next, he described Raghubir's grief,
And how he went to the shore of the lake.

He related the conversation between the Lord and Narad,
And the circumstances under which the Lord met Hanuman.
He then spoke of his alliance with Sugriv,
And of his taking Baali's life.   (66A)

He told of the Lord making the monkey king,
And taking up his abode upon Mount Pravarshana.
He described the season of rains and autumn,
Ram's wrath and Sugriv's fear.   (66B)

How the king of the monkeys sent out monkeys,
Who ran in every direction to search for Sita;

How they entered the cave in the ground,
And then how they met Sampati;
How, after hearing all that he had seen, Hanuman
Leapt over the boundless sea;
How the monkey entered Lanka,
And how he later reassured Sita;
How he laid waste the grove, lectured Ravan himself,
Set fire to the city, and leaped over the sea again;
How all the monkeys then went to Raghurai,
And told him of Vaidehi's well-being;
How Raghubir, with his army,
Went and made camp by the seashore;
How Vibhishan came to meet him,
And how the ocean was subdued—all this the crow related.

He spoke of how the bridge was built, and how
    the monkey army
Crossed the sea to the opposite side,
And how the valiant son of Baali
Went as an envoy to Ravan.   (67A)

The various battles between the demons and monkeys,
He described in much detail,
And the might and valour and ultimate destruction
Of Kumbhakaran and Meghnad.   (67B)

The killing of the Rakshasa hordes,
The battle between Raghupati and Ravan,
The death of Ravan, Mandodari's grief,
The enthronement of Vibhishan, the relief of the gods,
Then the meeting of Sita and Raghupati,
And how the gods sang their glory with folded hands,
How after that, the all-merciful Lord ascended the Pushpak
With the monkeys and set forth for Avadh,

And then how Ram arrived at his own city—
The crow sang of all these pure and glorious acts.
He then told of Ram's investiture as king.
He also described the city and its processes of kingly rule.
That entire story did Bhushundi tell,
Which I have told you, Bhavani.
When the king of the birds had heard the full story of Ram,
His heart filled with joy, and he said,

> "All my doubts have disappeared
> Upon hearing the full story of Raghupati,
> And by your grace, O best of crows,
> I have attained love for Ram's feet.   (68A)

> When I saw the Lord bound in battle,
> I had grown utterly confused—
> Ram is the sum of all bliss and knowledge,
> So how could he be in distress?   (68B)

When I saw his ways so close to those of mortal man,
Great doubt arose in my heart.
Now I regard that confusion as a favour,
Which the compassionate Lord bestowed upon me in his grace.
He alone who has been maddened by the intense heat of
     the sun
Can understand the blessing of the shade of a tree.
So had I not become so utterly bewildered and confused,
How should I have met you, Father,
And how heard the enchanting story of Hari,
Which you have recited so wonderfully and in such detail?
The Shastras, the Vedas and the Puranas all declare,
And the Siddhas and sages agree without doubt,
That only those upon whom Ram glances with favour
Ever find the company of true saints.

By Ram's favour, I have seen you,
And by your grace, all my doubts have disappeared."

> On hearing the words of the king of the birds,
> So full of humility and love,
> The crow was overcome with joy, so that
> His body trembled and his eyes filled with tears.   (69A)

> Uma, virtuous men, upon finding a listener
> Who is intelligent, courteous,
> Fond of pious tales, and a devotee of Hari,
> Reveal to him hidden mysteries.   (69B)

Then replied Kak Bhushundi,
Who had no little affection for the king of the birds,
"My lord, you are in every way entitled to my respect,
As the receptacle of Raghunayak's grace.
You had no doubts, no confusion nor illusion,
But in your grace, have done me a favour.
It was only a pretext, O king of the birds—
In sending you to me as overcome by delusion, Raghupati has done
    me great honour.
Yet there is nothing surprising, sire,
In that confusion of which you told me, lord of the birds.
Of Narad, Shiv, Brahma, Sanak and his brothers—
All great munis able to discourse on the essence of the soul—
Who has not been blinded by delusion,
Of whom has love not made a fool,
Who has not been maddened by desire,
And whose heart has not been consumed by wrath?

> Is there any sage, ascetic, or hero,
> Any poet, any learned or accomplished man
> In this world
> Whom greed has not mortified?   (70A)

Is there anyone whom the love of wealth has not
    made crooked,
Whom power has not made deaf,
Or whom the glance of a doe-eyed woman
Has not smitten like an arrow?   (70B)

Who has not been afflicted by the fever caused by the three gunas,
Or been untouched by pride and arrogance?
Whom has the fever of youth not made delirious,
And whose glory not been ruined by self-interest?
Who has not been stained by envy,
Or shaken by the fierce winds of grief?
Whom has the serpent of worry not bitten,
And who in this world is unaffected by maya?
Who is there so resolute that his body has not been wasted
    by longings
Like a piece of wood eaten away by insects?
Whose mind has not been sullied
By the threefold desires—for a son, for wealth and for
    worldly recognition?
All these make up Maya's army,
Powerful, and infinite in number.
Even Shiv and four-faced Brahma are afraid of her legions—
So of what account are other beings?

Maya's formidable army
Is spread over the whole world.
Lust and its companions are its commanders,
Deception, Trickery and Hypocrisy its warriors.   (71A)

This same Maya is Raghubir's servant maid.
Though once understood, she is seen to be a delusion,
She cannot be dispersed without Ram's favour.
My lord, I swear to this.   (71B)

This Maya, who makes the whole world dance to her tune,
And whose doings no one can understand,
Is herself set dancing with her attendants, like a dancer with
    her troupe,
By the play of the Lord's eyebrows.
Ram is the aggregation of truth, knowledge and bliss,
The uncreated, the embodiment of wisdom, the abode of strength
    and beauty,
The all-pervading, the permeable, the indivisible, the unending,
The complete, the supreme God of unfailing power,
Without attributes, beyond speech and the senses,
All-seeing, above reproach, invincible,
Indifferent, without form, without attachment,
Eternal, without passion, the accumulation of joy,
Transcending Nature, all-powerful, dwelling in every heart,
The actionless, passionless, imperishable Absolute.
In him, delusion can find no cause—
Can darkness ever face the sun?

    For the sake of his devotees,
    The divine Lord, Ram, became incarnate as a king,
    And performed deeds supremely holy
    In the manner of an ordinary man,   (72A)

    Like some actor upon a stage,
    Who assumes numerous disguises
    And plays different characters,
    While himself remaining the same.   (72B)

Such is Raghupati's marvellous sport, Uragari.
It bewilders the demons and delights his devotees.
Those dull of mind, absorbed in the pleasures of the senses,
Attribute delusion to the Lord, my master,
Like as when a man whose eyesight is faulty

Says the moon is yellow in colour,
Or when one confused about the points of the compass
Declares that the sun rises in the west,
Or when a man in a boat sees the world moving,
But mistakenly believes that he is standing still.
When children spin round and round in play, the houses and trees
    do not,
But they call each other liars for saying so—
Such also is the attribution of delusion to Hari, O bird,
For not even in dream is the Lord a subject of ignorance.
But the dull-witted wretches in the grip of delusion,
Whose hearts are surrounded by many walls,
Are the fools who stubbornly raise doubts
And lay their own ignorance upon Ram.

    Addicted to lust, anger, pride and greed,
    Engrossed in domestic affairs, the very nature of which
      is suffering,
    How can they know Raghupati,
    These fools who have fallen into a well of darkness?   (73A)

    The formless aspect of the Absolute is easy to understand,
    But no one can understand its incarnation.
    Even the minds of munis are perplexed
    Hearing of his many exploits, whether simple
      or profound.   (73B)

Hear, O king of the birds, of Raghupati's power,
As I relate, to the best of my ability, a delightful story.
I will also tell you the whole story, my lord,
Of how I was overcome by delusion.
You are a receptacle of Ram's grace, sire.
You cherish great love for Hari's perfections, and so give me great joy.
Therefore I will hide nothing from you,

But reveal to you a profound and charming secret.
Hear, too, of Ram's innate nature—
He does not tolerate pride in his devotees,
For pride is the root of rebirth, causes all kinds of pain,
And gives rise to every sorrow.
That is why, in his great affection for his devotees,
The merciful Lord gets rid of it
As when a boil appears on a child's body, my lord,
And the mother has it ruthlessly lanced.

> Although at first it hurts,
> And the child cries uncontrollably,
> The mother takes no notice of the little one's pain,
> Her purpose being to cure the affliction.   (74A)

> In the same way, for their own good,
> Raghupati cures his servants of pride.
> Who would not, abandoning all confusion,
> Worship such a Lord? So asks Tulsidas.   (74B)

O king of the birds, I will now tell you
Of Ram's grace and my own stupidity—listen with attention.
Whenever Ram takes on human form,
And, for the sake of his devotees, performs his countless playful acts,
I go to the city of Avadh,
And watch his childish acts with delight.
I go and attend the great festival of his birth,
And, charmed by his doings, stay there for five years.
My own chosen god is the child Ram,
In whose frame is contained the beauty of countless Kamdevs.
Ever gazing upon the face of my own Lord,
Uragari, I let my eyes be blessed.
Taking on the insignificant form of a crow, I stay with Hari,
And watch his various childish doings.

Wherever he wanders in childhood,
There I fly, close to him.
And for food I pick up and eat
Only the scraps that he lets fall in the courtyard.   (75A)

Once, Raghubir performed all his divine acts
With heightened intensity."
Remembering those playful doings of the Lord,
Bhushundi trembled with joy.   (75B)

"O king of the birds," he continued,
"Ram's deeds always give joy to his devotees.
The king's palace was beautiful in every way,
All of gold, and inlaid with precious stones of various kinds.
The lovely courtyard, where the four brothers
Daily played, defies description.
Here Raghurai romped about,
Performing the childish antics that delighted his mother.
His tender frame was as dark as an emerald,
Every part of it imbued with the beauty of countless Kamdevs.
His feet were soft, and pink like new-blooming lotuses,
With lovely toes and nails that had stolen the radiance of
     the moon,
And soles marked with the thunderbolt, elephant-goad,
     flag and lotus.
His pretty anklets made a sweet sound,
While around his waist a bright girdle of little bells, made of gold
     and studded with jewels,
Softly tinkled.

Three lines creased his beautiful belly,
His navel was pretty and deep.
His broad chest glittered with jewels
Befitting a child's attire.   (76)

His rosy palms, and nails and fingers were heart-enchanting,
And his long arms adorned with lovely ornaments.
He had the shoulders of a young lion, a conch-like neck,
A shapely chin, and a face the very extreme of beauty.
His speech was lisping, his lips were red,
And he had two perfect little white teeth above and below.
He had pretty cheeks, a beautiful nose,
And a smile that delighted all and was as radiant as the rays of the moon.
His blue-lotus eyes released one from rebirth,
And upon his forehead shone a gorochan tilak.
His brows were arched, his ears shapely,
And his curly hair black and beautiful.
A fine yellow tunic shone upon his body,
And his joyous shrieks and happy glances captivated me.
The beautiful child played in the king's courtyard,
Dancing at the sight of his own shadow.
He played all kinds of games with me,
Which I feel too bashful to describe.
When, laughing and shrieking, he would run to catch me,
I would fly away; then he would show me a sweet flour-cake.

> If I drew near, the Lord would laugh,
> And cry if I flew away.
> If I went up to him to touch his feet,
> He would run away, turning again and again to
>   look at me.   (77A)

> Seeing him play like an ordinary child,
> I became confused.
> What were these actions of the Lord,
> Who is the aggregation of knowledge and bliss?   (77B)

As soon as this doubt came into my mind, king of the birds,
Raghupati's delusive power, directed by him, overcame me.

But his maya did not trouble me,
Nor did it trap me in the cycle of birth and rebirth as it does
    other beings.
This, my lord, was because of a special reason—
Listen attentively to what it was, O steed of Hari!
Sita's beloved alone is absolute knowledge,
While every creature, moving or unmoving, is under the sway
    of maya.
If all were endowed with the same perfect knowledge,
Tell me, what would be the difference between God and the
    individual soul?
The individual soul in its arrogance is subject to maya,
And maya, the source of the three gunas, is subject to God.
The individual soul is dependent, the Deity is self-dependent;
The individual souls are many, Lakshmi's beloved is one.
Though these distinctions, which have been created by maya, are
    without purpose,
They do not disappear without Hari's grace, no matter what
    you try.

    He who seeks salvation
    Without prayer to Ramchandra,
    Is a beast without tail and horns,
    Whether he be wise or not.   (78A)

    Even if the moon were to rise in all its brilliance,
    With its entire entourage of stars,
    Or every forest on every mountain set ablaze,
    Night would not end without the sun.   (78B)

In the same way, O king of the birds, without the worship
    of Hari,
Mortals cannot be rid of their suffering.
Ignorance cannot prevail upon a servant of Hari's—

It is knowledge, impelled by the Lord, that pervades his
     whole being.
That is why, O noblest of birds, the servant is never destroyed,
But his devotion to the Lord grows ever stronger.
Ram laughed when he saw me bewildered and confused—
Now hear more of the wondrous act that followed.
The mystery of that playful deed no one ever knew,
Not his younger brothers, nor his mother or father.
The child, dark of form, with rosy palms and feet,
Upon his hands and knees, he rushed to catch me,
At that, Uragari, I took to flight,
And Ram stretched out his arms to catch me.
I flew higher and higher into the sky,
But still saw his arms as close to me as ever.

> I flew up into Brahma's realm,
> But when I looked back in my flight,
> Two fingers' breadth was all the distance, sire,
> Between Ram's arms and me.   (79A)

> Piercing the seven veils[5] of the world,
> I flew as high as I could.
> But when there too I saw the Lord's arms,
> I grew alarmed.   (79B)

Terrified, I closed my eyes,
And when I opened them again, I found myself in Ayodhya.
Ram looked at me with a smile,
And as he laughed, I instantly fell into his mouth.
Inside his belly, O king of the birds,
I saw innumerable clusters of universes,
And within those, many strange worlds,
Each more wonderful than the other.
There were countless Brahmas and Shivs,

Innumerable stars and suns and moons,
Innumerable guardians of the quarters and gods of death
    and time,
Innumerable mountains and vast plains,
Seas, rivers, lakes and forests without end,
And many more kinds of worlds spread out,
With gods, munis, Siddhas, serpents, men and Kinnaras,
And the four kinds of beings, moving and unmoving.

      Wonders that I had never seen, never heard of,
      And which had never entered my mind,
      All those marvels I saw there.
      How can I ever describe them?   (80A)

      In each universe I stayed
      One hundred years,
      And in this manner I wandered about
      Visiting numerous worlds.   (80B)

Each world had its own separate Creator,
Its own Vishnu, Shiv and Manu, its own deities guarding the
    points of the compass,
And men, Gandharvas, ghosts and goblins,
Kinnaras, demons, animals, birds and serpents,
And all the tribes of gods and Danavs.
Every creature was there, but different in form.
Each world, with its many rivers, seas, lakes, mountains,
Indeed each universe, was quite distinct.
In every universe I saw my own form,
And many other strange and extraordinary sights.
Every world had its own separate Ayodhya,
Its own Sarju, and its own, different, men and women.
And listen, sire, Dasharath and Kaushalya were there too,
And Bharat and the other brothers, different in each world.

In every universe, I witnessed Ram's descent
And his infinite childlike play.

> I saw everything separately and differently repeated—
> It was all quite extraordinary, O steed of Hari!
> But though I wandered through countless worlds,
> I did not see a different Ram, my lord.   (81A)

> The same childlike ways, the same beauty,
> The same gracious Raghubir
> Were what I saw as I went from world to world,
> Blown along by the fierce wind of delusion.   (81B)

In my wanderings through the numerous universes,
One hundred kalpas must have passed.
At last I came to my own hermitage,
And there I stayed for some time.
When I heard of my Lord's descent at Avadh,
I was overwhelmed with love and joy, and rushed there at once
To witness the great celebration of his birth
In the manner I have earlier described to you.
In Ram's belly I saw many worlds,
A sight to be seen, but beyond all telling.
There I beheld again the all-wise Ram,
Maya's master, the merciful God.
I reflected upon this again and again,
But my understanding was clouded by delusion.
I saw all this within the space of an hour,
And I was utterly confused and bewildered.

> When he saw me so troubled,
> The all-merciful Raghubir laughed,
> And the instant he laughed,
> I fell out of his mouth, O Garud,   (82A)

And Ram began to play his childlike games
With me again.
I tried to explain this to myself in a million ways,
But my mind knew no rest.   (82B)

Seeing his childlike doings now and recalling the supreme power I
          had just witnessed,
I lost awareness of my own body.
I fell to the ground, unable to utter a word
Except to cry, 'Save me, save me, O protector of the afflicted!'
When the Lord saw me so overcome with devotion,
He at once reined in the power of his maya.
Then the Lord, who is ever merciful to the lowly, placed his
          lotus hands
Upon my head and took away all my sorrow.
Ram, sum of compassion and the bestower of joy upon his devotees,
Thus rid me of all delusion.
As I reflected upon his great power that I had earlier glimpsed,
My heart filled with great joy.
Seeing his great tenderness towards his devotees,
Deep love sprang up in my heart.
With folded hands, and my eyes full of tears and my body
          trembling,
I paid him homage again and again.

Hearing my loving words,
And seeing in me his own humble servant,
He who dwells with Ramaa spoke words
That were pleasing, sweet and profound.   (83A)

'Kak Bhushundi, know me to be very pleased
And ask of me any boon,
Be it a mystic power like anima, boundless wealth,
Or freedom from rebirth, the source of all bliss.   (83B)

Or wisdom, knowledge, dispassion, discernment,
And all those many qualities that are difficult even for sages to
    attain in this world—
All these, without hesitation, I am ready to give you today. So ask
    whatever your heart desires.'
Upon hearing the Lord's words, I was filled with great love,
And I began to think to myself,
'The Lord, it is true, has offered to give me every blessing,
But he has not offered to grant me devotion to him.
Without devotion, all these virtues and blessings
Are like condiments without salt.
Without prayer, what use is any blessing?'
Having thus reflected, O king of the birds, I replied,
'If it is your pleasure, Lord, to give me a boon,
And bestow upon me your grace and love,
I ask the boon my heart desires, master,
For you are generous and know the inner secrets of all hearts.

    Unceasing and unalloyed faith in you,
    Of which the Vedas and Puranas sing,
    And for which the greatest ascetics and sages search
    But only a few, by your grace, find—   (84A)

    O Ram, wish-fulfilling Kalpataru to the devotee,
        friend of the suppliant,
    Ocean of mercy and abode of all bliss,
    Show me your grace, O Lord,
    And grant me that faith in you.'   (84B)

'So be it,' said the prince of the Raghu line,
And then spoke these most pleasing words,
'Listen, O crow, you are inherently wise,
So how could you have asked for any boon but this!
You have asked for devotion, the source of all blessing—

There is no one as fortunate as you in the world,
For even those munis who destroy their bodies in the fire of prayer
    and penance,
Cannot attain to it despite all their efforts.
I am delighted to see your shrewdness.
That you asked for devotion to me, pleased me greatly.
Listen now, bird, to the gifts I bestow upon you:
Every good quality will reside in your heart—
Devotion, wisdom, knowledge, dispassion,
The practice of abstract contemplation, and the mystery of my
    exploits and their classification.
You will understand the secret of all these,
And by my grace, will not need to suffer the hardship of
    spiritual endeavour.

All the confusions born of maya
Will no longer affect you.
Know me as brahm, the Supreme Absolute, without
    beginning or birth or attributes,
And endowed with every transcendent quality.   (85A)

Listen, O crow, devotees are always dear to me—
Remember this,
And in thought, word and deed,
Practise unwavering devotion to my feet.   (85B)

Now listen to this pure speech of mine,
Which is true and simple and has been explained in the Vedas and
    other scriptures.
I will reveal to you my own doctrine—
Listen to it with attention, and, abandoning all others, worship
    only me.
The world has come forth from my maya,
With all its diverse forms of life, moving and unmoving.

All are dear to me, for they have all sprung from me,
But man delights me the most.
And of men, Brahmans; of Brahmans, those who know
    the Vedas;
Of these, those who live according to the teachings of the
    sacred texts;
Amongst these, those free from worldly attachment are dear to me,
    and of these the wise;
And of the wise, I love most the spiritually wise,
And of them, the dearest to me are my own servants,
Who come to me and take shelter with no other.
Again and again I tell you this truth,
That there are none so dear to me as my own servants.
If Viranchi himself felt no devotion towards me,
He would be no dearer to me than any other creature;
And if the lowest, most insignificant creature had devotion
    towards me,
He would be as dear to me as life—this do I declare.

    Tell me, who would not like
    A true, kind and intelligent servant?
    The Vedas and Puranas, too, say this—
    So listen attentively, O crow.   (86)

A father has many sons,
Each with his individual qualities, temperament and behaviour.
One is learned, another an ascetic, another spiritually
    enlightened,
Another wealthy, or brave, or charitable,
One is all-knowing and wise, another intent on piety.
But the father loves them all equally.
Another is completely devoted to his father, in thought,
    word and deed,
And even in dream, knows no other duty.

This is the son the father loves as his own life,
Though he be utterly ignorant in every respect.
In the same way, all beings, moving or unmoving,
Including birds and beasts, gods, men and Asurs,
Indeed, the entire universe that I have fashioned—
I look upon it all with equal affection.
But amongst them all, if there be one who, abandoning pride
    and delusion,
Worships only me in thought, word and deed,

> Whether he be man or woman or of neither sex,
> Or any creature, moving or unmoving—
> If he, with all his being, sincerely worships me,
> He is my most beloved.   (87A)

> I tell you the truth, bird,
> A true servant is as dear to me as life.
> Understand this and worship only me,
> Relinquishing all other hope or assurance.   (87B)

Time will never affect you,
Remember and worship me without ceasing.'
I would never have tired of hearing the Lord's sweet words—
My body trembled and my heart filled with happiness.
My heart and my ears shared my joy,
But my tongue did not have the ability to relate it.
My eyes knew the joy of beholding the Lord's beauty,
But how can they describe it? They have no voice.
After delighting me with discourse,
He again began to play like a child.
With his eyes full of tears and his face downcast,
He looked at his mother as if he were hungry.
Seeing this, his mother rose and rushed to him,
And speaking soft words, clasped him to her bosom.

Then, holding him in her lap, she began to nurse him,
Singing all the while of Raghupati's charming deeds.

> That bliss, to attain which Purari, the giver of bliss to all,
> Assumed his unpleasing attire—
> In that joy do the men and women of Avadh
> Remain eternally immersed. (88A)

> Those wise and virtuous ones, O Garud,
> Who have experienced, even in dream,
> The smallest particle of that joy, hold of no account
> Even the bliss of becoming one with the Absolute. (88B)

I stayed in Avadh for some more time after this,
Observing his charming boyish play.
Then, having received the boon of faith by Ram's grace,
I bowed at the Lord's feet and came back to my own hermitage.
From the moment Raghunayak accepted me as his own,
Delusion has had no power over me.
I have now related to you my own personal story
Of how I was troubled and beguiled by Hari's delusive power.
From my own experience now I say to you, Garud,
That without the worship of Hari, suffering cannot be relieved.
Listen, O king of the birds, without Ram's grace,
Ram's power cannot be understood;
Without understanding, there is no confidence;
Without confidence, there is no love;
And without love, faith cannot be steady and unchanging,
But trickles away like water.

> Can there be knowledge without a guru,
> Or wisdom without dispassion?
> As the Vedas and the Puranas sing,
> Can happiness be attained without the worship of Hari? (89A)

Can anyone find peace, sire,
Without intrinsic contentment?
Can a boat move without water,
Though you strive and sweat till you die?   (89B)

Without contentment, desire cannot be destroyed,
And as long as there is desire, peace cannot be attained even in dream.
Can desire disappear without the worship of Ram?
Can a tree ever take root without soil?
Without wisdom, can equanimity be attained?
Can there be emptiness without sky?
Without faith there is no piety,
As there can be no smell without earth.
Can glory spread without penance,
Or there be any flavours in the world without water?
Can goodness be acquired without waiting upon the wise,
Or colours exist without light, sire?
Can the mind be still without internal happiness,
Or touch exist without air?
Without faith, success cannot be achieved,
Without prayer to Hari, the fear of rebirth cannot be destroyed.

Without faith, there can be no devotion;
Without devotion, Ram is not moved;
Without Ram's grace, no creature
Can attain peace even in dream.   (90A)

Thus reflecting, O steadfast one,
Abandon all doubt and false doctrine,
And worship the Raghu hero—
Ram, the compassionate, the beautiful, the beneficent.   (90B)

Thus, king of the birds, I have now declared to you,
The greatness of the Lord's power.

I have not been clever or inventive in my tale,
But have seen all that I have related with my own eyes.
Ram's greatness, his name, beauty and virtues
Are all boundless, and infinite himself is Raghunath.
The munis sing of Hari's perfections, each according to his
    understanding,
But not the Vedas, nor Sheshnag or Shiv, can completely
    comprehend them.
From you down to the mosquito, sire, all winged creatures
Fly across the sky but never find its end.
In the same way, Raghupati's greatness is unfathomable,
And none can reach its bottom.
Ram is as beautiful of form as countless Kamdevs,
And relentless as countless Durgas in the destruction of his foes.
His pomp and grandeur equal that of countless Indras,
And his vastness is as immeasurable as that of countless skies.

He has the strength of a myriad winds,
And the brilliance of a myriad suns.
He is as gentle as a myriad moons,
And soothes all the terrors of this existence.   (91A)

As insuperable, inaccessible and incomprehensible
As infinite deaths,
Is our divine Lord,
And as unassailable as infinite comets.   (91B)

The Lord is as unfathomable as innumerable underworlds
And as terrible as innumerable gods of death.
He is as sanctifying as countless millions of holy sites,
And his name destroys all the multitudes of sins.
Raghubir is as immoveable as ten million snowy peaks,
And as profound as ten million oceans,
The granter of every desire, the Lord

Is as munificent as ten million Kamdhenus.
He is as immeasurably intelligent as countless Sharadas,
As skilful in creation as countless Vidhis,
As nurturing a preserver as countless Vishnus,
And as powerful a destroyer as countless Rudras.
He is as wealthy as a billion gods of wealth,
Holds within himself as many universes as a billion Mayas,
And can bear as many worlds as a billion Sheshnags.
The lord of the universe, he is illimitable and beyond compare.

He is beyond compare and has no peer,
Ram alone is like Ram, the Vedas say.
If the sun be compared to fireflies, even a hundred million of them,
It would be diminished.
In the same way great munis have attempted to describe Hari
According to their own wit and understanding,
And the Lord lovingly listens to their descriptions and is pleased,
For he is kind and appreciates the sentiment of his devotees.

Ram is an unfathomable ocean of virtue,
Can anyone measure his depth?
I have told you whatever little
I heard from the saints.   (92A)

Abandon selfishness, vanity and pride
And ever worship Sita's beloved,
The great God who is moved by love,
The abode of bliss and compassion."   (92B)

The lord of the birds was delighted to hear
Bhushundi's pleasing words, and puffed up his feathers in joy.
With his eyes full of tears and his heart full of happiness,
He meditated upon the might of divine Raghupati.
He was filled with remorse upon remembering his former delusion,

When he had taken the eternal Supreme Spirit of the universe to
    be a mortal man.
Again and again he bowed his head at the crow's feet,
And regarding him the same as Ram, loved him even more.
No one can cross the ocean of existence without a guru,
Though he be equal to Viranchi or Shankar.
"The serpent of doubt had bitten me, dear Father,
And as a result of its venom, I was overcome by fits of delusion.
But Raghunayak, who bestows joy upon his devotees,
Appeared in your form as the antidote, and restored me to life.
By your favour, my delusion has been destroyed,
And I have learnt the incomparable mystery of Ram."

    After praising him in every way,
    And bowing his head before him with folded hands,
    Garud addressed him in gentle,
    Courteous and loving words.   (93A)

    "My lord, in my ignorance,
    I ask you a question.
    Instruct me, compassionate master,
    Knowing me to be your own servant.   (93B)

You are omniscient, and know the true nature of everything,
You are beyond the darkness of delusion, intelligent, good-natured,
    straightforward,
The abode of knowledge, wisdom and dispassion,
And Raghunayak's beloved servant.
What is the reason, then, for your having received such
    a form?
Explain this to me, sire.
Tell me also, O revered bird,
Where did you learn this beautiful story of Ram's exploits?
And master, I have heard from Shiv,

That you do not perish even at the destruction of all things.
The great god never utters an idle word,
And so there is a question in my mind.
The whole world, master, with all its creatures, moving and
    unmoving,
Serpents, men and gods, is Time's victim.
Time has destroyed countless universes,
And is ever implacable and strong.

    How is it that you alone are not affected
    By terrifying and formidable Time?
    Tell me, merciful one, is this the result
    Of spiritual wisdom or yogic power?   (94A)

    My lord, as soon as I came to your ashram,
    My confusion and delusion fled.
    What is the reason for that?
    In your kindness, master, explain it all to me."   (94B)

The crow, Uma, was delighted to hear Garud's words,
And replied with great affection,
"Blessed indeed is your mind, Uragari,
And your questions are very pleasing to me.
Listening to your agreeable and affectionate questions,
The memories of many previous births have come back to me.
I will now tell you my full story.
Listen to it, sire, with reverence and attention.
Prayer, penance, performing fire-sacrifices, self-restraint,
    undertaking sacred vows, acts of charity,
Dispassion, discernment, meditation and spiritual wisdom—
The goal of all these is love for Raghupati's feet,
Without which no one can attain well-being.
In was in this body that I found devotion to Ram,
That is why it is very dear to me.

Everyone has a special affection for that
Through which he has attained his purpose.

> O enemy of serpents, this is a maxim
> Accepted by the Vedas and endorsed by the saints—
> Show affection to the lowest creature
> If you know it to be your friend.   (95A)

> Silk is produced by worms,
> And from it is made lovely silken raiment.
> That is why all look after the worm,
> Supremely impure though it is, like they would their
>   own lives.   (95B)

The greatest advantage to any living creature
Is devotion to Ram in thought, word and deed.
That body alone is pure, and that alone is beautiful
In which one is able to worship Raghubir.
The learned and the wise never praise one who is against Ram,
Even if he acquires a body like Brahma's.
It was in my current body that devotion to Ram took root in
    my heart,
And that is why, sire, it is most dear to me.
Though I can choose when I die, I do not give up this body,
For without a body, as the Vedas declare, I cannot worship.
At first, delusion gave me great trouble,
And as long as I remained indifferent to Ram, I could not find
    peaceful repose.
Through different births I practised diverse actions—
Meditation, prayer, penance, sacrifice and almsgiving.
There is no womb in which I have not at some time taken birth
During my wanderings through the universe, O king of the birds!
I have done and experienced all kinds of deeds, master,
But I have never been as happy as I am now.

I remember many past births, my lord,
In which, by Shiv's grace, my mind has been free from delusion.

> Listen, O king of the birds, for I will now relate
> The story of my first birth.
> Hearing it will engender love for the Lord's feet,
> Through which all distress is dispelled.   (96A)

> In a former cycle of creation, my lord,
> The world was passing through an age of sin.
> In this Kaliyug, men and women, steeped in evil,
> Had all turned against the Vedas.   (96B)

In that Kaliyug, I was born in Koshal's city,
And in that birth, was given the body of a Shudra.
I was a devotee of Shiv in thought, word and deed,
But I was conceited and scoffed at all the other gods.
Intoxicated with the pride of wealth, I was a loudmouth,
Excessively aggressive, and with a heart full of deceit.
Though I lived in Raghupati's capital city,
I did not then understand its glory.
Now I have come to know Avadh's greatness.
The Vedas, Puranas and all the scriptures say
That anyone who has in any birth lived in Ayodhya,
Will eventually become a devotee of Ram.
A man comes to know the power of Ayodhya
When Ram, bow in hand, enters his heart.
That age of Kali was terrible, Uragari—
Every man and woman was immersed in sin.

> All virtue had been smothered by the sins of the age,
> And all the sacred books had been lost.
> Impostors proclaimed all kinds of creeds,
> Which they themselves had made up.   (97A)

People were overcome by delusion,
And all good deeds were stifled by greed.
Now listen, O all-wise steed of Hari,
As I tell you some of the practices of the age of Kali.   (97B)

The rules of caste were not followed, nor were the four stages of
    life observed,
And all men and women were intent on rebelling against
    the Vedas.
Brahmans sold the Vedas, kings consumed their own
    subjects,
And no one obeyed the injunctions of the scriptures.
The right path was the one that seemed the most appealing,
Those who bragged and boasted were considered learned,
And those who were pretentious or arrogant
Were acclaimed as saints by everyone.
He alone was considered clever who stole another's wealth,
Frauds and hypocrites were regarded as the most pious,
And one who knew how to lie or jest and joke,
In the age of Kali, he alone was considered a man of virtue.
An impious scoundrel who abandoned the path of the Vedas
Was, in the age of Kali, a man of wisdom and dispassion,
While anyone with long nails and matted hair,
Became renowned as an ascetic in that dark age.

They who put on unsightly rags and ornaments,
And devoured any kind of food, fit to be eaten or not,
Were the ascetics, the saints, the ones venerated
In that age of Kali.   (98A)

Those who harmed others
Were held in high esteem,
And rogues and liars in thought, word and deed
Were accepted as preachers in that Kaliyug.   (98B)

All men were subject to women, sire,
And danced to their tune like performing monkeys.
Shudras instructed the twice-born in spiritual wisdom,
And assuming the sacred thread took their contemptible alms.
All men were immersed in lust, greed and anger,
And hostile to the gods, the Brahmans, the Vedas and the saints.
Deserting their handsome and accomplished husbands,
Ill-starred women worshipped strange men.
Married women wore no ornaments,
While widows daily adorned themselves.
Disciples and gurus were like the deaf and the blind—
One did not listen, the other did not see.
A teacher who takes his pupil's money but does not rid him of
     his doubts
Falls into the deepest hell.
Mothers and fathers called their children to them,
And taught them only that which fills their bellies.

> Men and women spoke
> Only of spiritual wisdom,
> But would kill a Brahman or their guru
> Out of greed for a bit of money.   (99A)

> Shudras angrily argued with the twice-born,
> 'Are we any less than you?
> Anyone who understands the Absolute
> Is as good a Brahman as any!'   (99B)

Lusting after another's wife, deceitful and sly,
Enwrapped in delusion, violence and selfishness—
These were the men considered enlightened and wise.
Such are the practices I have seen in every Kaliyug.
Men who are themselves lost ruin those others too
Who follow the path of virtue.

Those who use logic to criticize the Vedas,
Spend a kalpa each in every hell.
Men of low caste, such as oilmen, potters,
Shvapachas, Kols, Kirats and distillers,
Upon losing their wives or their household property,
Shave their heads and turn into holy men.
They make the Brahmans worship them,
And so bring ruin upon themselves in this world and the next.
Brahmans are unlettered, greedy, lustful,
Dissolute, stupid and the husbands of unclean, low-born women.
Shudras practise prayer and penance, undertake sacred vows
    and fasts,
And discourse upon the Puranas from seats of honour.
All men behave according to their own way of thinking—
The unbounded wickedness cannot be described.

In the age of Kali, castes are mixed together,
And all men deviate from the sacred laws.
They practise sin, and in return receive
Suffering, fear, disease, sorrow and loss.   (100A)

The path of devotion to Hari is approved of by the Vedas
And is united with dispassion and discernment.
But men, overcome by delusion, do not follow this road
And walk, instead, along diverse paths they have
    themselves invented.   (100B)

Hermits build themselves homes at great expense,
Dispassion in them disappears, destroyed by lustfulness.
Ascetics become wealthy, householders poor—
The wonders of the Kali age, sire, are beyond telling.

Men throw out virtuous and well-born wives
And bring home some young servant-girl.

A son respects his mother and father
So long as he hasn't seen a woman's face.

From the moment his wife's kin become dear to him,
He begins to look upon his own family as enemies.
Kings are immersed in sin, and, discarding righteousness,
They tyrranize their subjects through daily punishment.

The wealthy, even if base-born, are considered high-born,
A sacred thread alone marks a Brahman, and any naked beggar is an ascetic.
Anyone who does not believe in the Puranas or the Vedas
Is regarded as a saint and Hari's true devotee in the Kali age.

There are multitudes of poets, but generous patrons are no longer heard
      of in the world.
There are many to criticize virtue, but no virtuous man to be found.
Famines occur again and again in the age of Kali,
And people die of starvation in large numbers.

>   Listen, O king of the birds, in the Kali age,
>   The whole universe is overwhelmed
>   By deceit, disobedience, hypocrisy, malice, heresy,
>   Arrogance, ignorance, lust, vanity and every other
>   evil passion.   (101A)

>   Men practise prayer, penance and fasting,
>   Perform sacrifices and give alms in spiritual darkness,
>   Gods do not shower the earth with rain,
>   And rice is sown but does not grow.   (101B)

Women have no ornament except their hair. Dissatisfied,
Poor and intensely selfish, they are always miserable.
The fools want happiness, but disdain righteousness,
Small-minded and hard-hearted, they know no tenderness.

Men are tormented by disease and find no rest anywhere,
But are arrogant and quarrelsome without any reason.
Their lives are short, about ten years and five,
But they think they'll outlive creation—such is their pride.

The age of Kali has driven mankind mad,
So that no one respects even a sister or a daughter.
There is no contentment, no consideration, no gentleness,
And everyone, high caste or low, has become a beggar.

Jealousy, insolence and greed are superabundant,
And equanimity of mind has disappeared.
All men are afflicted with sorrow and loss,
And rules and rituals of caste abandoned.

There is no self-restraint, almsgiving, compassion or good sense left,
But stupidity and dishonesty proliferate.
Men and women all indulge their bodies,
And those who speak ill of others are everywhere.

O enemy of snakes, the age of Kali
Is a storehouse of impurity and sin.
But this age has many virtues too, for in it
Salvation can be effortlessly attained.   (102A)

Liberation attained in the Krit, Treta and Dwapar ages,
Through prayer, fire-sacrifices and meditation,
May be reached in the age of Kali
Merely through Hari's name.   (102B)

In the Krityug, everyone is saintly and wise,
And men cross the ocean of existence by meditating upon Hari.
In the Tretayug, men perform many fire-sacrifices,
And cross the ocean of existence by dedicating their actions to the Lord.

In the Dwapar age, men cross the ocean of existence
By worshipping the feet of Raghupati, there is no other way.
And in the age of Kali men reach the other shore
Simply by singing of Hari's perfections.
In the age of Kali, neither meditation, sacrifice, nor wisdom is of use,
Man's only support is the singing of Ram's virtues.
He who worships Ram alone, giving up faith in all others,
And lovingly chants his praises,
Crosses the ocean of existence—of this there is no doubt.
The power of the name is thus manifest in the age of Kali.
The Kaliyug has this one sanctifying power—
Good intentions are rewarded, but bad ones are not.

> There is no age like the age of Kali,
> Provided a man has faith,
> For merely by singing of Ram's pure virtues,
> He can easily cross the ocean of existence.   (103A)

> Of the four parts of piety,[6]
> Only one is important in the Kaliyug—
> Charity practised in any way
> Leads to spiritual well-being.   (103B)

Directed by Ram's delusive power,
The distinguishing attributes of each age are ever present in
     all hearts.
Pure goodness, equanimity, wisdom
And cheerfulness are the effects of the Krityug.
An abundance of goodness mixed with strong emotion,
     love for action,
And a general feeling of happiness are the marks of the Tretayug.
Much passion, only a little goodness, some ignorance
And both joy and fear in the heart are characteristics of
     the Dwaparyug.

Great ignorance, some passion and hostility,
And antagonism everywhere is the effect of the Kaliyug.
The wise discern the characteristics of each age in their minds,
And renouncing wickedness, devote themselves to righteousness.
These attributes of the various ages have no effect on one
Who is utterly devoted to Raghupati's feet.
The illusion created by a magician is difficult to penetrate, king of
    the birds,
But the magician's servant is not deceived by his tricks.

The bad and good, created by Hari's maya,
Cannot be dispersed without the worship of Hari.
Bearing this in mind, abandon all desire,
And worship Ram.   (104A)

In that Kaliyug, king of the birds,
I lived in Avadh for many years.
Then a famine occurred, and overcome by adversity,
I was compelled to move to another land.   (104B)

I went to Ujjaini, O Uragari,
Miserable, sad, poor and suffering.
After some time had passed, I acquired some wealth,
And then began to devote myself to the worship of Shambhu.
There was a Brahman there who constantly worshipped Shiv
According to Vedic rites; he had no other occupation.
He was a very saintly man, one who knew the highest truth.
And though a worshipper of Shambhu, he did not disparage Hari.
I hypocritically served this kind Brahman,
Who was righteousness itself.
Seeing me outwardly so reverential, sire,
He instructed me like his own son.
The noble Brahman taught me a mantra sacred to Shiv,
And gave me every kind of good advice.

I would go to a Shiv temple and recite the mantra
With unbounded pride and arrogance in my heart.

> I, a vile wretch with a mind full of sin,
> Base-born, and in the grip of delusion,
> Would burn with envy at the sight of a Brahman
> Or worshipper of Hari, and rail at Lord Vishnu.   (105A)

> Distressed to see my behaviour,
> My guru would constantly admonish me.
> But I grew extremely angry—
> Does pride ever like good advice?   (105B)

One day my guru sent for me,
And instructed me for a long time on right behaviour.
'The fruit of worshipping Shiv, my son,
Is unceasing devotion to Ram's feet.
Shiv and Brahma both worship Ram,
So what is there to say of mortal man!
Do you wish for happiness, unfortunate one, by opposing him
Whose feet are adored by Brahma and Shiv?'
When I heard my guru speak of Har as Hari's servant,
My heart, king of the birds, burned with anger.
Though base-born, I had acquired learning
And become like a snake that has been fed on milk.
Arrogant, wicked, unfortunate, base-born,
I fought my guru day and night.
My guru, who was exceedingly kind, felt no anger,
But counselled me wisely again and again.
The first person a rogue kills and destroys
Is one from whom he has derived some benefit.
Smoke, which is born of fire, my friend,
Puts out that same fire when it attains the status of a cloud.
The dust lying upon the road is held in contempt,

And constantly endures being stepped upon by all;
But when blown aloft by the wind it first fills the air itself,
And then gets into the king's eyes or falls upon his crown.
Listen, king of the birds, realizing this state of affairs,
The wise do not keep company with the wicked.
Sages and scholars have ever laid down this rule—
Enmity with a bad man is not good, nor is friendship.
Stay ever aloof from them, my master,
Avoid the wicked as you would a dog.
I was a bad man, my heart full of deceit and falsehood,
And the guru's well-meant admonitions did not please me.

> One day, at a temple dedicated to Har,
> I was chanting his name
> When my guru came in, but in my pride
> I did not rise to salute him.   (106A)

> That gracious man did not say a word,
> Nor did he feel even a trace of anger in his heart.
> But the great god Shiv could not tolerate
> The grievous sin of disrespect to a guru.   (106B)

A voice from heaven was heard in the temple,
'You wretched and arrogant fool!
Though your guru has no anger,
Being so kind-hearted and truly wise,
Yet I pronounce a curse upon you, fool,
For I am not pleased by any transgression of what is right.
If I do not punish you, wretch,
The Vedic law that I follow will be broken.
The fools who bear malice against their gurus,
Fall into the worst abyss of hell for ten million ages.
They are then born from the wombs of beasts,
And suffer through ten thousand successive births.

You remained seated, unmoving like a python, vile sinner,
With your mind full of wickedness. So you shall become a snake!
Disappear into the hollow of some vast tree,
And there remain, you vilest of the vile, in that mean state.'

My guru cried out upon
Hearing Shiv's terrible curse.
Seeing me trembling with fear,
Great sorrow arose in his heart.   (107A)

Contemplating my horrible fate,
The Brahman devoutly prostrated himself
Before Shiv, and with folded hands,
And in a voice choking with emotion, he beseeched
    him thus: (107B)

*'I pay homage to the sovereign Lord of the northeast quarter, he who is
    salvation personified,*
The omnipresent and all-pervading Absolute, embodied in the Vedas.
*The self-contained, the unqualified, the unvarying, the undifferentiated
    and the indifferent,*
The all-pervading intelligence, who envelops all space and sky—
    I worship him.

*Incorporeal, the root of the sacred syllable Om, transcending all states
    and conditions,*
*Beyond all speech, understanding and perception by the senses, the Lord
    of the mountain,*
The terrible, the compassionate, the death of death itself,
The abode of all virtues, who is beyond birth and rebirth—
    I salute him.

As stern and white as the snow-clad Himalayas,
Radiant with the beauty of countless gods of Love,

With the lovely Ganga with her trembling waves glittering in his
    matted locks,
The crescent moon shining upon his forehead, and snakes around
    his neck,

With trembling ear-rings, shapely brows, large eyes,
Smiling face, and blue-stained throat; who is all-merciful,
And wears a tiger-skin and a garland of skulls—
Shankar, the beloved Lord of all. I worship him.

The wrathful, the exalted, the majestic, the Supreme Lord,
The indivisible, the unbegotten, with the radiance of countless suns,
Who roots out the threefold afflictions, and bears a trident in his hand—
Bhavani's beloved, accessible only through love. I adore him.

Beyond number, the blessed, the cause of universal destruction at
    the end of each kalpa,
The bestower of eternal joy upon the good, the slayer of the
    demon Tripur,
The aggregation of consciousness and bliss, the destroyer of all delusion,
Vanquisher of Love, be gracious to me, O Lord, be gracious.

So long as men do not worship the lotus feet of Uma's lord,
Neither in this world nor the next
Can they find peace or happiness, nor does their suffering end.
Therefore, O Lord, you who dwell in the inner hearts of all, have mercy.

I know nothing of meditation, prayer, or ritual worship,
But every moment and at all times I bow to you, O Shambhu.
Save me, Lord, a wretch afflicted by old age and the agony of rebirth—
O Shambhu, it is you alone I worship!'

The Brahmin uttered this eightfold prayer
In praise of Rudra to propitiate the great god.

To all those who repeat it with devotion,
Shambhu shows his favour.

> When the omniscient Shiv heard the Brahman's prayer
> And saw his loving devotion,
> A voice from heaven was heard in the temple again,
> 'Ask for a boon, best of Brahmans.'   (108A)

> 'If you are pleased with me, Lord,
> And would show your love to your servant,
> Grant me devotion to your feet, Lord
> And then another boon.   (108B)

> Overwhelmed by your maya, the foolish soul
> Wanders forever in error.
> So do not be angry with it,
> O all-compassionate God.   (108C)

> O merciful Shankar,
> Be gracious to this creature.
> After a little time, Lord,
> Let your curse become a kindness.   (108D)

O abode of mercy, now do only that, I pray,
Which will bring him the highest blessings.'
Upon hearing the Brahman's entreaty for the good of another,
The voice from heaven came again. 'So be it!' it replied.
'Even though he has committed a grievous sin,
And I in my anger have cursed him,
Yet seeing your goodness
I will do him a special favour.
They who are forgiving and helpful and kind to others
O Brahman, are as dear to me as Ram himself.
But my curse, Brahman, cannot be in vain—
He will have to be reborn a thousand times.

But the intolerable anguish of being born and dying
Will not affect him at all,
And in no birth will his knowledge of previous lives be lost.
Listen, Shudra, to my words unfailing—
You have been born in Raghupati's city,
And then you have devoted yourself to my worship.
By the power of the sacred city and by my grace,
Devotion to Ram will arise in your heart.
Now listen as I tell you the truth, my friend—
A vow to serve the Brahmans is the only way to please Hari.
Now do not ever insult a Brahman,
And regard a holy man as equal to the infinite Lord himself.
Indra's thunderbolt, my mighty trident,
Death's rod, and Hari's dreadful chakra—
He who does not die even when struck by these,
Is burnt to ashes in the fire of hostility to Brahmans.
Hold this true knowledge in your heart,
And nothing will be impossible for you in this world.
One other blessing I now bestow upon you—
You will be able to go wherever you wish unhindered.'

On hearing Shiv's words, my guru
Rejoiced, and cried, 'So be it!'
After admonishing me, he returned home,
Holding Shambhu's feet in his heart.   (109A)

Impelled by my doom, to the Vindhya mountains
I went, and was reborn a snake,
And then, after some time,
I effortlessly gave up that form.   (109B)

Whatever body I assumed, O steed of Hari,
I abandoned again with ease,
Like a man shedding his old clothes
When he puts on new ones.   (109C)

I assumed many forms, Garud,
But my knowledge never left me.
Thus Shiv honoured the Vedic laws,
And I suffered no pain.   (109D)

Whatever body I took on, whether animal, godly, or human,
I worshipped Ram in that form.
But one pain never left me—
The memory of my guru's kind and tender nature.
Finally I was born in a Brahman's body,
Difficult even for gods to attain—as the Vedas and Puranas declare.
In that body, whenever I joined other children at play,
I would act out all of Raghunayak's doings.
When I grew older, my father gave me lessons.
I would listen, understand and reflect on the lessons, but they failed
     to interest me.
All worldly desires left my heart,
And I became exclusively absorbed in my devotion to Ram's feet.
Tell me, king of the birds, is there anyone so foolish
As to abandon the cow of plenty and tend a donkey?
Immersed in love, nothing appealed to me,
And my father grew tired of trying to teach me.
When my father and mother passed away,
I left for the forest to worship Ram, defender of the devout.
Wherever I found any great munis living in the forest,
I would visit their ashrams and bow my head to them.
I would ask them to tell me about Ram's perfections,
And listen with delight to what they told me, Garud.
Thus, I roamed about, listening to recitations of Hari's virtues,
For by Shambhu's grace, I could go everywhere, unhindered.
The threefold longing for sons, wealth and fame left me,
And only one great desire remained in my heart—
To behold Ram's lotus feet,
For then I would consider my life to have been rewarded.

Every muni I asked replied thus to me:
'God is present in all things.'
But this view of the incorporeal God did not appeal to me,
And I grew ever more attached to the incarnate brahm.

Remembering my guru's words,
I became devoted to Ram's feet.
Singing Raghupati's praises, I wandered about,
My love every moment growing greater. (110A)

Upon Mount Meru's peak, under a banyan tree
Sat the muni, Lomas.
On seeing him, I bowed my head,
And very humbly addressed him. (110B)

When the gracious muni heard
My modest and gentle words, Garud,
He courteously asked me, 'Brahman,
With what purpose do you come here?' (110C)

I replied, 'O ocean of mercy,
You are omniscient and all-wise.
Teach me, blessed one,
How to worship the incarnate brahm.' (110D)

Then the noble muni reverently related
A few of Raghupati's perfections, Garud.
But being himself a sage devoted to true knowledge,
And seeing me as the most deserving,
He began to discourse upon the Absolute,
The unbegotten, without duality, without attributes, the sovereign
    of the heart,
The one, the passionless, the nameless and formless,
The indivisible, the incomparable, accessible only through experience,

Transcending the mind, beyond the senses, unblemished, indestructible,
Immutable, illimitable, the accumulation of bliss.
'You are It, there is no difference, It and You
Are one as waves and water are—so declare the Vedas.'
The muni explained it to me in many ways,
But this nirgun view did not stay in my heart.
I bowed my head at his feet and once more said,
'Tell me how to worship the incarnate brahm, noble muni!
Devotion to Ram is water, and my heart a fish—
How can they be separated, O wisest of munis?
Be gracious to me, and teach me how
I may see Raghurai with my own eyes.
When I have gazed upon the king of Avadh to my eyes' content,
I will listen to your discourse on the unembodied brahm.'
The muni once more related the incomparable story of Hari,
But, demolishing the sagun view, he discoursed upon the nirgun.
I rejected the nirgun view of the formless brahm,
And obstinately insisted upon its incarnate form.
For every answer I had another, and as I continued,
The muni began showing signs of anger.
I was so disrespectful, my lord,
That anger arose even in the heart of an enlightened soul.
Even sandalwood, with enough friction,
Will eventually burst into flame.

Again and again the muni angrily
Explained his theory of true knowledge,
While I, sitting there, began pondering
Various questions in my mind.   (111A)

Can anger exist without duality,
Or duality without ignorance?
Can the individual soul, dull, finite,
And subject to maya, ever be equal to God?   (111B)

Can one who helps others be afflicted with adversity,
Or one who holds the philosopher's stone be poor?
Can an oppressor be free from fear,
Or a libertine escape disgrace?
Can one's line prosper if one harms a Brahman?
Is objective action possible after attaining self-knowledge?
Can good sense arise from association with the wicked?
Can one who lusts after another's wife attain salvation?
Can those who have perceived the Supreme Spirit fall again into
      the cycle of rebirth,
Or those who revile Hari ever find happiness?
Can a kingdom endure without sound statesmanship,
Or sins persist in company with the narration of Hari's story?
Can unblemished fame be attained without virtuous action,
Or infamy attained without sin?
Is there any gain like devotion to Hari,
Which is sung by the Vedas, the saints and the Puranas?
Is there any loss in the whole world, brother,
Like not worshipping Ram even after receiving a human body?
Is there any wickedness like vilifying another,
O steed of Hari, or any virtue like compassion?
Thus I considered innumerable clever arguments in my mind,
And did not listen to the muni's discourse with any respect.
Again and again I defended the sagun form of worship,
Till at last the muni angrily declared,
'Fool, I am giving you the best possible instruction, but you refuse
      to accept it,
And persist with your countless arguments and counterarguments.
You have no belief in my words of truth,
But like a crow are afraid of everything.
You have a high regard for your own opinions, wretch—
So you shall be changed at once into an outcast bird!'
I took his curse upon my head,
But felt neither afraid nor demeaned.

I turned immediately into a crow,
And then, bowing my head at the muni's feet,
And invoking Ram, the jewel of the Raghu clan,
I joyfully flew away."   (112A)

Uma, those devoted to Ram's feet
And free of desire, pride and anger,
See their Lord present in the whole world—
So with whom can they quarrel?   (112B)

"Listen, O king of the birds, this was not the rishi's fault.
Ram, the ornament of the Raghu clan, directs the hearts of all,
And it was him, the ocean of mercy, who confused the muni's
    understanding
And thus put my love to the test.
When he saw that in thought, word and deed I was his servant,
The Almighty Lord restored the rishi to his senses again.
When the rishi saw my extraordinary fortitude
And my great belief in Ram's feet,
He was astonished, and, overcome with remorse,
He courteously called me to him.
The muni did all he could to console me,
And then gladly taught me the mantra sacred to Ram.
The sage in his mercy also taught me
How to meditate upon the child Ram.
The beauty and joy of this worship pleased me very much—
I told you this at the beginning.
The muni kept me with him for some time,
And then recited to me the *Ramcharitmanas*.
After reverently repeating this tale to me,
He spoke these gracious words:
'By Shambhu's grace, my son, I found
This secret and beautiful lake of Ram's acts.
I see that you are one of Ram's own devotees,

And so I have told you this story in full.
Never repeat this tale, dear son, in the presence of those
Who have no devotion for Ram in their hearts.'
The muni instructed me in many ways,
And I lovingly bowed my head at his feet.
Pleased, the great muni gave me his blessing,
Touching my head with his lotus hands.
'From now on, unceasing devotion to Ram
Will forever dwell in your heart by my grace.

You will always be Ram's favourite,
Endowed with every virtue, free from all pride,
Taking any shape you wish, choosing your own
      time to die,
And a treasure-house of wisdom and dispassion.   (113A)

Any hermitage where you may now live
Meditating upon the divine Lord,
Will be free from the effects of ignorance
For a distance of one yojan all around.   (113B)

Time, fate, virtue, sin, circumstance—
None of these sorrows shall ever torment you.
The many diverse and delightful mysteries of Ram,
Implicit or manifest in legends and the Puranas,
You shall come to know without any effort,
And your love for Ram's feet will be renewed afresh every day.
Whatever desire you may form in your heart,
Shall become easily attainable by Hari's grace.'
Hearing the muni's blessing, O Garud of steadfast mind,
A solemn voice was heard in the sky,
'May it be as you say, enlightened muni,
For he is my devotee in thought, word and deed.'
Hearing the voice from the sky, I was overcome with joy,

And, lost in love, all my doubts disappeared.
Then, receiving the muni's permission to depart,
I bowed my head at his feet again and again,
And joyfully came to this hermitage.
By the grace of the Lord, I had received a singular boon.
I have lived here now, O king of the birds,
For seven and twenty cycles of creation.
I unceasingly sing of Raghupati's perfections,
And the birds in their wisdom reverently listen.
Whenever Raghubir, for the sake of his devotees,
Assumes the body of a man in Avadh's city,
I go and stay at his capital
And delight myself by looking upon his childish pranks.
Then, holding Ram's child form in my heart,
I return, king of the birds, to my own ashram.
I have now told you the full story
Of how I took on the form of a crow,
And have answered all your questions, dear son.
The power of faith in Ram is great indeed.

> I love this body because it was in this form
> That I attained love for Ram's feet,
> And was favoured with the sight of my Lord
> So that all my doubts disappeared.   (114A)

> I stubbornly defended the doctrine of bhakti,
> For which the great rishi cursed me,
> But eventually I received a boon difficult even for
>   saints to obtain.
> See the power of devotion!   (114B)

They who knowingly abandon such bhakti
And strive only for knowledge are fools
Who disregard the wish-fulfilling cow tied up at home,

And wander instead in search of the milkweed for milk.
Listen, king of the birds—those who abandon the worship of Hari
And want happiness through other means
Are fools who stupidly seek to cross
The great ocean of existence without a boat."
Garud rejoiced to hear Bhushundi's words, Bhavani,
And said in gentle tones,
"By your grace, sire, in my heart remain
No doubt, sorrow, delusion, nor error.
Through your kindness, I have heard
The sanctifying tale of Ram's perfections and have attained peace.
But I have one more question, sire—
In your infinite mercy, please explain it to me.
The saints, the munis, the Vedas and the Puranas all say
There is nothing as difficult to attain as knowledge.
That is what that muni also said to you, sire,
But you did not respect knowledge as you did devotion.
What is the difference between knowledge and bhakti?
Explain it to me fully, O abode of compassion."
Pleased to hear Uragari's words
The wise crow courteously replied,
"There is no difference between bhakti and knowledge,
For both put an end to the distress born of this existence.
Great sages, though, tell of a difference between the two—
Listen to it carefully, O noblest of birds.
Wisdom, dispassion, contemplation, knowledge—
These are all masculine, Garud.
The power of the male is mighty in every way,
While the female is weak and inherently inferior.

> Only a man dispassionate and resolute of mind
> Can give up women,
> Not the libertine devoted to worldly pleasure
> Who has no regard for Raghubir's feet.   (115A)

But even such an enlightened muni
Falls under the spell of a doe-eyed woman
At the sight of her moon-bright face.
It is Vishnu's own delusive power, Garud, that becomes
      manifest as woman.   (115B)

I take no sides here, but merely state
The view of the Vedas, the Puranas and the saints.
A woman is never enamoured of another woman's beauty,
This, destroyer of serpents, is customary.
But listen to this—both maya and bhakti
Are of the feminine gender, as everyone knows.
Bhakti is beloved of Raghubir,
While poor Maya is only a dancing girl.
Ram is very favourably disposed towards Bhakti,
So Maya is terribly afraid of her.
Ram's Bhakti is incomparable and illimitable,
And Maya shrinks at the very sight of one
In whose heart Bhakti dwells unhindered—
She has no power over such a one.
Thus reflecting, enlightened munis
Desire only bhakti, the source of all bliss.

This mystery of Raghunath
No one comprehends all at once.
Whoever, by Raghupati's favour, does understand it,
Is never, even in dream, subject to any delusion.   (116A)

Now, O wise and clever Garud,
Listen more to the difference between knowledge
      and bhakti,
The hearing of which leads to everlasting
And uninterrupted love for Ram's feet.   (116B)

Listen, son, to this ineffable tale,
Which may only be understood but cannot be explained.
The soul is a tiny part of the Divine, indestructible,
Intelligent, pure and inherently blissful.
But it is in the grip of maya, sire,
And has trapped itself like a parrot or a monkey.[7]
The material and the spiritual have been tied together in
	a knot,
Which, though imaginary, is difficult to untie.
Thus the soul becomes caught in the cycle of rebirth,
And till that knot is untied, it can know no happiness.
The Vedas and Puranas suggest many means,
But the knot doesn't loosen and the entanglement increases.
The soul is filled with the darkness of delusion,
And cannot see how to loosen the knot.
Even when God creates favourable circumstances,
The knot remains difficult to untie.
If, by Hari's grace, the beautiful cow of true piety
Comes to dwell in one's heart,
She grazes upon the green grass
Of prayer, penance, fasts, self-restraint, internal purification,
And all the religious practices which the Vedas declare to be
	righteous conduct.
Her calf, for which her teats overflow with milk, is love.
Resignation is the rope which binds her hind legs, faith the vessel
	which catches the milk,
And the milkman a pure mind subject only to itself.
Once the milk of supreme righteousness has been obtained,
Let it be set to boil upon the fire of fulfilment.
Let it be cooled by the breath of contentment and forgiveness,
And set into curd with fortitude.
Let this be churned in the earthen pot of joy, with reflection for the
	churning-stick,

Self-restraint for the support, and truth and pleasant speech for
    the cords.
And by this churning extract the fresh butter of dispassion,
Clear, pure and sanctifying.

Let the butter be placed upon the fire of abstract
    contemplation,
Kindled with one's past actions, good and bad.
When the impurity of attachment is burned away,
Let the ghee of knowledge be cooled by reason.   (117A)

Let reason, the embodiment of worldly understanding,
Having obtained this pure ghee of knowledge,
Fill with it the lamp that is the intellect,
And set it firmly upon the stand of equanimity.   (117B)

From the raw cotton of the three states of consciousness[8]
    and the three gunas,
Let reason draw out the fibres of the fourth state of
    the soul[9]
And make out of them a wick
That is sturdy and strong.   (117C)

In this manner let it light the bright lamp
Of knowledge—
The moths of vanity and other vices
Are immediately consumed upon approaching it.   (117D)

'I am that brahm'—this indestructible awareness
Is the lamp's brightly burning flame.
The bliss that results from this self-realization is the
    shining light
That destroys the error of duality, the root of this existence.
Delusion and the other forms of infinite darkness

That depend on the prevalence of ignorance, all disappear,
Then reason, having thus found a light,
Sits in the chamber of the heart and tries to loosen the knot.
If it succeeds in untying that knot,
The soul realizes its purpose.
But when Maya sees it loosening the knot, Garud,
She creates many difficulties.
She sends forth the Riddhis and Siddhis, my friend,
Which tempt reason to avarice.
They draw near, by artifice, force, or fraud,
And blow out that lamp of knowledge by fanning it with
      their robes.
Reason, if it be clever and wise,
Refuses to look at them, realizing their hostile intent.
If reason is not hindered by these obstacles,
The gods proceed to create trouble.
The various senses are doorways and windows
At which the gods sit and keep watch.
If they see the wind of sensuality stirring,
They determinedly throw the doors and shutters open.
If that tempest blows into the heart,
The lamp of knowledge is put out.
The knot is not loosened, the light of self-realization is
      extinguished,
And reason is defeated by this wind of sensuality.
Neither the senses nor the gods like knowledge,
For they are ever enamoured of sensual pleasure.
And if reason has been fooled by this wind of sensuality,
Who can light that lamp again as before?

> Then the soul is again tormented
> By the manifold miseries of birth and rebirth.
> Hari's maya is very difficult to cross,
> It cannot be easily traversed.   (118A)

Discernment is difficult to explain, difficult to understand,
Difficult to achieve through practice,
And if, by some chance, one attains it,
There are many obstacles to retaining it.   (118B)

The path of knowledge is like the edge of a sword—
It is easy to fall from it, O king of the birds.
He who can walk this path without hindrance
Attains to the supreme state of eternal liberation.
But this supreme state of eternal freedom is difficult to attain—
So declare the saints, the Puranas, the Vedas and all the Shastras.
With the worship of Ram, sire, the same eternal liberation
Comes freely, of its own accord and even if not sought.
Just as water cannot stay without the ground beneath for support,
However many ways you may try to make it,
In the same way, O king of the birds,
The joy of salvation cannot stay without devotion to Hari.
Reflecting thus, the clever worshippers of Hari
Spurn salvation and crave devotion.
With bhakti, without any exertion or effort,
The ignorance that is the root of birth and rebirth is destroyed,
Just as we eat for our own satisfaction,
But it is the fire in our bellies that digests what is eaten.
Who is so foolish as to find no delight
In devotion to Hari that is so easy and pleasant?

'I am his servant, and the Lord is my master'—without this feeling
It is impossible to cross the ocean of this existence, Uragari.
Worship then Ram's lotus feet,
Keeping this truth in mind.   (119A)

In Raghunath is the power
To make the sentient inert,
And the inert sentient.
Blessed are they who worship him.   (119B)

I have explained the doctrine of knowledge to you,
Now listen to the power of the gem that is bhakti.
Devotion to Ram is a sparkling wish-fulfilling jewel,
Which shines with its own radiance night and day,
Needing neither lamp, nor ghee, nor wick.
Delusion and poverty do not come near him
Whose heart contains this jewel, Garud.
Nor can greed ever extinguish this light.
The deep darkness of ignorance is dispelled,
And the swarms of moths are all destroyed.
Lust and other evils do not approach him
In whose heart bhakti abides.
It changes poison into nectar, enemies into friends.
Without this jewel, no one can find happiness.
With it, those terrible diseases of the mind
Which cause all living beings to suffer, have no power.
He whose heart contains the jewel of devotion to Ram
Does not suffer, even in dream, the slightest trace of any sorrow.
They are the wisest of the wise in this world
Who strive ceaselessly to attain this precious gem.
Yet though this jewel is manifest in the world,
No can find it without Ram's grace.
There are easy ways to obtain it,
But luckless men reject them.
The Vedas and Puranas are sacred mountains,
And the legends of Ram their many glorious mines.
Good men are the miners, discernment their pickaxe,
And wisdom and dispassion their eyes, Uragari.
Anyone who searches for it with love,
Finds the jewel of bhakti, the source of all blessing.
My lord, I hold in my heart the firm conviction,
That one who serves Ram is greater than Ram himself.
Ram is the ocean, the good and the steadfast are the rainclouds;
Hari is the sandalwood tree, the pious are the breezes that spread
    its fragrance.

The fruit of all spiritual effort is firm devotion to Hari—
But no one has found it without the help of the saints.
Understanding this, he who seeks the company of saints,
Will find devotion to Ram easy to attain.

> Brahm is the ocean, knowledge is Mount Mandar,
> And the saints are the gods.
> Ram's story is the nectar they churn out
> Sweetened by bhakti.   (120A)

> With dispassion as its shield, and knowledge as
>   its sword,
> It is devotion to Hari that slays the enemies
> That are pride, greed and attachment, and triumphs
>   over them.
> Reflect, O king of the birds, and see this for yourself."   (120B)

Then the king of the birds affectionately replied,
"If you love me, gracious master,
Acknowledge me as your servant,
And answer these seven questions.
First tell me, my lord of steadfast mind,
What form is the most difficult to attain.
Next, consider and briefly explain to me,
What is the greatest suffering, and what the highest joy.
You know the essential qualities of the good and the bad,
So explain to me the inherent nature of both.
Tell me, what is the greatest virtue as declared by the Vedas,
And what the most dreadful sin.
Explain to me the diseases of the mind,
For you know all and are supremely compassionate."
"Listen, my son, with attention and affection,
As I briefly explain these rules of morality.
There is no other form like that of man,

Every living creature, moving or unmoving, desires it.

It is the ladder to hell, to heaven, and to ultimate liberation,

And bestows upon one the blessings of wisdom, dispassion
    and devotion.

Those who have attained this form, yet do not worship Hari

But remain immersed in the lowest of low lustful pleasures,

Have thrown away the philosopher's stone in their hands,

And are clutching at bits of glass instead.

There is no suffering in this world like poverty,

And no joy like communion with saints.

Helping others in thought, word, deed,

Is the innate nature of the good, O Garud.

The good endure pain for the benefit of others,

But the bad do so to give pain to others.

The good in their compassion are like the birch tree,[10]

Enduring the greatest suffering for the good of others.

But the bad, like hemp, to bind others,

Would have their skin removed and die in agony.

O destroyer of serpents, like snakes and rats,

The bad harm others without any purpose.

After ruining another's prosperity, they themselves perish,

Like hailstones dissolve after destroying the crops.

The rise of the wicked brings sorrow to the world,

Like the rising of the infamous Ketu.

The rise of the good always results in happiness,

Like the rising of the moon and the sun bringing joy to
    the world.

Non-violence is the greatest virtue as declared by the Vedas,

And there is no sin like speaking ill of others, O Garud.

He who reviles Shankar or his guru is reborn as a frog,

And retains that body through a thousand births.

He who insults a Brahman endures countless hells,

And then is reborn in the world in the body of a crow.

Arrogant souls who scorn the gods and the Vedas

Fall into the lowest hell,
While those who disrespect the good are reborn as owls
Who love the night of ignorance and for whom the sun of wisdom
    has set.
Fools who revile everyone
Are reborn again as bats.
Now listen, dear son, to the diseases of the mind,
From which all people suffer pain.
Ignorance is the root of all ailments,
And from these arise many pains.
Lust is wind, infinite greed is phlegm,
And anger is bile constantly burning the chest.
Should these three humours combine,
There results a most terrible fever.
The various, unattainable, sensual cravings
Are the many illnesses, too numerous to name.
Attachment is a ringworm, envy an itch,
Joy and sorrow, swollen glands in the throat.
There is the wasting disease that is burning jealousy at
    another's gain,
And the leprosy of wickedness and deceit.
Egoism is an excruciating pain in the joints,
While hypocrisy, dishonesty, vanity and pride are worms that infect
    the body.
There is the dropsy of ambition and avarice,
The dreadful ague of the threefold longing for sons, wealth
    and fame,
And the two fevers of selfishness and stupidity.
But why list all the many awful diseases?

    Men die even of a single disease,
    And these incurable diseases are many.
    They constantly torment the soul,
    So how can it find peace?   (121A)

There are countless different remedies—
Sacred vows and pious practice, abstract contemplation,
The pursuit of wisdom, the performance of sacrifices,
    prayer, almsgiving, and more—
But the diseases, O steed of Hari, do not yield.   (121B)

Thus every soul in the world is ill,
Suffering sorrow and joy, and fear and love and separation.
I have mentioned only some of the diseases of the mind—
They afflict all, but only a few are able to see them.
On being recognised, these tormentors of the faithful
Diminish, but are not completely destroyed.
If fed the unhealthy diet of sensual pleasure, they spring up
Even in the hearts of munis—so what can be said of mortal men?
All these diseases can be cured, if by Ram's grace,
These factors come together:
Confidence in the words of a true guru as the physician,
And abstinence from sensual pleasures as the diet strictly followed.
Devotion to Raghupati is the life-giving herb,
And faith the channel through which it is administered.
If these factors unite, these diseases are easily cured;
Without them, all efforts are in vain.
Regard the mind free of disease, my lord,
Only when it gathers strength through detachment,
Its appetite for good sense increases every day,
And its weakness for sensual pleasures disappears.
When the mind then bathes in the clear waters of knowledge,
It is filled with devotion to Ram.
Shiv, Brahma, Shukdev, Sanak and his three brothers, Narad
And other sages practiced in the contemplation of the divine,
All hold this same opinion, lord of the birds,
That one must practise love for Ram's lotus feet.
The Vedas, the Puranas and all the sacred books declare,
There can be no happiness without devotion to Raghupati.

Hair might grow upon a turtle's shell,
The son of a barren woman kill,
Or flowers of all kinds bloom in the sky,
But a soul can find no happiness if it be hostile to Hari.
Thirst might be quenched by drinking water from a mirage,
Horns sprout from the head of a hare,
Or darkness overcome the sun,
But the soul can find no joy if it be turned away from Ram.
Fire may appear from snow,
But no one opposed to Ram can find peace.

> Ghee might be churned from water,
> Or oil squeezed from a stone,
> But without the worship of Hari, liberation cannot
>   be attained—
> This is beyond debate.   (122A)

> The Lord can raise up a mosquito to be Viranchi,
> Or bring Viranchi down lower than a mosquito.
> Realizing this, and abandoning all doubt,
> The wise worship Ram alone.   (122B)

> I declare to you a definitive truth—
> And my words are never untrue—
> Only those who worship Hari
> Can cross the ocean of existence.   (122C)

I have told you, my lord, of Hari's incomparable doings,
In detail, and briefly, to the best of my understanding.
To worship Ram, forgetting all other duties, Garud,
This alone is the established truth of the Vedas.
Who else is worth serving, if not Raghupati,
Who has affection even for a fool such as me?
You are wisdom embodied, and beyond delusion,

Yet you have done me a great favour, my lord,
By asking me to tell you the sanctifying story of Ram,
The delight of Shambhu, Shuk, and Sanak and his brothers.
The company of the good is difficult to find in this world
Even once, whether for a second or an hour.
Reflect, Garud, and decide for yourself,
Whether I am fit to worship Raghubir.
Though I am the lowest of birds and impure in every way,
The Lord has made me known as one who purifies the world.

    Though I be the lowest of the low,
    Today I am exceedingly blessed,
    For acknowledging me as his own servant,
    Ram has bestowed on me the company of a saint. (123A)

    I have spoken, my lord, to the best of my ability,
    And have concealed nothing from you.
    But Raghunayak's story is an unfathomable ocean—
    Can anyone reach its bottom?" (123B)

As he reflected upon Ram's many qualities,
The wise Bhushundi rejoiced again and again.
"He whose glory the Vedas describe only as 'Not this, not this',
Whose might, majesty and greatness are unparalleled,
Whose feet Shiv and Brahma adore—that same Raghurai
Has, in his infinite gentleness, shown me his grace.
Nowhere have I heard of or seen such kindness—
So whom can I consider Raghupati's equal, O Garud?
Sadhus, saints, ascetics and those freed from rebirth,
Poets, scholars, sages and those who have renounced the world,
Mystics, heroes, hermits and those endowed with wisdom,
The devout, the learned and those who know the nature of all things—
Not even they can attain salvation without worshipping my master,
Ram—I pay him homage and bow again and again before him.

I adore the indestructible Lord, by seeking refuge in whom
Even wicked souls like me become pure.

> He whose name is the remedy for the disease that is
>   this existence
> And destroys the agony of the triple afflictions,
> May that compassionate God ever remain
> Gracious towards you and me."   (124A)

> Having heard Bhushundi's holy discourse,
> And seen his love for Ram's feet,
> Garud, now free of all doubt,
> Spoke in loving tones.   (124B)

"I have accomplished my purpose, now that I have heard
Your discourse steeped in devotion to Raghubir.
My love for Ram's feet has been renewed
And my distress born of maya has all gone.
You became my boat in the sea of delusion,
And have bestowed many blessings upon me, my lord.
I can never return this favour you have done me,
But again and again I prostrate myself at your feet.
A devotee of Ram, and with your every wish fulfilled,
You are so blessed, sire, there is none as fortunate as you.
Saints, trees, rivers, mountains and the earth—
Their business is only the good of others.
The heart of a saint is like fresh butter—
So the poets said, but did not say it right.
Butter melts only when it is itself heated,
But the most holy saints melt at the suffering of others.
My life and birth have been rewarded,
And by your grace, all my doubts have disappeared.
Know me ever to be your slave."
Again and again, Uma, did the lord of the birds speak thus.

After lovingly bowing his head at Bhushundi's feet,
And with Raghubir's image in his heart,
The steadfast Garud
Returned to Vaikunth.   (125A)

Girija, there is no gain
Like the company of saints.
It cannot be attained without Hari's grace—
So the Vedas and Puranas declare.   (125B)

I have now told you the most sanctifying story,
Upon the hearing of which the bonds of this existence fall away,
And there arises love for the lotus feet of Ram,
The sum of compassion and a wish-fulfilling tree to his suppliants.
Those who listen to this tale with full attention,
Are freed from all sins born of thought, word, or deed.
Pilgrimages and all the means of attaining salvation,
Meditation, detachment, the striving for spiritual knowledge,
The many pious practices, the sacred vows and the giving of alms,
Self-denial and restraint, prayer, penance and the performance of
    fire-sacrifices,
Compassion towards living beings, the service of Brahmans and
    one's guru,
Learning, humility and discernment—
All the expedients that the Vedas have described,
All have the same objective, which is devotion to Hari, Bhavani.
This devotion to Raghupati that the Vedas praise
Has rarely been attained by any, and then only by Ram's grace.

Though such devotion to Hari is difficult even for
    munis to realize,
It can be achieved without effort by those
Who continually listen to this story
With faith.   (126)

He is the man of perfect knowledge, endowed with wisdom and
      every virtue,
He is the ornament of the world, learned and beneficent,
He is the truly pious, the protector of his line,
Whose heart is utterly devoted to Ram's feet.
He is well versed in morality, and supremely wise,
He understands fully the truth of the Vedas,
He is a poet, a scholar and steadfast in battle,
Who worships Raghubir with sincerity.
Blessed is the land where flows the celestial Ganga,
Blessed is the woman who is devoted to her husband,
Blessed is the king who reigns with righteousness,
Blessed is the Brahman who swerves not from his duty.
Blessed is the wealth given away in charity,
Blessed is the intellect devoted to good deeds,
Blessed is the hour that brings the company of saints,
Blessed is the life unceasingly devoted to the Brahmans.

> Blessed is that family, O Uma,
> And worthy of worship throughout the world and most pure,
> In which is born
> A humble worshipper of the divine Raghubir.   (127)

I have now told you this story to the best of my understanding.
Though at first I had kept it secret,
When I saw the great devotion in your heart,
I told you Raghupati's story.
This tale must not be told to the foolish or the stubborn,
Or to those who do not listen with attention to Hari's playful deeds,
Nor to the greedy, the passionate, the lustful,
Who do not worship the master of creation, moving and unmoving.
This tale must never be repeated to one hostile to Brahmans,
Even if he be a king as mighty as the king of the gods.
Only those who hold dear the company of saints

Are worthy of hearing Ram's story.
Those who adore their guru's feet, and are devoted to righteousness
And the service of Brahmans are fit to hear this tale.
This tale will give especial delight
To one who loves Raghurai as his own life.

> One who seeks devotion at Ram's feet,
> Or liberation from rebirth,
> Should lovingly drink in this story
> From the cups of his ears.   (128)

Girija, I have related to you the story of Ram
That destroys the impurities of the Kali age and removes
     the impurities of the mind.
Ram's story is the life-giving herb that cures the disease
     that is rebirth—
As the Vedas and the learned declare.
It has seven beautiful parts,
Stairs leading to faith in Ram.
Only those who have Hari's special favour,
Can set foot upon these steps.
One who recites this tale without deceit,
Accomplishes all his heart desires.
Those who repeat it or hear it with delight,
Cross the ocean of existence as they would a puddle.'
Girija was delighted to have heard the whole story
And joyously replied,
'By my lord's favour, my doubts have disappeared
And my love for Ram's feet has sprung up anew.

> Through your grace, O Lord of the universe,
> I have now attained my desire—
> I now have unshakeable devotion to Ram,
> And all my sorrows have disappeared.'   (129)

This auspicious conversation between Shambhu and Uma
Results in happiness and destroys sorrow;
It puts an end to rebirth, removes doubt,
Gives joy to the faithful and is beloved of all good men.
To the worshippers of Ram in this world,
There is nothing more dear than the story of Ram.
By the grace of Raghupati, I have sung to the best of my ability
This beautiful and sanctifying tale.
In this age of Kali, there is no other means to salvation—
Not meditation, sacrifices, prayer, penance, fasting,
      nor ritual worship.
Remember only Ram, sing only of Ram,
And listen unceasingly to the recitation of Ram's virtues.
O heart, abandoning all guile, worship him
Whose special attribute it is to sanctify the fallen,
As poets, saints, the Vedas and Puranas declare.
Is there anyone who has worshipped Ram and not attained salvation?

Listen, my stupid heart! Is there anyone who has worshipped Ram,
The sanctifier of the fallen, and not attained salvation?
The prostitute, Ajamil, the robber, the vulture,
The elephant, and many other vile wretches have been redeemed by him.[11]
Abhirs, Jamanas, Kirats, Khashas, Shvapachas,
And others who are vileness personified,
Are sanctified if they but repeat once
The name of Ram, whom I adore.

Those who recite or listen or chant alone
This story of Ram, the ornament of the Raghu clan,
Wash away the impurities of the age of Kali and the impurities of
      their minds,
And attain Ram's abode without effort.
Anyone who sees the beauty of even five or six chaupais,
And holds them in his heart,

Is freed by Lord Raghubir from the distress
Born of the five forms of terrible ignorance.[12]

Ram alone is all-beautiful, all-wise,
Compassionate, and affectionate to the destitute—
Who else is as disinterested a benefactor
And bestower of salvation as he?
There is no other Lord like Ram,
By the slightest trace of whose favour
Even I, the dull-witted Tulsidas,
Have found supreme peace.

> There is no one as lowly as I am
> And no one as gracious to the lowly as you, Raghubir.
> Knowing this, O jewel of the Raghu clan,
> Take away my dreadful fear of rebirth.   (130A)

> As a woman is loved by her lover,
> And money by a miser, Raghunath—
> In the same manner may you ever be
> Dear to me, O Ram.   (130B)

Thus ends the seventh descent into the Manas lake of Ram's acts, that destroys all the impurities of the age of Kali.

Glossary

abir:

Red powder, thrown into the air in celebration.

Aditi:

The mother of the gods. In the Rig Veda, she is represented as being the mother of Daksh as well as the daughter of Daksh. She is addressed as 'the mother of the gods' and 'the mother of the world'. She gave birth to eight sons, of which she abandoned the eighth, the Sun. The other seven became the Adityas. In the Yajur Veda, she is called the wife of Vishnu, but in the Ramayana, the Mahabharata and the Puranas, Vishnu is called the son of Aditi; therefore, he is also sometimes called Aditya. In the Vishnu Purana, she is the daughter of Daksh and the wife of the sage Kashyap, by whom she was the mother of Vishnu in his Vaman, or dwarf, incarnation, and also of Indra. In the *Ramcharitmanas*, Aditi is reborn as Kaushalya and Kashyap as Dasharath, and in that form, they are the mother and father of Ram, who is Vishnu in his seventh incarnation.

Agahan:

The eighth month of the Hindu calendar equivalent to November–December.

Agastya:

A rishi, and the author of several hymns in the Rig Veda. It is said that he was born in a water-pitcher

323

as 'a fish of great lustre'. He is therefore also known as 'Ghatjoni' and 'Kumbhaj' or 'pitcher-born'. He is supposed to have drunk up the ocean because it had offended him, and because he wanted to help the gods in their wars with the Daityas when the latter had hidden themselves in the sea. He is therefore also called 'Samudra-chuluk' or 'ocean-drinker'.

ages of the world; yuga: The duration of the world is said to be 4,320,000,000 human years (equal to a day for Brahma); this period consists of a thousand epochs, and each epoch is made up of four ages, or yugas. These are: (i) Krit or Satyayug (the golden age); (ii) Tretayug (the silver age); (iii) Dwaparyug; (iv) Kaliyug. The first age comprises 1,728,000 years; the second 1,296,000 years; the third 864,000 years; and the fourth 432,000 years. The duration of the Dwapar is twice the length of the Kali, that of the Treta is thrice that of the Kali, and that of the Satyayug is four times that of the Kaliyug. In the current epoch, the first three ages have already elapsed, while the Kali is that in which we live. Ram's incarnation took place towards the end of the Tretayug.

Agni: Fire, one of the most ancient and sacred objects of worship in Hinduism. He appears in three places—in the sky as the sun, in air as lightning, and upon earth as ordinary fire. He is one of the chief deities of the Vedas, and, through the fire-sacrifices, the mediator between gods and men.

Ahalya: Wife of the Rishi Gautam, and a very beautiful woman. She was the first woman created by Brahma, who gave her to Gautam. Ahalya's exceptional beauty caught Indra's eye. Determined to seduce her, he enlisted the help of the moon, who turned into a cock and crowed at midnight.

Gautam, thinking it was time for his morning worship, went off to the river to bathe. Then Indra, taking the form of the rishi, entered his hermitage and seduced his unsuspecting wife. The sage, returning, caught him and in his fury cursed him. He also threw out Ahalya from the hermitage, and depriving her of the prerogative of being the most beautiful woman in the world, turned her into a block of stone. She was restored to life by the touch of Ram's feet.

Amaravati:	Indra's capital city, renowned for its magnificence and splendour.

amla:	The plant known as the Indian gooseberry and its fruit. The fruit is small and green and quite sour, but greatly valued for its medicinal properties. 'Holding an amla in the palm of your hand' signifies understanding something clearly and from every angle, just as the small and round amla fruit can be seen when held upon one's palm.

amrit:	Nectar conferring immortality, produced at the churning of the ocean by the gods and demons.

Anasuya:	The wife of the Rishi Atri, and by him, the mother of the sage, Durvasa. She was also one of the daughters of Daksh. She was exceedingly pious and practised intense austerities, which gave her miraculous powers.

anchal:	The flowing, free end of a sari.

Angad:	Son of Baali, the monkey king of Kishkindha.

apsara:	The apsaras are the nymphs of Indra's court. They are beautiful, fairy-like beings, and are the wives or mistresses of the Gandharvas. They are also famous for their liaisons with mortal men.

The Ramayana and the Puranas attribute their origin to the churning of the ocean. It is said that when they appeared out of the ocean, neither the gods nor the Asurs could have them, so they became common to all. They are also called Suranganas, or 'the wives of the gods'.

arghya: A libation of water and milk, flowers, kush grass and other auspicious ingredients made to a deity, or an honoured guest.

ark: The plant known as the crown flower. Native to India and South-east Asia, it grows to about 4 m in height, and has waxy white or lavender flowers. Its leaves and stem gives a thick, milky sap if broken. The seed follicles are small and hard. The plant is poisonous, but has several medicinal uses in Ayurveda. It is often grown in temple compounds and is believed to be particularly liked by Lord Shiva.

arti: A ceremony performed in welcome of an honoured guest, by moving circularly around his head a platter containing lamps, incense, flowers, etc.

Arundhati: The morning star, personified as the wife of the Rishi Vasishtha.

Ashvamedha: 'The sacrifice of a horse'; a sacrifice performed only by the greatest and most powerful of kings. It was believed that the performance of a hundred such sacrifices would enable a mortal king to overthrow Indra and become the ruler of the universe. A horse was selected and consecrated by the performance of certain ceremonies; it was then let loose to wander wherever it wanted for a year. The king, or his representative, followed the horse with an army, and if the horse entered another country, the ruler of that country had to either fight or submit. If the king who had released the horse was victorious over the kings through whose lands the horse passed, he would return home triumphant after a year, with the defeated kings behind him; if he failed in this, he was ridiculed and disgraced. After a king returned home successful, a great festival was held, during which the horse was sacrificed, either really or metaphorically.

Ashvins; Ashvin twins; Ashvinkumar:

Two Vedic deities, twin sons of the Sun by a nymph who concealed herself in the form of a mare (*ashva* in Sanskrit)—hence, Ashvini, and her sons, Ashvins. The Ashvins are ever young and handsome, and shine with the radiance of gold. Swift as falcons, they ride in a golden chariot drawn by horses or birds, and, as personifications of the morning twilight, they are the first bringers of light in the morning sky. They also have great healing powers, and are the physicians of heaven.

Astagiri:

This is the western mountain behind which the sun is supposed to set; it is also called Astachal.

Asur:

Literally, 'not a god', so 'enemy of the gods', or generally 'demons'. The word is used as a general term for the enemies of the gods, including Daityas and Danavs, who are descended from the sage Kashyap. It does not include the Rakshasas, who are descended from the sage Pulastya. The Asurs are in constant conflict with the gods.

Atri:

A rishi, and author of many Vedic hymns. In the Vedas, he appears in hymns in praise of Agni, Indra, and the Ashvins; later he is regarded as one of the ten Prajapatis, or lords of creation, engendered by Manu for the creation of the world; and still later, he appears as one of the mind-born sons of Brahma. He is also one of the Saptarishi, the seven great sages who preside over the world, and as one of them, he is one of the seven stars of the Great Bear. He married Anasuya, one of the daughters of Daksh, and their son was the sage Durvasa. In the Puranas, he was also the father of Soma, the moon, and the ascetic Dattatreya by Anasuya.

Ayodhya: The capital city of the kingdom of Koshal. It was the city from which ruled Ikshvaku, the founder of the solar dynasty. It later became the capital city of Dasharath and then of Ram. It is also the city of Ram's birth. It is also called Avadh.

Baali: The monkey-king of Kishkindha. He was the son of Indra, and said to have been born from his mother's hair (*baal*), hence his name. He was killed by Ram, and his kingdom given to his brother, Sugriv. His wife was Tara, and his sons were Angad and Tar.

Baitarni: '(The river) to be crossed'; it is the river that must be crossed before hell can be entered. The river is described as being filled with blood, excrement and all kinds of filth. It flows fast and with great force.

bakul: A medium evergreen tree native to India. The tree gives thick shade and bears fragrant flowers. Its fruit is also edible and is used in traditional medicine. It is also called maulsari.

Bali: A good and virtuous Daitya king, he was the son of Virochan, who was the son of Prahlad, the son of Kanakakasipu. Through devotion and penance, Bali became so powerful that he defeated Indra and the other gods, and extended his rule over the three worlds. The gods appealed to Vishnu for help, and he took on his Vaman or dwarf avatar to restrain the king. (See Vishnu, fifth avatar.) He asked the generous king for three steps of land. The king granted him the boon. Vishnu then stepped over the earth with his first step, the heavens with his second, and when he asked where he should place his foot for the third step, Bali offered his own head. Out of respect for Bali's goodness and generosity, Vishnu stopped short and gave him the infernal region of Patal to rule. Bali is also called Mahabali, and his capital city was Mahabalipuram.

Bana; Banasur: A powerful Daitya, the eldest son of the Daitya king, Bali; he had a thousand arms and was a devotee of Shiv and an enemy of Vishnu. He is also called Vairochi.

ber: The jujube tree and its fruit. This is cultivated as well as grows wild in India; every part of the tree has medicinal uses, and its small and somewhat acid fruit is very popular and is eaten pickled, cooked or raw. 'Holding a ber in the palm of your hand' signifies understanding something clearly and from every angle, just as the small and round ber fruit can be seen when held upon one's palm.

Bhadon: The sixth month of the Hindu calendar, equivalent to August–September.

Bhagirath: A king of the Ikshvaku dynasty, and a descendent of Sagar; he brought the sacred River Ganga to earth from heaven. King Sagar of Avadh married two women, the princess Keshini, and Sumati, the daughter of the sage Kashyap. With Keshini, he had one son, Asamanjas; through him the royal line was continued. With Sumati he had sixty-thousand sons. Now Asamanjas

grew up into such a wild and immoral man
that Sagar abandoned him. Unfortunately, the
sixty-thousand also followed in their brother's
footsteps, and became so known for their impiety
that the gods complained about them to Vishnu
and to the sage Kapil. Once, Sagar decided to
hold the Ashvamedha or horse-sacrifice. Though
the horse was guarded by his sixty-thousand sons,
it was carried off to Patal, the underworld. They
dug their way to the underworld, where they
saw the sage Kapil seated in meditation, and the
horse grazing close by. Thinking that he was the
thief, they threatened him with their weapons.
This disturbed the sage in his meditation, and
so enraged him that a single glance from him
reduced them to ashes. Their remains were
found by Anshumat, the son of Asamanjas, who
begged Kapil that his uncles be raised to heaven
through his favour. Kapil promised Anshumat's
grandson would be the means of accomplishing
this by bringing down Ganga, the river of
heaven. Anshumat returned to Sagar, who then
completed the sacrifice. The deep chasm that his
sons had dug became the ocean, which is called
'saagar' after his sons. The son of Anshumat was
Dilip, and his son was Bhagirath. Determined
to free the souls of his ancestors, Bhagirath left
his kingdom in the care of his ministers and
retreated to the Himalayas, where he practised
severe austerities in order to please Brahma. After
a thousand years of prayer and penance, Brahma
appeared before him. When Bhagirath told him
that he wanted to bring down the divine river,
Ganga, so that he may perform the appropriate
rites for his ancestors, Brahma told him to pray
to Shiv, for only he could withstand the force of
the river's descent. So Bhagirath prayed to Shiv.
The compassionate god was quickly pleased, and
agreed to help him, promising to hold the Ganga

in his matted locks and so reducing the force of her descent. Ganga agreed to come to earth, and as she fell, Shiv stood beneath her cascading waters and caught them in his hair, letting only a trickle escape. This trickle was as much as the earth could bear, and this became the mighty River Ganga upon earth. She followed Bhagirath, and he guided the river from the Himalayas, across the plains of northern India, into the sea, and from there to Patal, where the ashes of Sagar's sixty-thousand sons were washed with her waters and purified.

bhakti:	A many-nuanced idea meaning at one time all or any one of the following: faith, belief; devotion, adoration, worship; attachment, devotedness, service. In the Hindu context, it means devotion to and love for a personal god. There are nine forms of bhakti, which are explained by Ram to Sabari in the Aranyakand (35-36).
Bharadvaj:	An eminent rishi to whom are attributed many hymns from the Vedas.
Bharat:	'He who supports, bears, or carries'; son of Dasharath and Kaikeyi, younger brother to Ram.
Bhogavati:	The magnificent, subterranean capital city of the Nagas in Patal.
Bhrigu:	A Vedic sage. He is one of the Prajapatis and the great Rishis, and regarded as the founder of the race of Bhrigus or Bhargavas, in which were born Jamadagni and his son, Parashuram. He officiated at Daksh's sacrifice.
Bhringi:	A sage, especially devoted to Shiv. It is said that Bhringi was so deeply devoted to Shiv that he even refused to honour Parvati, maintaining

that he would worship Shiv and Shiv alone. He attempted to circle Shiv in homage, leaving out Parvati, so Shiv took Parvati upon his lap; Bhringi then turned himself into a snake and tried to slither between the two. At that, Shiv made Parvati a part of himself, taking on the form of Ardhanarishvar. Bhringi then turned himself into a bee and tried to separate the two. At this Parvati was so angry that she cursed him, so that he lost all flesh and blood and, turning into a bag of bones, collapsed upon the ground. Bhringi then realized that he could not separate Shiv from Parvati, for they were not separate, but together made up the whole. Bhringi was forgiven, and given a third leg by which to support himself.

Bhushundi;
Kak Bhushundi:

The crow, Bhushundi. He is a sage in a crow's body, and a great devotee of Ram. He is also one of the four narrators of the *Ramcharitmanas*, and relates the story of Ram to Garud.

birth, modes of:

According to Hindu tradition, there are four modes of birth: (i) born from the womb (such as man and other mammals); (ii) born of an egg (such as birds, fish and so on); (iii) engendered by heat and moisture (such worms, insects, lice, etc.); and (iv) born by sprouting or germinating (trees, plants, vegetables, etc.). From these four modes of birth are generated eighty-four lakh (1 lakh = 100,000) forms of life.

blue-throat:

The Indian roller. This bird has a blue crown and blue wings and tail, and a pale-brown breast. Though it does not have a blue throat, it is called nil-kanth (literally 'blue-throat' in Hindi), which is also a name for Shiv. It can be easily seen in India, and is believed by many to be sacred to Vishnu.

brahm:

The Absolute, the Eternal, the Self-existent, the divine essence and source of all being from which all created things emanate and to which they all return (not to be confused with Brahma who is the Supreme Spirit personified as the Creator).

Brahma:

The Supreme Spirit manifested as the Creator of the universe. He is the first god of the Hindu triad of the Creator, the Preserver and the Destroyer. He is represented as red in colour, with four heads. He wears a pointed beard, usually white in colour. He has four arms, in which he variously holds his sceptre, a spoon, a rosary of beads, a waterpot, a lotus, his bow Parivita and the Vedas. His consort is the goddess Sarasvati. His vehicle is the hansa, or swan. Brahma is also called 'Aj', the unborn; Chaturanan or Chaturmukh, 'having four faces'; Sanat, 'the ancient'; Vidhi, as providence, or the one who ordains what will be; Vidhatra or Vidhata 'disposer' or 'arranger'; Viranchi, the Creator.

Brahman:

The first of the four castes of Hinduism. It is the priestly caste, though its members may not necessarily be priests. In Hindu belief, a Brahman is the chief of all created beings. His person is inviolate, he is entitled to every honour and causing harm to a Brahman results in the severest consequences, in this life and the next. The chief duty of a Brahman is the study and teaching of the Vedas, and the performance of fire-sacrifices and other ceremonies. Hindus believe that there are two kinds of gods: the gods themselves, and then the Brahmans who have learnt the Vedas—they are gods upon earth.

chakor; chakori (f.):

A mythical bird, which is believed to subsist only upon moonbeams and to eat fire at the full moon.

chatak; chataki (f.):	A mythical bird that subsists only on raindrops that fall in autumn, when the sun is at the same longitude as the star Svati.
Chintamani:	The 'wish-jewel'. It has the power of granting all desires. It belongs to Brahma, who is himself sometimes called by this name.
Chitrakut:	'Bright peak'; one of the peaks of the Vindhya range, and the first dwelling-place of Ram and Sita during their exile.
Dadhichi:	A Vedic rishi. Once, Indra had been driven out of his kingdom by the Asur, Vritra, who was invulnerable to any known weapon. Vritra also stole all the water in the world for his own use and that of his army. Indra turned to Vishnu for help, who revealed that Vritra could be defeated only by a weapon made from the bones of the sage Dadhichi, who was practising penance in the Naimisha forest. Indra and the other gods went to Dadhichi and appealed to him for help. The sage agreed, and gave up his life immediately. From his bones, Vishvakarma, the smith of the gods, fashioned the thunderbolt and other weapons, with which Indra and the gods defeated Vritra and his army.
Daityas:	A race of demons and giants, the sons of Diti, daughter of Daksh, by the sage Kashyap. They warred against the gods, and were often victorious. They are very similar to their cousins, the Danavs.
Daksh:	'Competent, intelligent'; Daksh is one of the mind-born sons of Brahma, and is generally associated with male energy or creative power. Depending on the source consulted, he had twenty-four, fifty, or sixty daughters. The Ramayana and the Mahabharata agree on the larger number. According to the Mahabharata, ten of his

daughters married Dharma, and thirteen married the sage Kashyap, becoming the mothers of gods and demons, men, birds, serpents and all living things. Twenty-seven married Soma, the Moon, and these became the twenty-seven Nakshatras or lunar asterisms. His daughter Sati married Shiv and killed herself because of a quarrel between her father and her husband. Daksh was also one of the Prajapatis, and is often regarded as their chief. He is also called Prajesh (lord of creatures).

damru: A small drum shaped like an hour-glass, which is held in one hand; it is said to have been created by Shiv, and by beating it, Shiv produced the very first sounds. Shiv also performs his cosmic dance of regeneration to the beat of the damru.

Danav; Danuj: A clan of demons, giants who warred against the gods; they are the sons of Danu, daughter of Daksh, by the sage Kashyap. They are associated with and very similar to the Daityas.

Dandak: A vast forest between the rivers Godavari and Narmada. Some passages in Valmiki's Ramayana describe it as beginning immediately south of the Jamuna. It is described as a wilderness, with scattered hermitages, and full of wild beasts and Rakshasas.

Dasharath: A prince of the solar dynasty, descendant of Ishkvaku, the king of Koshal, and the father of Ram and his brothers, Bharat, Lakshman and Shatrughna. Dasharath had three wives, Kaushalya, Sumitra and Kaikeyi.

Dharma: Literally, 'that which is to be held fast or kept'. It is a many-layered concept, and can variously mean statute, law, rule, or custom; customary observances of caste, sect, or social class;

prescribed course of conduct, duty, or obligation; virtue, morality, morals; righteousness, good works; religion, piety, or religious observances.

Dhruv: The Pole star; son of Uttanapad and his wife Suniti, he was a staunch devotee of Vishnu. According to the Vishnu Purana, King Uttanapada was one of the sons of Manu Swayambhuva. He had two wives: Suruchi, who was his favourite, and was haughty and cruel, and Suniti, the second queen, who was gentle and kind. Suruchi had a son called Uttam, and Suniti's son was Dhruv. Suruchi demanded that her son Uttam should alone succeed to the throne. Uttanapad agreed, and Suniti and Dhruv left the palace for the forest. Dhruv, rejected by his father, declared he wanted no honours except those that he attained by his own actions. In his grief he meditated upon Vishnu, and in return for his unwavering devotion, Vishnu raised him up to the heavens as the Pole star.

Diti: One of the daughters of Daksh, wife of Kashyap, and mother of the Daityas.

Durvasa: 'Ill-clothed'; a sage known for his fiery temper and irascible nature. According to some sources, he is the son of Atri and Anasuya; but some authorities say that he is a son or an emanation of Shiv. Many fell under the curse of his anger, including Indra, whom he cursed for disrespecting him, and by his curse, the gods under Indra became weak and were overpowered by the Asurs. This state of affairs ultimately led to the churning of the ocean by the gods and demons to recover amrit and other precious things.

Dushan: A man-eating Rakshasa, the younger brother of Ravan; he was killed by Ram.

elephants, celestial: The eight elephants who protect the earth and support it at the eight points of the compass. They are Airavat, Pundarik, Vaaman, Kumud, Anjan, Pushpadant, Sarvabhaum and Supratik. (See also guardians of the eight quarters).

food, flavours of: There are six kinds of flavours in food. These are: sweet, sour, salt, bitter, acrid and astringent.

food, kinds of: There are four kinds of food, classified according to the way in which they are ingested: (i) food that is chewed; (ii) food that is swallowed; (iii) food that is sucked; and (iv) food that is lapped up or drunk.

Galav: A pupil of Rishi Vishvamitra. At the end of his studies, he asked Vishvamitra what fee he should give him. Vishvamitra refused to ask for anything, but when Galav insisted, he grew annoyed, and to get rid of him, asked him to bring him a thousand white horses with one black ear. After a long search, Galav found three kings who each had two hundred of the kind of horses he wanted. The kings, all of whom were childless, agreed to let him have the horses if he could somehow ensure they had a son. Galav appealed to Garud for help, who took him to see King Yayati. The king gave him his daughter, Madhavi, who, by a special boon, was able to bear sons and still remain a virgin. Galav gave her in marriage one after another to the three childless kings, Haryashwa, king of Ayodhya, Divodas, king of Kashi, and Ushinar, king of Bhoj; to each of the kings, Madhavi bore a son, and in return, Galav received 200 of the horses he wanted. Galav then presented Madhavi and the 600 horses to Vishvamitra. The sage accepted them and had a son by Madhavi, who was named Ashtaka. When Vishvamitra retired to the forest, he gave his hermitage and the horses

	to Ashtaka. And Galav, having taken Madhavi back to her father, also retired to the forest, like his guru.
Gandharva:	The Gandharvas are heavenly beings, who have their home in the sky or atmosphere; many of them live in Indra's heaven. They are entrusted with the task of preparing soma for the gods, are skilled in medicine, and are singers and musicians.
Ganesh:	Lord of the ganas, the troops of lesser deities attendant upon Shiv; the son of Shiv and Parvati. As the god of wisdom and the remover of obstacles, he is propitiated at the beginning of any endeavour. He is represented as a short man, with a yellow body, four hands, and the head of an elephant, with one tusk. He has a pot belly, signifying his love of food. In one hand he holds a shell, in another a discus, in the third a club, and in the fourth a lotus. His steed is a rat. He is also called Ganpati, 'chief of the ganas'; Ganraja, 'king of the ganas', Gajanan, 'elephant-faced'; Vinayak, 'leader of the Shiv's retinue' or 'remover of obstacles'.
Ganga:	The sacred river Ganges. According to the Puranas, the river flows from the toe of Vishnu, and was brought down to earth by the actions of Bhagirath, to purify the ashes of the sixty-thousand sons of King Sagar, who were burnt by the angry glance of the sage Kapil. Thus the river is also called Bhaagirathi. To save the earth from the shock of her fall, Shiv caught the river upon his head and checked the force of her waters with his matted hair. (See also Bhagirath.) Personified as a goddess, she is the daughter of Himvat and Maina, and her sister is Uma, the goddess Parvati.

Garud:

King of the birds and the steed of Vishnu. He is represented with the head, wings, talons and beaks of an eagle, and the body and limbs of a man. His face is white, his wings red and his body golden. When he was born, he was so bright that people mistook him for Agni. He is the son of the rishi Kashyap and Vinata, one of the daughters of Daksh. From his mother he is called Vainateya, 'Vinata's son'; as Vishnu's mount he is called 'Hariyan'; as the enemy and devourer of snakes he is called Urugari, Uragari, Pannagari, Uragad; and as king of the birds he is Khagesh, Khagapati.

Godavari:

Revered by Hindus, this is India's second-longest river after the Ganga; it rises in Trimbakeshwar in Maharashtra and flows east for 1465 kilometres to empty into the Bay of Bengal.

Gomati:

River in northern India; it is a tributary of the Sarju. It is also called the Dhenumati.

gorochan:

A bright yellow pigment, found as a bezoar in cattle; this is considered very rare and holy and has various ritual uses in Hindu practice, and is specially used for marking the foreheads of Hindus with the tilak. It is also supposed to have medicinal properties, including as a sedative and an antidote to poisons.

guardians of the eight quarters:

The eight points of the compass (the four cardinal and four intermediate points) are guarded and presided over by eight guardian deities. They are: (i) Indra, king of the gods, guards the east; (ii) Agni, or Fire, the south-east; (iii) Yama, god of death, the south; (iv) Surya, the Sun, the south-west; (v) Varun, the Sky, the west; (vi) Vayu, the Wind, the north-west; (vii) Kuber, god of wealth, the north; (viii) Soma, the Moon, the north-east. Some substitute Shiv in his form as Ishan, for Soma.

Each of these guardian deities has an elephant who helps to defend and protect the quarter; together these eight celestial elephants support the earth upon their backs. Indra's elephant at the east is Airavat; Agni's elephant at the south-east is Pundarik; Yama's at the south is Vaaman; Surya's at the south-west is Kumud; Varun's at the west is Anjan; Vayu's at the north-west is Pushpadant; Kuber's at the north is Sarvabhaum; and Soma's elephant at the north-east is Supratik.

Guha: Chief of the Nishads, and a devotee and friend of Ram.

guna: A quality, or an ingredient or constituent of nature, of which there are three in particular, viz., Sattva, Rajas, and Tamas, or 'goodness, passion, and darkness', or 'virtue, foulness, and ignorance'.

gunj seeds: The tiny, bright red and black seeds of the shrub known as the jequirity bean or the rosary pea; they form the smallest of a jeweller's weights.

Hanuman; Hanumant;   Literally, 'he who has large jaws'; the monkey
Hanumat: chief who helped Ram in his search for Sita and fought with him in his war against Ravan. The son of Pavan, the Wind, he was of divine origin and endowed with magical powers. His mother was Anjana, the wife of a monkey called Kesari. He was enormously strong, he could also fly and change his size at will. In his true form he is as vast as a mountain and tall as a tower. His body is yellow and glows like molten gold. His face is as red as a ruby and his tail is so long that no one can measure its length. At the end of the war with Ravan, he went back with Ram to Ayodhya; there, Ram gave him the reward of perpetual life and youth. He epitomizes devotion to Ram. He is known by many names. For setting Lanka on

fire, he is called Lankadahi; as the son of the wind he has the patronymics Pavanputra, Anili and Maruti; from his mother he is called Anjaneya; for his magic powers and knowledge of the healing arts, he is called Yogachara and Rajat-dyuti, 'the brilliant'. He is also a grammarian, and rivals Brihaspati, the guru of the gods, in his knowledge of all the sciences.

Harishchandra: Son of Trishanku and king of Ayodhya, the twenty-eighth in descent from Ishkvaku, founder of the solar dynasty. He was a just and virtuous king, and famed for his generosity. There are several legends about him. The Mahabharata says that he was raised to Indra's heaven for his performance of the Rajasuya sacrifice (a fire-sacrifice that may be performed only by the greatest of kings) and his immense generosity. The Markandeya Purana gives a fuller version of the story: One day, while Harishchandra was out hunting, he heard the cries of several women in distress. The king rushed to help, but the cries were an illusion created by Vighnaraj, the god of obstacles. At that time, the sage Vishvamitra was observing strict penance in the forest. Vighnaraj, to test Harishchandra's goodness, entered his body, and the moment he did so, the king lost his temper and began to loudly curse and hurl abuse at Vishvamitra. This angered the sage, who, because of his anger lost all the power he had acquired through years of penance. Vishvamitra was now furious with Harishchandra, and the king, seeing his wrath, begged for forgiveness. In return, the sage demanded the sacrificial gift that would be due to him as a Brahman for the performance of a Rajasuya sacrifice. The king agreed, and promised to give him whatever he would choose to ask. Vishvamitra demanded that the king give him everything he possessed. The king agreed and handed over all his material possessions to the sage, including his kingdom and the clothes he wore, so that he had remaining only his own body, a garment of bark, his wife, Shaivya, and his son, Rohit. The king, now destitute, left for the city of Banaras. But the sage was waiting for him there, and demanded that the gift be completed. In despair, Harishchandra sold his wife and his son, and handed over the proceeds to Vishvamitra. Now there remained only himself. Just then, Dharma, the god of justice, appeared in the form of a low-caste Chandal, and offered to buy him. When Vishvamitra still insisted upon the completion of his gift, the king sold himself to the Chandal and gave the money to the sage. His new master put Harishchandra in charge of a cremation ground, with strict instructions to be always present there and to allow cremation only after the payment of a toll. The honest king did exactly as his master commanded. As the months passed, his appearance grew dishevelled, and he lost all hope of ever seeing his wife and son again. One day, Rohit was bitten by a snake and died. His grieving mother carried his body to the cremation ground. The king and the queen recognized each other, and exchanging stories, were overcome with grief. They decided to immolate themselves upon the funeral pyre of their son. Harishchandra made ready a great pyre upon which he placed Rohit's body, and once all was done, he lost himself in contemplation of Vishnu. At this, the gods all appeared and asked him to stop, and bringing Rohit back to life, told him that he, his wife and his son had all won a place in heaven because of his steadfastness in fulfilling his promise to Vishvamitra. But Harishchandra was hesitant. He could not go to heaven without his master, the Chandal's permission. At this, the Chandal appeared and revealed himself to be Dharma. Harishchandra still refused, saying he could not leave behind his faithful subjects, in turmoil without a king. So Indra, Dharma and Vishvamitra took the king, his wife and his son to Ayodhya. There, Vishvamitra crowned Rohit king of Koshal, after which Harishchandra and his wife Shaivya were taken to heaven.

Hataklochan: 'The golden-eyed', a powerful Daitya chief, son of Diti by the sage Kashyap, and twin brother of Kanakakasipu; he was killed by Vishnu in his third, Boar, incarnation. Hataklochan had dragged the earth to the bottom of the sea. In order to recover the earth, Vishnu took the form of a boar, and after a battle that lasted a thousand years, he killed Hataklochan and carried the earth back to the surface on his tusks. He is also known as Hiranyaksh and Kanakalochan.

Himvat; Himvant; Himalaya: 'Snow-clad'; the personification of the Himalaya mountains, husband of Maina, and father of Ganga and Uma (Parvati). He is also called Himachal, Himbhudar, Himgiri, Tuhinachal, Tuhingiri, 'snowy mountain'; Girish, 'mountain king' or 'king of the mountain', a title he sometimes shares with Shiv.

humours of the body: In the Indian Ayurvedic system of medicine, the body is regarded as having three humours (or bodily fluids) in addition to blood. The three humours are vat or (wind), pitt (bile) and kaph (phlegm). All organic disorders of the body arise from an imbalance in these humours.

Ikshvaku: Founder of the solar dynasty, and king of Ayodhya at the beginning of the Tretayug or second age of the world. He had a hundred sons, of whom one was Nimi, who founded the Mithila dynasty.

Indra: God of the firmament, personification of the
atmosphere; king of the gods. His consort is
Indrani (also known as Shachi); he has a son by
her, called Jayant. His heaven is Swarga; his capital
is Amaravati; his elephant is Airavat; and his
horse is Uchchaihsravas. His charioteer is Matali.
In the Vedas, he is one of the most important of
the gods, though he is not unbegotten/uncreated
but has a father and a mother. He is described in
the Vedas as a being of golden colour, with arms
of enormous length. His forms are infinite and he
can take any shape at will. He rides in a golden
chariot drawn by two ruddy horses with flowing
tails and manes. His weapon is the thunderbolt,
which he carries in his right hand; he also uses
arrows, a hook and a net in which he entangles
his enemies. His chief delight is soma ras, the
extremely potent juice of the soma plant, which
he drinks in enormous quantities. He controls the
weather, dispenses rain, and sends down lightning
and thunder. He is constantly at war with Vritra,
the demon of drought and bad weather, whom
he ultimately overcomes with his thunderbolts.
In the later centuries, Indra's importance decreased.
He became less than the triad of Brahma, Vishnu
and Shiv, but remained chief of all the other
gods. According to the Mahabharata, he is the
son of Aditi by Kashyap, and the foremost of the
Adityas. He is the regent of the atmosphere and
the guardian of the east quarter of the compass. He
sends the lightning and hurls the thunderbolt, and
the rainbow is his bow. He is represented as a fair-
skinned man, riding a white horse or an elephant,
and holding the thunderbolt in his hand. He is
constantly at war with the Asurs, and is often
defeated by them. He killed Vritra, but because
Vritra was a Brahman, Indra had to go into hiding
and perform penance till his guilt was purged away.
There are many stories of his lack of self-restraint.
He became infatuated with Ahalya, the beautiful

and virtuous wife of the sage Gautam, and in his arrogance, decided to seduce her. He tricked the sage to leave the hermitage, and then taking on his form, seduced the unsuspecting Ahalya. The sage returned to see him leaving his house, and in fury cursed him so that he would be covered with the marks of a thousand yonis (the female organs of reproduction). Thus he was called Sa-yoni. But these marks were later changed to eyes, because of which he is also called Netra-yoni or Sahasraksha 'the thousand-eyed'. He was defeated and carried off to Lanka by Ravan's son, Meghnad (who thus received the title of Indrajit, 'vanquisher of Indra'). Brahma and the other gods had to beg Meghnad to release him, which Meghnad did, in return for the boon of immortality. Brahma then tells Indra that his defeat was his punishment for seducing Ahalya. He is also known as Sakr, 'the powerful'; Purandar, 'destroyer of cities'; Pakripu, 'destroyer of the demon Pak'; Maghva or Maghvan, 'endowed with riches, wealthy'; Basav or Vasava, 'lord of the Vasus'.

Jabali:	A Brahman, and a priest of King Dasharath. He is also called Javall.
Jadu:	One of the sons of King Yayati, from his wife Devyani. Jadu (or Yadu) refused to relieve his father of the curse of old age passed on to him by the Rishi Sukra, and was therefore cursed in turn by Yayati that his children will not have a kingdom to rule. He was the founder of the line of Jadavas (or Yadavas), in which Krishna was born. He did ultimately receive the southern part of his father's kingdom, which the Jadavas went on to successfully rule.
Jagbalik:	A celebrated sage. To him is attributed the code of law called *Yajnavalkyasmriti* (from 'Yajnavalkya', the Sanskrit rendering of his name). He is believed

to have flourished at the court of Janak, king of Videha and Sita's father.

Jam, Jamraj; Yam, Yamraj:	The god of death. He is the son of the sun god Surya and his wife Saranyu, and twin brother of the river Jamuna. He is represented as a man green in colour and clothed in red; he is armed with a huge mace and a noose. He rides upon a buffalo, because of which he is also called as Mahishesh, 'the god whose steed is a mahish, or buffalo'. He is sometimes also called Shaman, 'the destroyer'.
jamana:	From the Sanskrit *yavana*; originally denoted a Greek, an Ionian, and then came to mean any barbaric foreigner from the West.
jambu:	The rose-apple tree, also called jamun in Hindi.
Jamuna; Yamuna:	The river Jamuna (or Yamuna) is the daughter of the sun god Surya and his wife Saranyu, and the twin sister of Jam (or Yama), the god of death. While Jamraj is death, Jamuna is life and bathing in her waters absolves one of sin.
Jamvant:	King of the bears. With his army of bears, he helped Ram in his war against Ravan and was always ready with sage advice and good counsel. He is also called Jambavat.
Janak:	A prince of the solar dynasty, king of Mithila/ Videha, and the father of Sita. Amongst his ancestors are the kings Ishkvaku and Nimi. Janak was known for his great knowledge and good works. It is said that Janak refused to submit to the hierarchical superiority of the Brahmans and insisted upon his right to perform fire-sacrifices without their intervention. He is also called Siradhwaja, 'he whose banner is the plough',

because his daughter Sita appeared as a baby in the furrow he was ploughing in preparation for a fire-sacrifice to obtain children. He is also known as Videh, the title used for the kings of Videha. 'Janak' is also the name of a royal dynasty of Mithila to which he belonged. He is therefore also called Janakpati, or 'lord of the Janak dynasty'.

Jatayu: King of the vultures, and son of Garud, Vishnu's steed. He is a friend of King Dasharath, and became an ally of Ram. He saw Ravan carrying away Sita and tried to stop him. In the ensuing battle, he was mortally wounded. Ram found him in time to hear his dying words and learn what had happened to Sita. Ram and Lakshman performed his last rites, and he ascended to heaven in a chariot of fire.

javas: The camel thorn. A small and prickly plant, it grows to about four feet in height. It has long spines along its branches and bright pink or reddish flowers. It is said to wilt at the coming of the rains and flourish only in dry soil.

Jayant: Son of Indra, also called Jaya.

jiva: The individual soul.

jubaraj: Literally 'young king'; an heir-apparent associated with the reigning sovereign, who assumes kingly duties while the king is still living.

Kabandh: A hideous Rakshasa killed by Ram. He was originally a Gandharva, the son of the goddess Lakshmi. He is described as being covered with hair, as huge as a mountain, without head or neck, a mouth full of immense teeth in the middle of his belly and a single eye in his breast. According to some accounts, he was turned into this hideous monster as the result of a quarrel with Indra, who struck him with his thunderbolt and drove his head and thighs into his body. Another account says that he was cursed by the sage Durvasa. When mortally wounded, he asked Ram to burn him, and from that fire he came out in his original form as a Gandharva. He is also called Danu.

kadamb: A tall, evergreen tree, with fragrant, globe-shaped orange flowers which are used in the preparation of perfumes; the tree also has great mythological and religious significance in India.

Kadru: A daughter of Daksh, and one of the thirteen wives of the sage Kashyap. She is the mother of the serpents, including Sheshnag. Her offspring bear the metronymic Kadraveya.

Kaikeya: A kingdom in the west, beyond the rivers Saraswati and Beas, and from which came Dasharath's queen, Kaikeyi.

Kaikeyi: A princess of Kaikeya, King Dasharath's favourite queen, and the mother of Bharat, his second son.

Kailash: A mountain in the Himalayas, north of the Mansarovar; it is the abode of Shiv, and also of Kuber, the god of wealth.

Kalnemi: A Rakshasa, and Ravan's uncle. At Ravan's behest, he attempts to kill Hanuman.

kalpa: A period of 4,320,000,000 years, equal to a day for Brahma. This is one cosmic cycle of creation, and is made up of a thousand cycles of the four ages, or yugas. (See also 'ages of the world'.) According to the Puranas, there are innumerable such cycles of creation, and within them, in each cycle of the four yugas, there occurs one incarnation of Ram.

Kalpataru: A tree in Indra's paradise that grants all desires. It is also called Kamtaru, 'tree of desire'.

Kam: Literally, wish, desire, longing; affection, love, passion; sexual passion; lust; love of pleasure; and personified, the god of love, Kamdev. He is the son of Vishnu by Rukmini, and the husband of Rati, the goddess of desire. He is lord of the celestial nymphs, the apsaras. He is armed with a bow and five arrows: the bow is of sugarcane, the bowstring a line of bees, and each of his five arrows is tipped with a particular flower (the white lotus, the ashok flower, the mango blossom, the jasmine and the blue lotus), which pierce the heart through the five senses; his favourite arrow is the one tipped with the mango blossom. His helpers are Vasant or Spring, and Malayanil, the southern winds or the cool and fragrant winds that blow from the Malay mountain. He is usually represented as a handsome young man riding on a parrot, and attended by apsaras; one of the apsaras bears his banner, which displays the Makar (a fabulous sea creature that represents Capricorn in the Hindu zodiac, and is depicted with the head and forelegs of an antelope and the body and tail of a fish), or a fish on a red background. He is therefore also called Jhashketu, 'one with a fish on his banner'. Once, as Shiv sat in meditation, Kamdev inspired him with thoughts of Parvati; Shiv, greatly angered by this impertinence, opened his third eye and reduced Kamdev to ashes. Later, Shiv relented and allowed him to be reborn as feelings. Kamdev therefore does not have a substantial form or body. He is thus called Anang and Atanu, or 'bodiless'. He is also known as Hridayniket, 'one whose abode is the heart'; Mayan or Madan, 'passion, lust or love (or the act of intoxicating or exhilarating, or gladdening)'; Manmath, 'he who churns the heart'; Manobhav, 'mind-born'; Manoj, 'born of the mind'; Mansij, 'born or generated in the mind, mind-born, heart-born'; Mar, the passion of love, personified. As husband to Rati, he is known as Ratinath, 'Rati's lord'. He is also called Kandarp.

Kamadgiri: Literally, 'the mountain that fulfils all desires'; the hill in Chitrakut upon which Ram stayed.

Kamdhenu: 'The cow that grants all desires'; she belongs to the sage Vasishtha and was one of the fourteen precious objects recovered at the churning of the ocean.

Kanakakasipu: 'Golden-robed'; a powerful Daitya chief, son of the sage Kashyap and his wife Diti, and twin brother to Hataklochan. As the result of practising severe austerities, he obtained from Shiv sovereignty over the three worlds for a million years, as well as immunity from death by man and beast. He grew so arrogant in his power that he declared that no one may worship any god but him. When his son, Prahlad, remained steadfastly devoted to Vishnu, he punished him and tried to kill him several times, but in vain. He was finally killed by Vishnu in his fourth avatar as Narsingh or Narkeshari, who was half-man, half-lion, and thus neither man nor beast. He is also called Hiranyakashipu.

kanji: A sour drink made by steeping mustard seeds in water and letting it ferment.

Kapil: A celebrated sage, the founder of the Sankhya philosophy. He reduced the sixty-thousand sons of King Sagar to ashes with a single glance.

kapila cow: A brown or reddish-coloured cow, considered in Hinduism to be the most sacred of all cows. A number of Hindu pilgrimage sites are linked to cows, some specifically to the brown cow. Several of these sites are mentioned in the Mahabharata and the Puranas. According to the Puranas, the gift of a kapila cow is equal to the giving away of a whole world in charity and confers upon the giver an assured place in Vishnu's heaven for as many thousand years as there are hairs upon the body of that cow and her calf, and after that time is over, it guarantees rebirth into a rich and wealthy family. Gifts of land, horses, gold, etc., do not equal in virtue even a sixteenth of the gift of a kapila cow.

Karamnasa: A river that flows through the holy city of Kashi; bathing in its waters destroys all merit (as opposed to bathing in the waters of the Ganga, which destroys all sin).

karila: A thorny, leafless shrub that grows in arid regions.

karma: Fate, or the certain consequence of previous acts; destiny.

Kashi: The city of Varanasi. It is sacred to Shiv, and one of the most holy of all pilgrimage places for Hindus. It is believed that those who die in Kashi immediately attain liberation from the cycle of birth and rebirth.

Kashyap: A Vedic sage, to whom are attributed some of the Vedic hymns. According to the Atharva Veda, he was 'self-born' and sprang into existence from Time. According to the Mahabharata, the Ramayana, and the Puranas, he was descended from Brahma. All authorities agree that he played a significant role in creation. The Mahabharata and later sources say that he married Aditi, and twelve other daughters of Daksh. From Aditi were born the celestial Adityas, headed by Indra, and also Visaswat, from whom was born Manu, the progenitor of all mankind. The Ramayana and Vishnu Purana state that Vishnu in his dwarf incarnation was the son of Aditi and Kashyap. From Kashyap's twelve other wives were born demons, serpents, reptiles, birds and all living things. He is also one of the Saptarishi, the seven great sages.

Kaushalya: King Dasharath's chief queen, and Ram's mother.

Kaustubh: A precious jewel, obtained at the churning of the ocean and worn by Vishnu upon his breast.

Ketu: A comet or meteor, and the ninth of the planets; and in Vedic astronomy, the descending lunar node, represented by a dragon's tail. He is personified in mythology as the lower half of the Danav, Rahu. See Rahu.

Khar: A man-eating Rakshasa, the younger brother of Ravan; he was killed by Ram.

Khasiya: A tribal, hill people of northern India.

Kinnara: Literally, 'What men?' in Sanskrit; they are mythical beings with the body of a man and the head of a horse. They are singers and musicians, and live in the paradise of Kuber, the god of wealth, on Mt Kailash. According to some sources, they sprang from the toe of Brahma together with the Yakshas; but others say that they are the sons of Kashyap.

kinshuk: A tree native to India. When in bloom, it is covered with a profusion of bright red, flame-coloured flowers. It is also known as the palash, the dhak, or the flame-of-the-forest.

Kirat: A mountain tribe that lives by hunting; a man of that tribe.

kodo: A kind of small grain (like millet), considered inferior to rice and usually eaten by the poor.

kok; koki (f.):   These birds are a symbol of love and fidelity. Legend says that they are doomed to spend every night apart because of a curse pronounced upon them by a sadhu. They spend the day together, but every night they must separate; the birds spend the night calling to each in sad and mournful tones. Since they can be together only during the day, the birds are full of joy in the light of the sun, and grow sorrowful in the light of the moon. They are also called chakravak birds, or chakwa (male) and chakwi (female). They are also identified with the rathang birds, the ruddy or Brahmany geese.

kokil; koel: The black or Indian cuckoo. This bird is prominent in Indian poetry; its musical cry is supposed to inspire pleasing and tender emotions.

Kol: A tribe that lives the hills and forests of central India; a man of that tribe.

kos: A measure of distance, equivalent to about 2 miles.

Koshal: A country on the Sarju river, with Avadh its capital city. This was the kingdom ruled by Dasharath, and later by Ram.

Kshatriya: The second of the four castes of Hinduism. It is the regal or warrior caste.

Kuber: The god of wealth, and the king of the Yakshas. He is also regent of the north, and the keeper of gold and silver, pearls and precious stones, and all the treasures of the earth. He is the son of Vishravas (the son of the sage Pulastya), and the half-brother of Ravan. His consort is called

Yakshi. Kuber's city is Alaka in the Himalayas, and his garden is on Mount Mandar, where he is waited upon by the Kinnaras. Some authorities place his abode on Mount Kailash, in a palace built by the divine architect, Vishvakarma. According to the Ramayana and Mahabharata, he once ruled in the city of Lanka, also built by Vishvakarma, and from which he was thrown out by Ravan. He is the owner of the self-moving flying chariot, Pushpak, given to him by Brahma. He is also the keeper of the nine Nidhis, nine treasures considered precious beyond compare. They are called padma or the lotus flower, maha-padma, sankha, makar, kachhapa, mukunda, kunda, nila, kharba. Their nature and purpose are not clearly defined. Each treasure is also personified as a spirit that is also the guardian of that particular treasure. These guardian spirits are worshipped by some tantrics. Kuber is represented as a fair-skinned man, deformed in body, with three legs and only eight teeth. His body is covered with jewelled ornaments. He receives no worship. He is also known as Dhanesh, 'god of wealth'; Dhandhari, 'holder of wealth'; and 'Dhanad, 'one who grants wealth, the munificent'.

Kumbhakaran: A Rakshasa, the son of Vishravas (the son of the sage Pulastya), and brother of Ravan. As the result of a boon (or, as variously told, a curse) by Brahma, he slept for six months at a time and remained awake for only a single day.

kush: A kind of grass used in sacrifices and rituals. It is also called darbh.

Kushaketu: King Janak's younger brother, the father of the princesses Mandavi and Shrutakirti. He is also known as Kushadhvaja.

Lakshman:	'Possessed of lucky signs or marks, fortunate, prosperous'; son of Dasharath and Sumitra, Ram's younger brother and Shatrughna's twin. For his mother, Sumitra, he is also called Saumitri, 'Sumitra's son'. He is often considered to be the incarnation of the celestial serpent, Sheshnag.
Lakshmi:	The goddess of wealth and beauty, Vishnu's consort, and the mother of Kamdev, the god of love. According to the Ramayana, she sprang from the the froth of the ocean, in all her beauty, when it was churned by the gods and the Asurs. The Vishnu Purana says that she accompanied Vishnu in all his incarnations, and when Vishnu was born as Ram, she became Sita. She is also known as Shri; Indira; and Ramaa, 'Ram's consort'.
Lanka:	Ravan's kingdom. Also known as Singhal.
life, ends, fruits, rewards of:	These are four: (i) kama or sensual pleasure; (ii) artha or wealth; (iii) dharma or religious merit; and (iv) moksha or nirvana, i.e., liberation from worldly existence and rebirth.
life, four stages of:	For traditional Hindus, life is divided into four stages: (i) Brahmacharya, the student life, spent in study and obedience to one's guru; (ii) Grihastha, the stage of a householder, the married man living with his wife, and engaged in the ordinary duties of everyday life; (iii) Vanaprastha, the phase of a 'forest-dweller', who has discharged his duties in this world, and who, handing over his responsibilities to the next generation, has retired to the forest to devote himself to a life of simplicity and contemplation of the divine; and (iv) Sannyas, the period spent as a religious mendicant, who has renounced all worldly goods and desires and attained complete detachment from this material existence; freed from all forms and observances,

	he wanders about, subsisting only on alms, and striving for ultimate absorption into the divine.
lila:	Literally 'play, sport, pastime'. In Hindu belief, all creation is the Lord's lila, his sport or pastime.
Madhav:	Krishna (Vishnu) in his role as presiding deity of Prayag.
Magh:	The tenth month of the Hindu calendar, corresponding to January–February.
Mahishasur:	Literally, 'the buffalo demon', an Asur killed by the goddess Parvati in her form as Durga. Through intense austerities, he received a boon from Brahma and asked to be made immortal. Brahma refused the boon of immortality, but granted him the boon that no man would be able to kill him. The gods were powerless against him and were soundly defeated by him in battle. Then the goddess Parvati, who was Shiv's Shakti, the feminine manifestation of Shiv's cosmic energy, took on one of her fierce forms and killed him.
Mai:	A Daitya, the architect of the Asurs, as Vishvakarma was of the gods. He was the father of the demon Mayavi, and of Mandodari, Ravan's wife.
Maina:	The wife of Himalaya, and the mother of Parvati.
Mainak:	A winged mountain.
Makar:	Makar (equivalent to Capricorn) is the tenth sign of the zodiac, and is represented by a water-animal with the body and tail of a fish, and the forelegs, neck and head of an antelope.
Malaya, mountain range:	One of the seven mountain ranges mentioned in the Puranas; they are supposedly the southernmost

mountains of the Western Ghats in peninsular India. The mountains were famous for their sandal trees, which yielded the finest sandalwood in the world.

Manas; Manas lake; Mansarovar:

A freshwater lake in modern Tibet, at the foot of Mt Kailash, the abode of Shiv. The lake is sacred to Hindus, Buddhists and Jains, and an important place of pilgrimage for them.

Mandakini:

A sacred river that flowed by the hill of Chitrakut, where Ram and Sita spent part of their forest exile. It is also called Payasvini, 'water-giving'. It is said that the river was brought down from heaven to Chitrakut by Anasuya, the wife of the sage Atri, in order to alleviate a drought.

Mandar:

The sacred mountain with which the ocean is said to have been churned by the gods and Asurs for the recovery of amrit and thirteen other precious things lost during the great flood.

Mandavi:

Sita's cousin, the eldest daughter of Janak's younger brother Kushadhvaj (Kushaketu); she was married to Bharat.

Mandodari:

The daughter of the Daitya Mai, she was Ravan's favourite wife, and the mother of Meghnad.

Manthara:

Queen Kaikeyi's hunch-backed bondswoman, who roused the queen's jealousy and set her against Ram, which led to him being banished to the forest for fourteen years.

Manu:

From the root *man*, 'to think'; this name belongs to fourteen mythological progenitors of mankind and rulers of the earth, each of whom rules for the period called a Manwantara (Manu-antara: the life or period of a Manu). There are fourteen

Manwantaras in any kalpa. The gods, the seven great sages (Saptarishis) and Indra change from one Manwantara to another. The first of these Manus was Svayambhuva, who sprang from Swayambhu, the self-existent.

Mar:
The passion of love; personified, it is another name for Kamdev, the god of love.

Marich; Marichi:
A Rakshasa, son of Taraka; he was also one of Ravan's ministers, and helped him to kidnap Sita from the forest hermitage.

Maruts:
Marut
The storm gods. They are armed with thunderbolts and ride on the whirlwind and direct the storm. Many origins are assigned to them – they are the sons of Rudra, the sons or brothers of Indra, sons of the ocean, sons of the earth. Their number varies—according to one source they are twenty-nine in number, according to another, three times sixty; in the *Ramcharitmanas*, Tulsi says they are forty-nine in number. In the singular, Marut is also the god of the wind, and the presiding deity of the north-west quarter.

Matali:
Indra's charioteer.

maya; Maya:
Illusion, deception; the unreality of worldly things; in Hindu belief, a deception dependent on the power of the Supreme Being, through which mankind believes in the existence of the world which is in fact mere illusion without reality. Personified, Maya is a woman, the consort of the Supreme Being, and the immediate operative cause of the creation. It also means magical or supernatural power, such as that possessed by the Rakshasa, Ravan.

Meghnad:
Literally, 'the rumbling or thundering of clouds'; he was Ravan's eldest son by his chief queen,

Mandodari. When Ravan attacked Indra's forces, Meghnad accompanied him and fought most valiantly. He used the power of invisibility given to him by Shiv to capture, tie up and carry off Indra to Lanka where he kept him a prisoner. The gods, led by Brahma, went to Lanka to secure Indra's release, and Brahma gave Meghnad the title of 'Indrajit', 'conqueror of Indra'. He is also called Arindam, 'the destroyer of enemies'.

Mekal: A part of the Vindhya mountain range, in which rise the headwaters and several tributaries of the Narmada river.

Meru: A fabulous mountain in the centre of the earth, upon which is situated Swarga, Indra's heaven, containing the cities of the gods. It is also known as Sumeru.

Mithila: The capital city of Videha, the kingdom of King Janak; also known as Janakpur, or Janak's city, Tirhut, and Terahuti.

moksha: Ultimate freedom from birth and rebirth. There are four kinds of moksha possible: (i) living in the same world as the Supreme Being; (ii) living in close proximity to the Supreme Being; (iii) attaining a form similar to that of the Supreme Being; and (iv) complete union with the Supreme Being.

mridang: A double drum, broader in the middle than at the ends.

muni: A sage, a holy man who has attained almost divine status through penance and meditation. The term is also used as a title for the seven great Rishis and for other wise and learned men.

Naga: A semi-divine being belonging to the serpent
                      race, with a human face, the tale of a snake and
                      the expanded neck of the cobra. The Nagas are
                      said to have sprung from Kadru, one of the wives
                      of the sage Kashyap, for the purpose of populating
                      the underworld, Patal, where they rule in great
                      splendour.

Nahush: The son of Pururavas, and the father of Yayati;
                      he came into conflict with the Brahmans. His
                      story is told, with variations, in the Mahabharata
                      and the Puranas. Nahush was a good and
                      righteous king, and, through prayer and penance
                      and sacred study, he acquired the sovereignty
                      of the three worlds. Once, when Indra had
                      temporarily gone into hiding (for having killed
                      the demon Vritra, who was a Brahman), leaving
                      his throne vacant, Nahush was chosen to reign
                      in his stead. He ruled over the heavens wisely
                      and well for many years, but as time went by,
                      he became arrogant and haughty. One day, he
                      caught sight of Shachi, Indra's beautiful consort,
                      and wanted her for himself. Shachi, known for
                      her love and fidelity to Indra, was angered and
                      distressed by his advances, and complained to
                      the sage Brihaspati and sought his protection.
                      The gods remonstrated with Nahush, but
                      blinded by desire, he refused to listen to them,
                      and insisted upon having Shachi as his consort.
                      Brihaspati then advised Shachi to lay down a
                      condition—that she would accept Nahush as her
                      husband if he would come to her in a palanquin
                      carried by sages. Nahush, who had lost all sense
                      of propriety and was guided only by his stubborn
                      desire to possess Shachi, agreed at once. He
                      somehow convinced the rishis to carry him to
                      Shachi on his shoulders. The sages were not very
                      strong men, and walked slowly with frequent
                      stops. The king grew impatient, and kicked the

sage Agastya, who was one of the sages carrying him. The sage cried out in anger, 'Fall, you serpent!' and Nahush fell from his palanquin and turned into a huge python. Horrified, he begged Agastya to forgive him; relenting, Agastya put a limit on the curse, saying that he would regain his human form when he had learnt how to be a good king. According to one version of the story, he was released from his curse by the eldest Pandava, Yudhishthira, who lectured him on the qualities of a good king. Nahush, understanding these at last, was released from his serpent form and ascended to heaven.

Nar and Narayan: Two ancient sages; twin sons of Dharma (Brahma's son) and his wife Ahimsa (daughter of Daksh). The brothers are considered by some to be the fourth avatar of Vishnu.

Narad: A Devarshi, or divine sage or saint akin to a demigod, to whom some of the hymns of the Rig-Veda are ascribed. Various sources have different accounts of his life. He is regarded as one of the four sons of Brahma, and one of the ten principal and original Munis or Rishis. He is also the inventor of the vina or lute and lord of the celestial musicians, the Gandharvas. He was also one of the great writers on law, the author of the *Naradiya Dharmashastra*. Later, he is connected to the legend of Krishna. He is also regarded as somewhat of a mischief-maker, causing frequent quarrels among the gods by bearing tales.

Narmada: A sacred river, said to rise from the Mekal hills, and because of which the river is also known as 'Mekal's daughter'.

Nimi: Son of Ikshvaku, and the founder of the dynasty of Mithila. According to the Vishnu Purana, he was cursed by the sage Vasishtha to lose his corporeal form, and in response, he pronounced the same curse upon the sage. Both then abandoned their bodily forms. Though Vasishtha took birth again, Nimi's corpse was embalmed and preserved in death as he had been in life. The gods offered to restore him back to life, but Nimi refused, saying that the separation of the soul from the body was so painful that he did not want to have to experience it again. The gods respected his wishes, and instead, placed him in the eyes of every living creature, because of which their eyelids are always blinking. (A blink of the eye is called 'nimish'.)

nine poetic sentiments (navras):

The nine poetic sentiments or moods are: erotic, humorous, compassionate, astonishing, frightening, peaceful, disgusting, wrathful and heroic.

nirgun:

Devoid of all qualities or properties, without attributes; the Supreme Being, who has no attributes of any kind.

Nishad:

A forest tribe who lived along the banks of the Ganga; their main occupation was hunting and fishing.

Ocean of Milk:

In Hindu cosmology, one of the seven seas surrounding directional space.

ocean, churning of:

One of the most well-known stories in Indian mythology; from this was produced, amongst other things, amrit, the nectar of immortality, and Lakshmi, the goddess of wealth and beauty. Once, Indra displeased the sage Durvasa, who in his anger, cursed Indra that he and all the gods would lose their strength, energy and good fortune. Weakened by the sage's curse, the gods were defeated in battle by the Asurs, who now gained control over the universe. In despair, the gods appealed to Vishnu. Vishnu directed them to churn the ocean and thus to obtain from it the nectar of immortality—this, if consumed, would restore to them their strength and power. The gods, rendered powerless by Durvasa's curse, were unable to accomplish this task on their own, and on Vishnu's advice, enlisted the Asurs to help them, agreeing to divide with them whatever was retrieved from the ocean. Vishnu assured the gods that he would make sure that the nectar of immortality would remain with the gods. The ocean was then churned, with Mount Mandar as the churning stick, and Sheshnag, the celestial serpent as the rope wound round it. The Asurs held the head of the serpent, and the gods the tail, and as they pulled back and forth on the serpent, Mount Mandar began to sink into the waters. So Vishnu took on the form of a kurma or tortoise (his second avatar), and slipping into the waters, supported Mount Mandar on his back. From the churning of the ocean were produced many precious objects, Lakshmi, precious gems, the horse Uchhaishravas, and a deadly poison (which Shiv swallowed and held in his throat). At last, there arose from the waters Dhanvantari (who became the physician of the gods), bearing in his hands the pot of amrit. The Asurs demanded their share of it, but Vishnu's steed, Garud, grabbed the pot and flew away with it. Then Vishnu took on the form of the beautiful enchantress, Mohini, and distributed the amrit amongst the gods, who drank it and regained their strength. Only one of the Asurs, called Rahu, managed to drink some of the amrit, and though his head was cut off by Vishnu as punishment, he had already attained immortality and was thus placed amongst the stars. (See Rahu, and Vishnu—second avatar).

paan: Betel leaves prepared with areca nuts, etc., used as a mouth-freshener after a meal and served to honoured guests.

pakar: The Indian fig tree, also called gular in Hindi.

Panchavati: A place in the Dandak forest, near the River Godavari, where Ram lived for a long period during his exile. It was here that Lakshman cut off Supanakha's nose (nasika). Hence, it is often identified with the modern city of Nasik.

Parashuram: 'Ram with the axe', the sixth avatar of Vishnu. He was born in the Tretayug, as the son of the Brahman, Jamadagni, to deliver the world from the tyranny of the Kshatriyas. His weapon is the axe. The Mahabharata relates that, at the command of his father, he cut off his mother's head. She had so infuriated her husband by her thoughts that he had asked each of his sons in turn to kill her. They had all refused, except Parashuram. His obedience pleased his father so much that he told him to ask a boon. Parashuram asked that his mother be restored to life, and that he himself become invincible in combat and enjoy a long life. When his father was pitilessly slain by the sons of Sahasrabahu (Kartavirya), king of the Haihayas, Parashuram vowed to wipe out the whole Kshatriya race. It is said that he cleared the earth of Kshatriyas twenty-one times. (See also 'Sahasrabahu'.) As foremost amongst the descendants of Bhrigu, he is also called Bhrigupati, Bhrigunath and Bhrigunayak, 'lord of the Bhrigus'; and Bhrigubar, 'the best of the Bhrigus'. He is also known as Parashudhar, 'he who holds an axe'.

Parvati:	'Of the mountains'. She is the daughter of Himvat (the Himalaya mountains personified), and his wife Maina. She is the consort of Shiv, the reincarnation of his first wife Sati. She is also Shiv's cosmic energy or Shakti. She is worshipped in different forms and is known by different names. Her forms and names invoked by Tulsidas include Ambika, 'the compassionate'; Aparna, 'deprived of leaves'; Bhavani, consort of Bhav (Shiv); Gauri, 'the brilliant goddess'; Girija or Shailaja, 'born of the mountain', and Girinandini, 'daughter of the mountain'. She is also Shakti Shiv's cosmic energy; Shivaa, consort of Shiv; and Uma, 'light' or 'splendour'. In her fierce, demon-slaying form she is called Kalika, or Durga. As the supreme goddess, she is called Jagadamba or Jagadambika, 'mother of the world'.
Patal:	One of the seven subterranean regions, and the abode of the Nagas; hell.
pathin:	A large freshwater fish native to India; it is also known as the pahina or parhina fish.
Payasvini:	'Water-giving'; another name for the River Mandakini.
persuasion, methods of:	There are four methods of persuasion: (i) sama (argument, calm words to win someone over to one's own point of view); (ii) dana (inducement in the form of money or gifts); (iii) danda (punishment, corporal chastisement); (iv) bheda (by causing dissension).
pipal:	The holy fig-tree, *Ficus reliogiosa*.
Prahlad:	The son of the Daitya king Kanakakasipu, and an ardent devotee of Vishnu. Kanakakasipu grew so powerful that he declared that his subjects must

worship him, and him alone. Prahlad refused, and continued to steadfastly worship Vishnu, despite all the punishment that his father heaped upon him. In his fourth avatar, as Narsingh or Narkeshari (half-man, half-lion), Vishnu killed Kanakakasipu, and made Prahlad king of the Daityas as a reward for his devotion. Prahlad was also given a status equal to Indra for his life, and finally united with Vishnu upon death.

Prajapati: 'lord of created beings', the ten mind-born sons of Brahma, from whom all mankind has descended.

Prayag: The modern city of Allahabad, the confluence of the rivers Ganga, Jamuna and the subterranean Sarasvati, and one of the most important places of pilgrimage for Hindus. Krishna, as Madhav, is its presiding deity. Prayag is also supposed to be the site of a banyan tree famous in legend to be imperishable.

Prithuraj: In the Vedas and the Puranas, he is the first consecrated king. He taught men agriculture and to cultivate the earth, and it is from him that the earth derives her name of Prithivi. It is said that he prayed for hearing as sharp as though he had ten thousand ears so that he could hear all of the glory of God.

Priyavrat: A son of Svayambhuva Manu and Satarupa. He was dissatisfied that only half the earth was illuminated by the sun at any one point, and so followed the sun seven times around the earth in his own flaming chariot. The ruts made by the wheels of his chariot became the seven oceans; and so the seven continents were formed.

Pulastya:

One of the Prajapatis or mind-born sons of Brahma, and one of the great Rishis. He was the medium through which the Vishnu Purana was communicated to man. He was the father of Visravas, who, through three handmaidens, became the father of Ravan and Kumbhakaran, of Vibhishan, and of Supnakha; all the Rakshasas are supposed to have sprung from him.

Purana:

Literally, 'old', hence an ancient legend or tale. The Puranas are sacred works comprising the whole body of modern Hindu theology and mythology. The Puranas come much later than the epics, and must be distinguished from them. While the epics tell the stories of heroes as mortal men, the Puranas tell of the deeds of gods. There are eighteen acknowledged Puranas. The Vayu Purana is regarded as the oldest, and dates back to the sixth century CE; other Puranas are considered to be as recent as the thirteenth or even the sixteenth century.

Pushpak:

A self-flying magical chariot, so large that it contains within it a palace or a city. Brahma gave it as a gift to Kuber, but it was carried away by Ravan, who then used it as his chief mode of conveyance. After Ravan had been defeated and killed by Ram, the latter used the Pushpak to carry himself and Sita back to Ayodhya. He then returned it to Kuber.

Raghu:

A prince of the solar dynasty. In Kalidasa's poem *Raghuvansa,* on the ancestry and life of Ram, Raghu is said to be the son of Dilip and the great grandfather of Ram; it is from him that Ram gets the patronymic Raghav, and the title Raghupati, or chief of the dynasty of Raghu.

Rahu:

The ascending lunar node in Vedic astrology, and the cause of eclipses. He is also considered as one of the nine planets, the king of meteors and guardian of the south-west quarter. In mythology, Rahu is a Danav who seizes the Sun and the Moon and swallows them, thus causing eclipses. He is the son of Viprachitti and Sinhika, and is known by his metronymic, Sainhikeya. He had four arms, and his lower part ended in a tail. At the churning of the ocean, amongst the many precious objects that were produced was amrit, the nectar of immortality. The gods decided to keep this for themselves, and when it was time to distribute it, the demons were left out. Rahu, assuming a godlike form, seated himself amongst the gods and drank some of the amrit. The Sun and the Moon realized who he was and informed Vishnu, who cut off his head and two of his arms. But, since he had already become immortal by drinking the amrit, he was placed amongst the stars. His upper parts, represented by a dragon's head, being the ascending lunar node, and his lower parts, known as Ketu and represented by a dragon's tail, being the descending node. Since then, Rahu wreaks his vengeance on the Sun and the Moon by occasionally swallowing them. Rahu and Ketu are usually paired together.

Rakshasa; Rakshasi (f.):

A race of demons, of whom Ravan was king. According to some sources, they are the descendants of the sage Pulastya, like Ravana is himself; others say they sprang from the foot of Brahma. They are usually portrayed as huge, ugly, terrifying beings. They are skilled and powerful warriors, with magical powers and the ability to change shape at will. Most of them can fly and many of them are man-eaters who haunt cemeteries, forests and lonely places at night.

They disturb fire-sacrifices, harass pious men and make life difficult for mankind in all sorts of ways. There are good Rakshasas too, such as Ravan's brother, Vibhishan.

Ram; Ramchandra: 'Pleasing, beautiful, charming'; the eldest son of King Dasharath of Avadh, and his chief queen Kaushalya. His wife is Sita, princess of Mithila. He is the seventh avatar of Vishnu, and the protagonist of the Ramayana. As a descendant of the prince Raghu, he is called Raghav or Raghunandan. He is also called Raghunath or Raghupati, lord of the Raghus; Raghunayak, chief of the Raghus; Raghuraj, 'king of the Raghus', Raghubar, 'best of the Raghus'; Raghubir, 'hero of the Raghus'; Raghuchand, 'moon of the dynasty of Raghu'. As Sita's husband, he is also called Sitanath, 'Sita's lord'; Janakinath, 'Janak's lord'. Sita is the incarnation of the goddess Lakshmi, who is also called Ramaa or Shri—as her husband or beloved he is therefore also known as Ramaakant, Ramaaraman, Shrikant, Shriraman. He is also addressed by all the names of Vishnu.

Rambha: An apsara who emerged at the churning of the ocean; she is the epitome of perfect womanhood.

Rantidev: A king of the Lunar dynasty; he was renowned for his piety and generosity. He was a great devotee of Vishnu, and believed that all he had came from him. He was enormously rich and extremely generous, and offered so many cattle in sacrifice that their blood formed the Chambhal river. He saw himself as Vishnu's instrument to serve the poor and needy. According to the Mahabharata, he had 200,000 cooks and had 2000 cattle and as many other animals slaughtered daily for use in his kitchens, and had the meat fed to innumerable poor and needy people. One day, the gods visited

Vishnu in Vaikunth and in casual conversation asked him, 'Who do you think is your greatest devotee?' Without hesitation, Vishnu replied that it was Rantidev. The gods, intrigued, decided to test Rantidev's devotion, and caused a great famine to overcome his kingdom. The king, with his characteristic generosity and piety, opened the royal granary and treasury to his people. But the famine continued. The king then opened his palace to the people, and gave away all that he possessed. He shared whatever food he had with them, but soon even that finished. The people were starving, and, at his wits' end, the king turned to Vishnu for help. Giving up all food and drink, he began to meditate on Vishnu. For forty-eight days he prayed and fasted. On the forty-ninth day, his ministers persuaded him to take some food, and brought him water and a dish made of rice boiled in milk. Just as he was about to eat the rice and milk, a Brahman appeared, hungry and starving. The king gave away part of the food to the Brahman. He was just about to begin eating again when a poor man appeared begging for food. The king gave away another portion of the food to him. Just then, a Shudra appeared before him, begging for food for himself and his dogs. The king gave away the rest of the food to him. He now had only water left, just enough to slake his thirst. As he was about to drink the water, a Chandal, an outcast, appeared and begged for water. The king gave even that away. The Chandal drank the water, and as he did so, the king felt refreshed and strengthened. He opened his eyes in surprise, to see the gods before him. They acknowledged him as Vishnu's greatest devotee, and reversed the famine and its effects, restoring his kingdom to prosperity. And Vishnu, to honour his devotee, took him unto himself. Rantidev merged with his Lord, thus attaining the highest state. An alternative version of the story states that Rantidev, in his generosity, would every now and then hold a great sacrifice and give away all that he possessed. On one occasion, having given away everything he owned, he and his family remained without food or water for forty-eight days. The king accepted his condition, and lived only upon what he received without asking. On the forty-ninth day, as he lay on the ground, starving and semi-conscious, he was given some water and a dish made of rice boiled in milk. As he was about to share this food with his wife and children the gods appeared to test him, in the guise of the Brahman, the Shudra, the low-born man with his dogs and the Chandal.

Rati: 'Love, desire'; the goddess of desire and sexual pleasure, the consort of Kamdev, and daughter of Daksh.

Ravan: The evil and powerful Rakshasa king of Lanka; the son of Vishravas by the Rakshasi Nikasha; grandson of the sage Pulastya. His chief queen was Mandodari. He was the half-brother of Kuber, and as Kuber was king of the Yakshas, Ravan was king of the Rakshasas. Through penance and prayer to Brahma, Ravan received the boon of invulnerability to gods and demons, but was doomed to die because of a woman. He was also able to take any form he pleased. He is described as having ten heads and twenty arms, copper-coloured eyes and teeth as bright as the moon. He was as dark as a cloud, and as enormous as a mountain. His body bore all the marks of royalty, but was marked by the scars of the wounds he had received in his battles against the gods. It was scarred by the thunderbolt of Indra, by the tusks of Indra's elephant, Airavat, and by Vishnu's discus. Tall as a mountain peak, he could stop the sun and the moon in their course across the sky. His strength was so great that he could lift up Mount Kailash in play. He terrorized gods and men with his evil deeds, till at last they appealed to Vishnu for help. Since he had been too arrogant to ask for invincibility against men, Vishnu took birth as Ramchandra, son of Dasharath, for the sole purpose of destroying him; the gods became incarnate as bears and monkeys to help him in this enterprise. For his ten heads, he is called Dashashish. He is also called Dashanan, 'ten-faced'; Dashkandhar or Dashkanth, 'ten-necked'; Dashmukh, 'ten-faced'. As the enemy of the gods, he is known as Surari; as the king of Lanka, he is called Lankesh.

riddhi; Riddhi: Prosperity, affluence, accomplishment. Riddhi is also prosperity, personified as Kuber's wife, or, in some instances, as one of Ganesh's wives. In the plural, the Riddhis refer to some of the attendants of Kuber, and signify riches.

rishi: A sage; the inspired sages to whom the hymns of the Vedas were revealed; also used as a title for the seven great sages, and other wise and learned men.

Rishyamuk: A mountain in the south, near the source of the Pampa river and the lake Pampa, upon which lived the monkey Sugriv and his followers. Ram stayed there for a while with the monkeys.

Sabar; Shabar: A tribal people of southern India.

Sabari; Shabari: A woman of the Sabar tribe (hence her name). The daughter of a hunter, she was a devotee of Ram. She sought salvation upon the death of her guru, the sage, Matanga; just before he died, Matanga assured her that she would indeed attain salvation, and that Ram himself would grant it to her. Sabari waited faithfully for Ram, living for many years as an ascetic in the forest. During his exile, Ram, hearing of her devotion to him, visited her in her hermitage. There, she offered him fruits that she had collected especially for him in the forest, and which she had tasted herself before offering to check their sweetness. Lakshman protested that since she had bitten into the fruit, Ram should not eat them. But Ram saw only her devotion and ate the fruits she offered. He then granted her salvation.

sachchidanand: Literally 'Existence (or being or entity) or truth, thought (or knowledge or consciousness), and happiness (or bliss)'—a name for the Supreme Spirit.

Sagar: A prince of the solar dynasty; king of Avadh. From Sumati, the second of his two wives, he had sixty-thousand sons. During the performance of the Ashvamedha, or horse-sacrifice, the king ordered his sixty-thousand sons to retrieve the sacrificial horse, which had been carried off to the underworld. They dug their way to Patal, where they found the horse grazing and the sage Kapil seated close by in meditation. Thinking him to be the thief, the sons of Sagar began to accuse and threaten him. This so enraged the saint that he reduced all of them to ashes. Their souls were finally liberated by the actions of Bhagirath, who brought the Ganga to earth in order to purify their ashes. Sagar finally completed his sacrifice, and gave the name 'saagar' to the chasm which this sons had dug (saagar means ocean).

sagun: 'With attributes'; possessing a form that has qualities, hence, the incarnate form of the Supreme Spirit.

Sahasrabahu:

'The thousand-armed'; he was king of the Haihaya tribe, and is better known by his patronymic, Kartavirya. As a result of penance and prayer, the divine saint Dattatreya granted him a thousand arms, a golden chariot to take him wherever he wished to go, the power of righting wrongs by dispensing justice, the conquest of the earth and the disposition to rule it righteously, invincibility and finally, death at the hands of a man renowned the whole world over. He ruled wisely and well for 85,000 years. He was a contemporary of Ravan, and when Ravan came to conquer his capital city, Mahishmati, he took him prisoner effortlessly; he let Ravan go on the request of the rishi, Pulastya. One day, when out hunting, Sahasrabahu reached the hermitage of the sage Jamadagni. The sage and the sons were out, but his wife, recognizing the king, treated him with due respect. But instead of acknowledging the hospitality he had received, the king in his arrogance carried off the calf of the sacred cow, Surabhi, which Jamadagni had acquired through penance. When Jamadagni's son, Parashuram, returned and heard what the king had done, he followed the king, cut off his thousand arms with his arrows and killed him. Sahasrabahu's sons, in retaliation, attacked Jamadagni in his hermitage and killed him. When Parashuram found his father's lifeless body, he laid it on a pyre and vowed to wipe out the whole of the Kshatriya race. He killed all the sons of Sahasrabahu, and cleared the earth of Kshatriyas twenty-one times. Sahasrabahu's death at the hands of Parashuram was as per the boon granted him—to be killed by a man renowned the world over.

samadhi:

A state of profound meditation restraining the senses and confining the mind to contemplation.

Sampati:

A vulture, the eldest son of Arun, the charioteer of the Sun, and the older brother of the vulture, Jatayu.

Sanak; Sanandan;
Sanatan; Sanatkumar:

The four Kumars, the four mind-born sons of Brahma; declining to create progeny, they remained forever boys, and forever pure and innocent. Sanatkumar was the most prominent of them all. They are also known by their patronymic Vaidhatra (from Vidhatra, or Brahma).

Sanjivani:

In mythology, a life-giving herb that is said to restore the dead to life.

sanyasi:

One who has renounced the world, abandoning all attachment; according to Hindu scripture, sannyasa is the last and fourth stage of life for a man.

Saptarishi:

The seven Rishis, the mind-born sons of Brahma. They form, in astronomy, the constellation of the Great Bear.

Sarasvati:

'Watery'. In the Vedas, Sarasvati is primarily a river, as sacred as the Ganga is today. Though now lost, it was the third stream that met the Ganga and the Jamuna at their confluence at Prayag. Sarasvati was also a deity, the personification of the river, and as a river goddess she was the bestower of fertility and wealth. In the Brahmanas and the Mahabharata, she is recognized as Vach, the goddess of speech and eloquence. In later times, she is the goddess of learning, inventor of the Sanskrit language and the Devanagari script, and patron of the arts and sciences. She is also the wife of Brahma. She is represented as a beautiful and graceful young woman, white in colour, wearing a crescent on her brow. She is often shown as holding the vina in her hands. Her steed is the swan. In her form as the goddess of speech and eloquence, she is known as Bharati, 'articulate'; Brahmi or Brahmani, 'Brahma's consort'; Gira, 'speech'; Sharada, 'one who bears a vina'; Vani or Bani, literally 'sound, speech, language, voice'. As the consort of Brahma (Vidhatra), she is known as Vidhatri.

Sarju; Sarayu:	A sacred river, that flows past Ram's city of Avadh; it is believed to rise from the sacred Manas lake.
Sati:	A daughter of Daksh, and Shiv's first wife; she killed herself because of her father's anger against Shiv. She was subsequently reincarnated as the goddess Parvati, the daughter of Himvat and Maina.
Savan:	The fifth month of the Hindu calendar, corresponding to July–August.
ser:	A measure of weight, roughly equivalent to a kilogram.
Shachi:	Indra's consort.
Shakti:	Cosmic energy; it denotes the energy or active power of a deity personified as his consort, as Parvati of Shiv, Lakshmi of Vishnu, Sarasvati of Brahma, etc.
Shatanand:	Janak's guru and family priest.
Shatrughna:	'Foe-destroyer'; he is Lakshman's twin and the youngest of Ram's three brothers. He is also called Ripusudan, Ripuhan, 'destroyer of enemies; and Ripudaman or Ripudavan, 'subduer of enemies'.
shehnai:	A wind instrument, somewhat like a clarinet; its sound is considered auspicious and it is especially played at weddings.

Shesh; Sheshnag: Shesh, or Sheshnag, is the king of the Nagas or
the serpent race. His kingdom is Patal, abode of
the Nagas. He is represented as a serpent with a
thousand heads; his coils form the couch upon
which Vishnu lies, and his thousand hoods the
canopy which shelter him whilst he sleeps during
the intervals of creation. He sometimes bears the
entire world upon one of his heads. He is also
called Anant, 'the endless', and is regarded as the
symbol of eternity.

Shibi: Shibi was a pious and generous king, famed for his
large-heartedness and his upholding of dharma.
One day the gods decided to put him to the test.
Agni took on the form of a dove, and Indra that of
a hawk, and as the king sat in court one morning,
the dove flew into his lap and nestled there. The
hawk followed and claimed the dove as its rightful
prey. The king refused to give up the dove, since it
had sought shelter with him, but he also realized
the legitimacy of the hawk's demand. He offered
the hawk anything he wanted in place of the dove,
but the hawk would be satisfied with nothing
except a piece of the king's own flesh, equal in
weight to the dove. So the king had a pair of scales
brought, and placing the dove on one side, he
began hacking off pieces of his own flesh, which
he put on the other side. But no matter how
much of his own flesh he cut off, the dove was
always heavier. At last, he climbed on to the scales
himself and would have cut off his own head,
but the gods intervened, and Agni and Indra,
appearing in their own forms, acknowledged his
generosity and made him whole again.

Shiv: Auspicious, propitious, fortunate; the Destroyer,
the great and powerful third deity in the Hindu
triad; he is described as the destructive power,
but his powers and attributes are much wider. As
the great god of dissolution, he is called Rudra or

Mahakal; but in Hindu philosophy, dissolution is coupled with regeneration, so as Shiv or Shankar, he is the reproductive power that perpetually restores that which has been destroyed. He is thus also called Ishvar, and Mahadev, 'the great god'. As the restorer, he is worshipped in the form of a linga or phallus, or as the linga combined with a yoni, the female reproductive organ representative of his Shakti, or female energy. He is also the supreme ascetic, the epitome of penance and abstract meditation through which unlimited powers are acquired, the highest spiritual knowledge is gained, and union with the Supreme Absolute achieved. In this form he is represented as a naked ascetic, with matted hair, his body smeared with ashes. He is also the lord of goblins and ghosts, and in this form he wears serpents wound around his neck and a necklace of skulls. He is a handsome man, fair-complexioned, with five faces and four arms, and is usually represented sitting upon a tiger skin in profound meditation. He has a third eye in the middle of his forehead, and surmounted by the crescent moon. His third eye, if opened, has great destructive power—it reduced Kamdev, the god of love, to ashes, and periodically destroys creation in the cycle of destruction and regeneration. His matted locks are coiled upon his head, and within it is held the River Ganga, which he caught and contained as she descended from heaven upon earth (and because of which he is called Gangadhar, 'he who holds the Ganga'). He is often attired in the skin of a tiger, a deer, or an elephant. In his four hands he carries a deer, the bow Ajagav, a damru (small hour-glass–shaped drum) or the Khatwang (a club with a skull at the end), or a cord for binding offenders. He is usually accompanied by his bull, Nandi. His consort is the goddess Parvati. As lord of all creation, he is called Akhileshvar, and as lord of the universe he is called Vishvanath and Jagadish; as the Destroyer, he is also called Har. As lord of Mt Kailash, he is known as Girinath and Girish, 'lord of the mountain'. The city of Kashi is sacred to him; thus he is also called Kashinath, 'lord of Kashi'. As regent of the north-east quarter, he is called Ish or Ishan. For his action of reducing Kamdev, the god of love to ashes, he is known as Anangarati, 'enemy of Anang (Kamdev)'; Kamari, 'the foe or conqueror of Kam'; Kamripu, 'the foe of Kam'. In his androgynous form he is known as Ardhanarishvar, 'the god who is half a woman'. He has a bull (brish) on his banner (ketu), and is therefore also known as Brishketu. When vish or poison was thrown up amongst the treasures retrieved at the churning of the ocean, Shiv swallowed it and held it safely in his throat, which turned blue as a result; from this he is called Nilkanth, 'blue-throated' (See ocean, churning of). As the destroyer of the demon known as Tripurasur, he is also called Purari and Tripurari. An alternative explanation is that he destroyed the triple city known as Tripur, which belonged to a trio of demons collectively called Tripurasur. Since he bears the crescent moon on his brow, he is also called Shashibhushan, 'one who has the moon as his ornament' and Chandramauli, 'the moon-crested one'. For the garland of skulls that he wears around his neck, he is known as Kapali, 'the one who wears a necklace of skulls'. He is also known as Ashutosh, 'he who is quickly pleased'; Bhav, 'existence'; Shambhu, 'one who causes happiness'; Shankar, 'one who causes tranquillity' or 'auspicious'; Mahesh or Mahadev, 'the great god'; Sarv, 'complete, entire, universal'; Sadashiv, 'always happy or prosperous'.

shivaling: A phallic representation of Shiv.

Shringber; Shringberpur: The town of Shringber, it lay on the left bank of the Ganga. It was on the border of Koshal with

Bhil country. The area around was inhabited by the Nishad tribe; their chief was Guha. The town has been identified with modern Singraur.

Shringi:

'The deer-horned'; a hermit, and son of the sage Vibhandaka. Shringi or Rishyashringa as he was called, performed the fire-sacrifice that resulted in the birth of Ram and his brothers. One version of his story says that his mother was a doe, and he was therefore born with antlers; another version says that his mother was the apsara, Urvashi, who abandoned her infant son and his father, her lover, after the child's birth. Rishyashringa was brought up by his father in the forest, in complete isolation from all other human beings. He was endowed with magical and mystical powers. Once, when the kingdom of Anga was struck by intense drought, its king, Lomapad, was told that he must hold a sacrifice conducted by a priest who was perfectly chaste. The only such priest that could be found was Rishyashringa, who had grown up with no knowledge of women at all. He was persuaded to come to Anga and perform the sacrifice, which successfully ended the drought in Anga. Rishyashringa then married Shanta, the daughter of Lomapad. (Shanta was actually the adopted daughter of Lomapad; her real father was King Dasharath.)

Shrutakirti:

Sita's cousin, the younger daughter of Janak's younger brother Kushadhvaj (Kushaketu); she was married to Shatrughna.

Shudra:

The fourth, and lowest, of the four castes of Hinduism. This is the servile class, whose duty it was to serve the three higher castes.

Shuk; Shukdev:

An eminent rishi, he was the son of Vyas and the main narrator of the Bhagavat Purana.

Shvapach:	Literally, 'one who eats dog-meat', and thus refers to one belonging to the lowest, most degraded caste.
Siddha:	'Accomplished', a semi-divine being, of great purity and holiness, and said to be specially characterized by the eight siddhis or supernatural faculties, which he acquires by the performance of intense austerities or certain mystical rites or processes. The Siddhas, together with the Munis, and other holy and accomplished beings, inhabit the Bhuvarlok or middle region between the earth and the sun. The term 'Siddha' is also used for a great sage or ascetic who has attained the eight siddhis, usually through intense austerities and yogic practice.
Siddhi; siddhi:	Success or accomplishment personified; one of Ganesh's wives. In northern Indian tradition, Ganesh's two consorts are Siddhi (Success) and Buddhi (Wisdom). In one recounting, they are said to have been born of Brahma's mind, who then offered them to Ganesh as his brides; in another they are regarded as having been summoned by Ganesh himself, and then offered to him by Brahma. Buddhi is also sometimes called Riddhi—she is spiritual success, as opposed to the material success that is her sister Siddhi. In the plural, the siddhis are supernatural faculties. They are usually stated to be eight in number. They are: (i) anima, the faculty of making oneself infinitesimally small; (ii) mahima, the faculty of making oneself infinitely great; (iii) laghima, the faculty of becoming infinitely light; (iv) garima, the faculty of becoming infinitely heavy; (v) prapti, the faculty of obtaining whatever one wishes; (vi) prakamya, the faculty of doing whatever one wishes; (vii) ishitva, the power of absolute supremacy; (viii) vashitva, the power of absolute subjugation.

sindur:	Vermilion; applied on the head of a woman it indicates that she is married; it is applied to the head of the bride for the first time by the bridegroom upon the completion of the wedding rites.
sinsupa:	The ashok tree.
siris blossom:	The flower of the tree Acacia sirissa; the flower is exceptionally fragile and delicate-looking, with pale, slender filament-like petals.
Sita:	'A furrow'; in the Vedas, Sita is the furrow, or farming personified and is worshipped as the goddess of agriculture and fruits. In the Ramayana, she is the daughter of Janak, the king of Videha, and the wife of Ram. Remnants of old Vedic belief can still be seen in the story of her birth. It is related that one day, as King Janak was ploughing the field in preparation for a great fire-sacrifice to obtain children, there sprang from his plough a baby girl, whom he adopted. He named her 'Sita', which means 'furrow', and took her home to his palace, where she grew up as his beloved daughter. From her father, she is known as 'Janaki'. So, from the manner of her birth, Sita is also called Avanikumari, 'daughter of the earth'. She is also known as Vaidehi, 'daughter of Videh, king of Videha' or 'princess of Videha'; and Maithili, 'princess of Mithila'.
sixteen ways of honouring a guest:	In Hindu tradition, a guest is considered equal to a god, and he is honoured by being given the following sixteen things: (i) asana, a seat; (ii) arghya, a libation of water with milk, flowers, etc.; (iii) padya, water to wash the feet; (iv) achamaniya, water to drink; (v) snaniya, water to bathe and for ablutions; (vi) gandhakshak, sandal paste and rice grains; (vii) vastra, fresh clothes; (viii) pushpa,

flowers; (ix) dhupa, incense; (x) dipa, light or lamps; (xi) naivedya, food; (xii) mukhasta jal, water to rinse the mouth with; (xiii) tambula, betel leaves; (xiv) dakshina, a gift; (xv) pradakshina, circumambulation; and (xvi) nirajana, a worship with lighted lamps.

Skand:
The god of war, the planet Mars, and the commander of the divine armies. He was born miraculously from the seed of Shiv, for the express purpose of destroying the Asur Tarak. It is said that Shiv cast his seed into fire, and it was afterwards received by the river Ganga. From her waters came forth Skand, in the form of a beautiful baby boy. He was found by the six Krittikas (the Pleiades), and each claimed the baby for herself, and each wanted to nurse him. In order to please them, Skand grew six heads. He is shown as riding on a peacock, with a bow in one hand and an arrow in the other. He is also known as Shanmukh, 'one with six-faces'.

Sone:
A river in central India, it is a tributary of the Ganga.

spheres, fourteen:
According to Hindu scripture, the universe is divided into fourteen spheres, seven ascending and seven descending. The seven higher spheres, in ascending order, are: Bhuh, Bhuvah, Svah, Mahah, Janah, Tapah and Satyam; the lower sphere, in descending order, are: Atal, Vital, Sutal, Talatal, Mahatal, Rasatal, Patal.

states of being, four:
The four states of being are: (i) jagrat or waking; (ii) svapna or sleeping/dreaming; (iii) sushupti or deep repose; and (iv) turiya or the state in which the soul has become one with the Supreme Spirit. These four feminine states are each paired with a male consort; these are: (i) vishva or creation;

(ii) tejas or power; (iii) pragya or wisdom; and (iv) brahm, the universal Absolute.

Subahu: A Rakshasa. He defiled and interrupted the fire-sacrifices of the sage Vishvamitra; for this, he was killed by Ram.

Sugriv: King of the monkeys, and brother of Baali. He is also called Sukanth.

Sukarkhet: A town, identified with the town of Soron in northern India. It is located on the river Ganga, about thirty-two miles south of modern-day Ayodhya. It is an important place of pilgrimage for Hindus.

Sumantra: Dasharath's trusted minister and charioteer.

Sumitra: One of Dasharath's queens, the mother of the twins Lakshman and Shatrughna.

Supnakha; Surpanakha: Literally, 'having finger-nails like winnowing fans'; a Rakshasi, Ravan's sister.

Surasa: A goddess, the mother of the Nagas, she was asked by the gods to test Hanuman's strength and courage as he flew across the ocean to Lanka.

Sutikshna: A hermit who lived in the Dandak forest and met Ram and Sita during their exile. He was a disciple of the sage Agastya.

Svati: The star Arcturus, as forming the fifteenth nakshatra, or lunar asterism. According to popular belief, the rain that falls under this lunar asterism is endowed with special properties including the attribute that if a drop of it falls into a seashell, it becomes a pearl. The chatak subsists only on the rain that falls during autumn, under the influence of this nakshatra.

svayamvar:

The public ceremony of a young girl or princess selecting a husband of rank from an assembled gathering of suitors; this ceremony is usually restricted to the Kshatriya caste. Sometimes, a task may be set by the bride's family for her suitors to accomplish, as in the case of Sita's svayamvar, where the successful suitor had to string and break Shiv's bow.

tamal:

A tree found across India; it has very dark bark and white blossoms.

Tamas; Tamasa:

A tributary of the Ganga.

Tara:

Wife of Baali, king of the monkeys, and the mother of Angad. After Baali was killed by Ram, she was taken by Baali's younger brother, Sugriv, as his wife.

Tarak:

A Daitya, whose austerities made him formidable to the gods, and for whose destruction Shiv's son, Skand, the god of war, was born.

Taraka:

The daughter of the Yaksha, Suketu; turned into a Rakshasi by the sage Agastya, she lived in the forest at the confluence of the Ganga and the Sarju and ravaged the surrounding land and terrorized the rishis in the forest. Vishvamitra wanted Ram to kill her, to stop her from doing further harm. But Ram was reluctant to kill a woman. So deciding to deprive her of the power to do harm, he cut off her two arms. Lakshman cut off her nose and ears. But using her magic powers, she pelted Ram and Lakshman with a shower of rocks and boulders, so that finally, at Vishvamitra's command, Ram killed her with a single arrow. Her son was the Rakshasa Marich, who later helped Ravan in his abduction of Sita.

three afflictions or the triple fires:

These are mental and physical distress, distress caused by the acts of God, and distress caused by others.

tilak:

A ceremonial mark made with vermilion or sandalwood paste upon the forehead between the eyebrows upon installation to office, coronation of a king, betrothal, etc.

triveni:

'Triple-braid'; the confluence of the three sacred rivers Ganga, Jamuna and the subterranean Sarasvati at the city of Prayag (modern Allahabad). The waters of the Jamuna are dark, and of the Ganga light. The stream of the Sarasvati is invisible.

Trijata:

A Rakshasi who befriended Sita when she was Ravan's prisoner in Lanka. She is also called Dharamagya.

Trishanku:

The name given to Satyavrata, a prince of the solar dynasty, and king of Avadh. Satyavrata was a good king, but in his arrogance he decided to ascend to heaven in corporeal form. He therefore asked the sage Vasishtha to perform the sacrifice by means of which he could attain this end. Vasishtha declined to perform the ceremony, declaring that what the king wanted was impossible. Satyavrata then appealed to Vasishtha's sons, who refused, saying that he wanted to make trouble between them and their father and, for his presumption, cursed him to become a Chandal. While in Chandal form, and having nothing to eat one day, Satyavrata killed Vasishtha's cow, the Kamadhenu, and ate her. For these three sins, of pride, making trouble between father and sons, and killing a cow, Vasishtha gave him the name 'Trishanku' (from *tri* or 'three', and *shanku* or 'sin'). He then turned to Vishvamitra, who agreed to perform the sacrifice and send him to heaven in his current body. The sons of Vasishtha opposed the sacrifice, for which Vishvamitra reduced them all to ashes. He then began the sacrifice, but as Trishanku ascended to heaven, Indra and the other gods opposed his entry and hurled him down to earth. Trishanku fell head first, and hung upside down in the sky, midway between the earth and heaven. It was finally agreed that that is where he should stay. He can still be seen in the sky, as the constellation Trishanku in the southern hemisphere. The saliva that dropped from his mouth is said to be the River Karamnasa, the waters of which, if touched, destroy all religious merit.

Trishira: Literally, 'three-headed'; a Rakshasa, and a brother, son, or friend of Ravan, killed by Ram.

twice-born: A man of any one of the three upper Hindu castes (but particularly a Brahman), whose investiture with the sacred thread upon puberty constitutes, religiously and metaphorically, his second birth.

Udayagiri: This is the eastern mountain from behind which the sun is supposed to rise; it is also called Udayachal.

Urmila: Janak's and Sunayana's daughter, Sita's younger sister; she was married to Lakshman.

Vaikunth: The paradise or heaven of Vishnu; its site is sometimes described as in the Northern Ocean, sometimes it is said to be located on the eastern peak of Mount Meru. Vishnu himself is also sometimes designated by this term.

Valmik; Valmiki:	The author of the Sanskrit Ramayana. Regarded as the first, or original poet, he is said to have invented poetry when he began to compose the Ramayana. Tradition maintains that before he became a sage and the author of the Ramayana, Valmiki was the dacoit Ratnakar, who would waylay travellers and then rob and mercilessly kill them. One day, he ran into the sage Narad, who asked him why he did what he did. Ratnakar replied that it was for his family; Narad asked him whether his family appreciated the burden of sin that he was accumulating for their sakes and whether they would share it. Ratnakar staunchly replied that they would, but when he asked his wife and children, they refused to accept the burden of his crimes. Ratnakar realized the folly of his ways and begged for forgiveness. Narad then gave him the mantra of Ram's name, but since this was a mantra that could not be given to thieves and murderers, Narad told him to recite it backwards. Ratnakar did so, and meditated on the name, sitting so still and for so long that anthills grew around him. He continued his penance for many long years, till finally a divine voice declared him to be free of the guilt of his crimes, and renamed him Valmiki, or 'the one born of anthills'.
Vamdev:	A prominent rishi, attached to Dasharath's court.
Varun:	Amongst the oldest of the Vedic gods, Varun is the personification of the sky, the maker of earth and heaven. He is described as being furnished with snares and nooses, with which he seizes and binds evildoers. No mortal can escape from Varun's snares.
Vasishtha:	A celebrated Vedic sage, to whom many hymns are ascribed. According to the Vishnu Purana, he was the family priest of the house of Ishkvaku;

he was contemporary not only with Ishkvaku himself, but with his descendants down to the sixty-first generation, including Dasharath and Ram.

Veda; Vedas:

From *vid*, 'know'; hence 'divine knowledge'. The Vedas, composed in verse in an ancient form of Sanskrit some time between 1500 and 1000 BCE (though opinions vary considerably about their age, and many scholars believe that they can be pushed back at least another thousand years), are the foundation of Hindu belief and practice. It is believed that the Vedas emanated as the breath of the Supreme Being. It is agreed that they were revealed orally to the sages whose names they bear, and thus the whole body of the Veda—the entire body of divine knowledge—is known as 'Sruti' or 'what was heard'. The Vedas are four in number: Rig, Yajur, Sama, Atharva. The Rig Veda is the oldest; in fact, it is the original Veda, from which the Yajur and Sama Vedas are mostly derived. The Atharva Veda was composed much later.

Vedant:

'End of the Veda'; name of the complete Veda; name of a certain system of philosophy and theology based particularly on the Upanishads; and of works concerning this philosophy and in support of it.

Vedashira:

One of the seven great rishis (Saptarishi), associated with the fourth Manwantara. (See Manu.)

vedi:

A quadrangular space, with the sacred fire in the centre, where wedding rites are conducted.

vedika:

Ground prepared for a sacrifice or ceremony, usually consisting of a raised floor or platform and covered with a roof supported by pillars.

Vena: Son of Anga by his queen, Sunita, and a descendant of Manu Swayambhuva. Vena grew up to be a cruel and vicious man, so much so that his father, unable to bear his atrocities, left the kingdom and disappeared, no one knew where. Seeing the kingdom without a king, the sages decided to put Vena upon the throne. Royal power made him worse, and in his arrogance, he banned offerings and performance of sacrifices to the gods, declaring that he alone was worthy of such worship. The sages reasoned with him, but he refused to listen; they admonished him more strongly, but he would not change his mind. Finally, they killed him with blades of consecrated grass. After his death, the sages saw clouds of dust in the distance, and were told that these were raised by men who had begun to loot and plunder because the country was now without a king. Since Vena was childless, the sages rubbed his left thigh to produce a son; from this arose a short, dark man with a flat nose. He was asked to sit, 'nishida'; he did so and thus became a Nishad, from which sprang the tribe living in the Vindhya mountains. The sages then rubbed the right hand of Vena, and from this came forth his son Prithu. (See Prithuraj.) Vena's story is told a little differently in the Padma Purana. This states that Vena was a good king at the start of his rule, but soon turned to the teachings of the Jains. For this heresy, the sages attacked and beat him, till from his left thigh came forth the Nishad tribe, and from his right arm came Prithu. Being freed of sin by the birth of the Nishad, he gave up his kingdom and retired to an ashram on the Narmada, where he engaged in penance. For this, Vishnu forgave him and made him one with himself.

Vibhishan: 'The terrible'; a younger brother of Ravan, and ally of Ram. He was raised to the throne of Lanka by Ram after the defeat and death of Ravan.

Videh: 'Bodiless'; the title born by the kings of the kingdom of Videha, including King Janak, Sita's father.

Videha: The kingdom of King Janak, Sita's father. Its capital city was the city of Mithila.

vina: An ancient multi-stringed musical instrument; it is supposed to have been invented by Narad.

Vinata: A daughter of Daksh, one of the thirteen wives of the sage Kashyap, and mother of Garud. From her were born all the birds.

Viradh: Also known as Tumburu, he was a Gandharva cursed by Kuber to become a horrible, man-eating Rakshasa. He is described as being as tall as a mountain peak, deformed, of dreadful aspect, clad in a tiger's skin, smeared with fat, soaked in blood, like death with an open mouth, bearing three lions, four tigers, two wolves, ten deer and the great head of an elephant with tusks on the point of an iron pike. He had obtained from Brahma the boon of invulnerability. Ram, with Lakshman and Sita, encountered him in the Dandak forest. (This incident is told in detail in Valmiki's Ramayana.) Viradh cursed and taunted the brothers, and grabbed Sita. Ram and Lakshman shot him with their arrows, proving that he was not invulnerable. But he caught them and throwing them over his shoulder, ran off with them as easily as if they had been children. They broke both his arms, beat him with their fists and threw him to the ground, but they could not kill him. So they dug a deep hole and buried him alive. Then there arose from the earth a beautiful form, who said he was a Gandharva cursed by Kuber to take on the form of a Rakshasa. Ram released him from the curse and sent him back to his own realm.

Vishnu: From *vish*, to pervade. The preserver and
            restorer, he is the second of the Hindu triad. He
            is also called Hari. In the Rig Veda, Vishnu is
            the manifestation of solar energy, and does not
            have the importance he acquired later as the
            great preserver of the universe. In the Puranas
            and the Mahabharata, he is the embodiment of
            mercy and goodness, which manifests itself as
            the preserving power, which is self-existent and
            all-pervading. He is therefore associated with
            water, which was everywhere before the creation
            of the world. He is represented in human form
            as reclining upon the serpent Shesh, and floating
            upon the Ocean of Milk. He is therefore also
            called Narayan or 'floating upon the waters'. His
            consort is Lakshmi, the goddess of wealth and
            beauty. The river Ganga is said to spring from his
            toe. Vishnu is represented with four hands; one
            holds the Panchajanya, a shankha or conch-shell;
            the second the Sudarshan or Vajranabha, which
            is a chakra or discus; the third holds Kaumodaki,
            a gada or club; and the fourth holds a Padma,
            or lotus. As the husband of Lakshmi (who is
            also known as Shri, Ramaa and Kamla), he
            is known as Shripati, Ramapati and Kamlapati; as
            the one who dwells with Lakshmi, he is known
            as Shrinivas, Ramanivas and Ramaniket. He is
            also known as Sarangpani, 'the one who bears the
            bow called Sarang'. As the slayer of the demon
            Khar in his incarnation as Ramchandra, he is
            known as Kharari, 'enemy of Khar'; as the slayer
            of the demons Madhu and Kaitabh he is known
            as Madhusudan and Kaitabhajit respectively. As
            the giver of liberation, he is called Mukund. He
            is also known as Anant, 'the infinite'. Vishnu
            has 'descended' to earth, or taken incarnate form
            several times. His 'descents', or avatars, are usually
            said to be ten in number, though the Bhagavata
            Purana says that they are twenty-two, or

innumerable. Vishnu's ten avatars are as follows: (i) Matsya, 'the fish': this avatar is connected with the Hindu legend of the flood. The objective was to save Vaivaswata, the seventh Manu, who became the progenitor of all mankind. One day Manu found in the water he used for his ablutions a little fish which spoke to him and warned him of a great flood that was coming which would destroy all living creatures, and said that it would save him. The fish grew and grew till it was so huge that it had to be put into the ocean. The fish then instructed Manu to build a ship, and to take refuge in it when the flood came. Manu did so, and when the flood came, Manu embarked in the ship. The fish then swam to Manu, who, using the serpent Sheshnag tied the ship to the fish's horn, and was towed to safety; (ii) Kurma, 'the tortoise': when the great flood subsided, the gods realized that many valuable things had been lost at the bottom of the ocean. So Vishnu appeared as a tortoise, and placed himself at the bottom of the Ocean of Milk, and took upon his back the mountain Mandar. The gods and demons wound the serpent Vasuki around the mountain. The gods took one end of the serpent, the demons the other, and in this way they churned the ocean until they recovered the lost objects; (iii) Varah, 'the boar': a Daitya called Hataklochan had dragged the earth to the bottom of the sea. In order to recover the earth, Vishnu took the form of a boar, and after a battle that lasted a thousand years, he killed the Daitya and carried the earth back to the surface on his tusks; (iv) Narsingh, Narhari, or Narkeshari 'the man-lion': Vishnu took on the form of half-lion, half-man to deliver the world from the Daitya Kanakakasipu. Kananakasipu's son, Prahlad, was a devotee of Vishnu, and refused to obey his father's order that he should worship him and not Vishnu. When

Prahlad declared that Vishnu was all-pervading
and everywhere, Kanakakasipu demanded to
know if he was present even in the stone pillar in
the hall of his palace. At this, to avenge Prahlad,
Vishnu appeared out of the pillar in the form
of Narsingh, half-man, half lion, and therefore
neither man nor beast, and killed Kanakakasipu.
The first four avatars are said to have taken place
during the Satyayug, the first age of the world; (v)
Vaman, 'the dwarf': in the Tretayug (the second
age of the world), the Daitya king Bali became so
powerful that he became king of the three worlds.
The gods asked Vishnu to help them, so that
may once again regain their pre-eminence in the
world. So Vishnu descended to earth as a dwarf,
and the son of Kashyap and Aditi. The dwarf
begged Bali to give him as much land as he could
cover in three strides. Bali, with his characteristic
generosity, agreed. The dwarf took two strides by
which he covered heaven and earth. Recognizing
Bali's virtue, he refrained from taking the third
step, and left Patal, or the underworld to Bali. This
avatar is also known as Tribikram or Trivikrama,
literally 'three strides'; (vi) Parashuram, 'Ram
with the axe': he was born in the Tretayug, as
the son of the Brahman Jamadagni, and his wife,
Renuka. From his father's side he was descended
from Bhrigu. He appeared in the world for
repressing the tyranny and violence of the
Kshatriya or warrior caste. Though he appeared
in this world before Ramchandra, Vishnu's
seventh avatar and the hero of the Ramayana,
they were both living in this world at the same
time. His weapon was the parashu or axe; (vii)
Ram, or Ramchandra, the hero of the Ramayana
and of Tulsi's *Ramcharitmanas*, he was born in
the Tretayug to destroy the demon Ravan. He
was the son of Dasharath, king of Ayodhya;
(viii) Krishna, 'the dark': he is considered to be

the most perfect of all of Vishnu's avatars. He is often regarded not as an avatar, but as Vishnu himself, when his elder brother Balram takes his place as the eighth avatar; (ix) Buddha: Buddha's far-reaching influence as a religious leader caused the Hindu Brahmins to adopt him as an avatar of Vishnu, who encourages wicked men to disregard the Vedas and the gods, and so bring about their own destruction. In eastern India, the ninth avatar is Jagannath, 'lord of the world', a form of Krishna; (x) Kalki, 'the white horse': the last and tenth avatar is yet to come. Vishnu will appear at the end of the Kaliyug, the last and fourth age, mounted on a white horse, and carrying a fiery sword. He will finally destroy the wicked and rid the world of evil, and the cycle of creation will begin again with piety restored.

Vishvakarma: A son of Brahma, and the chief architect and artist of the gods.

Vishvamitra: A celebrated sage, and the companion and counsellor of the young Ram. He was born a Kshatriya, and was the king of Kanauj, but through long and intense austerities, successfully elevated himself to the caste of Brahman and became one of the seven great Rishis. According to the Rig Veda, he was the son of a king named Kushika, because of which he is called Kaushik. Later sources make him the son of Gadhi, king of Kanyakubja and a descendant of Puru. He is therefore also called Gadhij, 'born of Gadhi' or, Gadhinandan, 'Gadhi's son'.

Vyas: Literally, 'an arranger', this title is common to many ancient authors, but is especially applied to Veda Vyas, the arranger of the Vedas. The name is also given to the compiler of the Mahabharata, and the arranger of the Puranas.

Yaksha: Yakshas are semi-divine beings who protect
                     forests and other wild places, and are generally
                     harmless, though they may, on rare occasions, be
                     evil. They are the attendants of the god of wealth,
                     Kuber.

Yayati: Son of Nahush, and the fifth king of the Lunar
                     dynasty. He had two wives, Devyani and
                     Sarmishtha. From Devyani was born his son Yadu,
                     and from Sarmishtha his son Puru, the respective
                     founders of the Yadavas and the Pauravas. In all
                     he had five sons, the three others being Druhyu,
                     Turvasu and Anu. Yayati was fond of women,
                     and for his infidelity to Devyani, he was cursed
                     with old age and infirmity by her father, Shukra.
                     This curse Shukra consented to transfer to any of
                     his sons who would agree to bear it. All refused,
                     except Puru, who gave up his youth to his father
                     and took on his curse of decrepitude. Yayati spent
                     a thousand years enjoying the pleasures of the
                     senses, after which he restored his youth to Puru
                     and made him his successor. This story is told in
                     the Mahabharata, as well as in the Vishnu Purana.
                     The version in the Padma Purana is different.
                     Yayati was invited to heaven by Indra, who sent his
                     charioteer Matali to fetch him. On the way, they
                     had a philosophical discussion, which had such an
                     impact on Yayati that when he returned to earth,
                     he, by his virtuous rule, made all his subjects free
                     from passion and decay. Yama, the god of Death,
                     complained that men no longer died. So Indra
                     sent Kamdev, the god of love, and his daughter,
                     Asruvindumati, to tempt Yayati with desire. They
                     succeeded, and Yayati, deeply enamoured of the
                     youthful Asruvindumati and in order to become
                     a fit husband for her, asked each of his sons to
                     exchange their youth for his old age. All refused,
                     except Puru, who gave his manly vigour to his
                     father and assumed his decrepitude. After some

time, Asruvindumati persuaded Yayati to return to heaven, and he then gave Puru back his youth. According to the Mahabharata, King Yayati, at the end of his life, gave up his throne to Puru and retired to the forest to lead the life of an ascetic. There, the king lived on fruits and roots for some time, and practised austerities, attaining complete control of his mind and his senses. He also performed fire sacrifices to honour his ancestors and the gods, and followed every prescribed rite and tradition for one in the third or forest-dwelling stage of life (See four stages of life). He then lived on scattered seeds that he gathered for a thousand years, and then for another year observing the vow of silence and living upon air alone and without sleep. He passed another year practising the most severe austerities, with four fires burning around him and the sun above, and then, living upon air alone, stood upon one leg for six months. These austerities earned him a place in heaven. He lived in heaven for a long time, where he was held in great reverence by the gods and other celestial beings. One day, Yayati went to meet Indra, the king of the gods, and in the course of conversation, Indra asked him to whom he was equal in the austerities he had practised. Yayati's boastful answer, that he did not, in the matter of austerities, behold any who was his equal amongst men, gods, Gandharvas and rishis, led to a diminishing of his virtues, and he was hurled from the heavens back into the world of men.

yojan: A measure of distance, equivalent to 4 kos or about 9 miles.

Acknowledgements

Many people have stood by me in the five long years it has taken to complete this translation. Of these, my thanks first and foremost to R. Sivapriya, who made this project possible, and to Ambar Sahil Chatterjee, who has seen this through from the very beginning to the end. My gratitude also, to Shantanu Rai Chaudhuri, for his patient and meticulous editing.

I would also like to thank my teacher, Mrs Chandrakanta Chandra, who first introduced me to the literary genius of Tulsidas and the wonders of medieval Hindi literature in school, and whose help, in resolving nuances of language or understanding points of Tulsi's philosophy or ideology, has been invaluable to me on this journey of discovery and translation.

As always, my profound thanks to Dr Rupert Snell, my guru and guide, without whose encouragement I may not have had the courage to take up this project, and who has been ever present with help, advice, and support every step of the way.

My very special thanks to my daughters, Vipasha Bansal and Vidisha Jain, who bore the brunt of my obsession with this work. Vipasha patiently rescued me from innumerable tangles of grammar and syntax, and Vidisha was unfailing in her encouragement and support.

And finally, to my long-suffering family and friends—in particular Usha Bubna, Dr Asha Maheshwari, Anil Ratti and Shaiontoni Bose—for their patience and support, my undying gratitude.

Notes

Introduction

1. Though even at the time that Valmiki composed his epic, two other, very different, tellings of the Ram story existed—one was the Buddhist *Dasaratha Jataka*, in which Ram and Sita are brother and sister and rule as consorts, and the other the Jain *Paumchariya* by Vimalasuri, who sets the story in the court of the historical king Srinika and depicts the Rakshasas not as demons, but as normal human beings.

2. This reference to Tulsi is found in the *Bhaktamal*, a collection of short biographies composed by Nabhadas, possibly around 1585.

3. For a detailed discussion on the spread and circulation of the *Ramcharitmanas*, see Philip Lutgendorf, 'The Quest for the Legendary Tulsidas', *According to Tradition: Hagiographical Writing in India*, edited by Winand M. Callewaert and Rupert Snell.

4. For a discussion on available biographies of Tulsidas, see Philip Lutgendorf, 'The Quest for the Legendary Tulsidas', *According to Tradition: Hagiographical Writing in India,* edited by Winand M. Callewaert and Rupert Snell.

5. *Balkand*, 34.

6. *Balkand*, 30A, 31.

7. *Balkand*, 14D.

8. *Balkand*, Mangalacharan 7.

9. The relevant passages are contained in Book 3, *Aranyakand*, 24, where Sita conceals herself in the fire and substitutes her shadow; and in Book 6, *Lankakand*, 108–09, where the shadow Sita is destroyed and the real Sita steps forth out of the fire.

10. *Balkand*, 16.
11. *Balkand*, 14.
12. *Balkand*, 227–36.
13. Philip Lutgendorf, *The Life of a Text: Performing the* Ramcaritmanas *of Tulsidas*, University of California Press, 1991, p. 7.
14. *Aranyakand*, 34–36.
15. *Balkand*, 30.
16. *Balkand*, 124A.
17. For a more detailed discussion on the title, see Philip Lutgendorf, *The Life of a Text: Performing the* Ramcaritmanas *of Tulsidas*, University of California Press, 1991, pp. 19–20.
18. *Balkand*, 35–36.
19. *Balkand*, 36–37.
20. As an example, see *Uttarkand*, 113.
21. *Ayodhyakand*, 0; this doha, numbered 0, is the first doha after the Sanskrit mangalacharan; from this the Avadhi text of the second book begins.

Book IV: KISHKINDHAKAND (KISHKINDHA)

1. The Daitya, Mayavi, had a younger brother called Dundhubi, who had earlier taken on the form of a buffalo and attacked Baali. Baali had killed him and hurled his gigantic corpse far away from his capital city. A few drops of blood had fallen upon the hermitage of Rishi Matanga on the Rishyamuk mountain. This had enraged the rishi, who had then declared that he who had desecrated his hermitage by spilling blood there would have his head shattered to pieces if he came near his hermitage. So, Baali could not step upon the Rishyamuk mountain.
2. The full incident is related in Valmiki's Ramayana: Sugriv showed Ram Dundhubi's massive skeleton, and Ram sent it flying hundreds of miles through the air. But Sugriv was still not convinced of his strength, for Baali had thrown it the same distance when it was still covered in flesh and therefore heavier. So, Ram, to convince him, took an arrow from his quiver and shot it so that it passed through seven palm trees which stood in a row one behind the other, pierced the hill behind them, continued downwards towards the lowest hell and returned to Ram's quiver.
3. The babul is the gum-acacia, a small tree with sharp spines. 'To plant a babul tree' is to do something conducive to harm or to a bad end.
4. Kash is a species of grass native to the Indian subcontinent. It grows to about 3 m high and bears long feathery white flowers in the autumn. So, in Tulsi's metaphor, these white flowers are like the white hairs of the rainy season, which is now old and spent.

5. The star Agastya (or Canopus), which drinks up the water after the rainy season, in the same way that Rishi Agastya drank up the ocean.

6. In Valmiki's Ramayana, she is called Swayamprabha —'self-luminous'. An ascetic, and unmarried, she and Ravan's sister, Surpanakha (as Supnakha is called in Sanskrit) are the only two unmarried women in the Ramayana. While Surpanakha flaunts her sexuality without apology, Swayamprabha is an ascetic, deriving power from her asceticism. The cavern, she explains, has been built by the Danav Mai, the architect of the Asurs, and no one who enters it may leave it alive. But she knows the purpose of the monkeys' mission, and agrees to help them escape.

7. Tribikram (literally 'three strides')—this alludes to Trivikrama or Vaman, Vishnu's fifth avatar as the dwarf, who with three strides broke the power of the Daitya king, Bali.

Book V: SUNDARKAND (THE BEAUTIFUL)

1. Once, all mountains had wings and could fly through the air. Then Indra clipped their wings with his thunderbolt, and they became fixed to the earth. The only mountain to escape this fate was Mainak, who, helped by the Wind god, was able to fly faster than Indra's thunderbolt, and hide himself in the sea. The ocean now asks Mainak to hide no longer, but to rise out of the waters and help the Wind god's son by allowing him to rest upon its peak.

2. Lankini is often regarded as the personification of the city of Lanka itself.

3. Tulsi plants are used extensively in the worship of Vishnu, and therefore Ram—so their presence signified the home of a believer.

4. A single braid is a sign of mourning for an absent husband.

5. Chandrahas, literally, 'deriding the moon'; hence, a glittering sword that ridicules the moon by its own, greater, brilliance.

6. South is the direction in which lies the abode of Yamraj, the god of death, so dreaming of a person travelling towards the south is considered to foretell that person's death.

7. The serpent snare was a special kind of noose to entangle an enemy, and was stolen by Ravan from Varun.

8. Ram is the Supreme Spirit, and Brahma, Vishnu and Shiv its part-manifestations—each of the countless universes that Ram's maya brings forth has its own triad of the three gods.

9. Once, Ravan tried to conquer King Sahasrabahu's capital city, but the king took him prisoner effortlessly; he let Ravan go on the request of the rishi, Pulastya. And once, as Baali, king of the monkeys, was deep in prayer, Ravan tried to sneak up behind him and grab him, but instead, Baali caught him

under his armpit and kept him pinned there while he completed his worship; he let him go only when Brahma interceded on Ravan's behalf.

10. According to Hindu belief, there are forty-nine winds, each presided over by its own deity. Collectively these forty-nine deities are known as the Maruts. It is only at the time of dissolution, when creation comes to an end, that all forty-nine of the winds blow together.

11. This is often taken to give weight to the belief that Hanuman was actually an incarnation of Shiv—that since Shiv himself had been Hanuman, as he remembered that moment, he was once again immersed in bliss.

12. This refers to the legend that says that once all the mountains had wings and could fly and move about, till one day Indra clipped their wings. Sumeru, chief of all the mountains, also had its wings cut off by Indra.

13. Sagar was a king of the solar race, and so one of Ram's ancestors. It is said that his sixty-one thousand sons dug the bed of the ocean and so, it is from his name that the ocean is also called 'sagar'.

14. This incident is properly explained in Valmiki's Ramayana. The ocean complains that on his north shore live the people of the Abhira tribe, who are so impure a people that he cannot bear to receive into his bosom any river or stream from which they have drunk. So Ram, with his arrow of fire, dries up every river and stream in their land, but gives them instead a never-ending supply of subterranean water and makes the region exempt from disease.

Book VI: LANKAKAND (LANKA)

1. Madhu and Kaitabh were two demons who sprang from the ear of Vishnu as he lay asleep at the end of a cycle of creation, and were about to kill Brahma, who lay asleep on a lotus that grew from Vishnu's navel. Vishnu killed them—and hence he is also known as Kaitabhajit, and Madhusudan.

2. Ghamoi is a prickly shrub that bears yellow flowers, and which, it is believed, destroys bamboo. So Prahast is as destructive to their lineage as ghamoi is to bamboo. Ghamoi is also small and easily destroyed, while bamboo is tall and strong and resilient—so, according to some commentators, this metaphor means that Prahast is as unlike his father, Ravan, as possible.

3. A game similar to hockey, but played on horseback.

4. In some versions of the story, it is stated that when Lakshman left to follow Ram into the forest in pursuit of the golden deer, he drew a line in the earth which he told Sita not to cross for her own safety. When Ravan came to her forest dwelling disguised as an ascetic, he first asked

her for food, and when she offered it to him, he insisted she step out of her hut, and step over the line, which he did not dare cross. Tulsi does not mention this incident of Lakshman drawing a line in Aranyakand, but interestingly, refers to it here.

5. When in bloom, the kinshuk tree is covered with bright red flowers.

6. Brahma had granted Meghnad the boon that he could not be killed except by one who had forsaken food and sleep for twelve years. (He was finally killed by Lakshman, who had known neither hunger nor rest in the twelve years that he had served Ram in exile.)

7. In this case, it is Lakshman who is referred to as the Lord—reminding the audience that he, too, is divine, and along with Ram, a part incarnation of Vishnu.

8. This was the mark of the sage, Bhrigu's foot. See Balkand, stanza 199, for the full story.

9. These are the Pramaths. Some of them are ascetics and yogis, but many are lovers of sensual pleasures and these are attendant on Shiv. According to the Puranas, the Pramaths in Shiv's service number 36 crore.

10. Dying people were often taken by friends and relatives and laid on the banks of sacred streams and rivers, half in, half out, so that they may be washed by the sacred water in their last moments.

11. Joginis are witches or female demons with magical powers, created by and attendant on the goddess Parvati in her form as Durga. Chamundas are also female attendants of Durga. They are often portrayed as terrifying, black-bodied women wearing garlands of skulls around their necks.

12. Kalikas are female attendants of the goddess Kali (Parvati in her most terrible and terrifying form).

13. Dasharath does not wish to become one with the Lord—for if he becomes one with him, he cannot adore him. Therefore he had set his heart on 'separation and devotion'.

14. To think of Ram at the moment of death, even if the thoughts be hostile, ensures salvation and union with Ram, who is the Absolute incarnate. This is what happened to the demons—at the point of death, their minds were focused on Ram. And they took on the form of Ram, i.e., their spirits were absorbed into Ram and became one with him.

Book VII: UTTARKAND (EPILOGUE)

1. 'A home near me'—i.e., liberation by proximity to the Lord.

2. The four coats of bark are the four states of consciousness—waking, dreaming, dreamless sleep, and the state in which the soul has become

one with the Absolute; the six trunks are the six stages of existence—conception, birth, childhood, manhood, old age and death; the twenty-five branches are the twenty-five categories of matter of which the material world is composed—Prakriti or primordial matter, Mahat or cosmic reason, Ahankara or cosmic ego, Manas or cosmic mind, Chitta or cosmic thought, the five sense perceptions of hearing, sight, taste, smell and touch, with the five sense-organs, the five Tanmatras or subtle elements corresponding to these, and the five gross elements or Mahabhutas of ether, earth, fire, water and sky. The innumerable leaves are the innumerable desires, the innumerable flowers are the innumerable actions to attain these desires, the two kinds of fruit are pain and pleasure, and the creeper clinging to it is maya.

3. The Ashvamedha was the horse sacrifice, which was performed only by the greatest and most powerful of kings.

4. Just as the Rishi Kumbhaj (Agastya) drank up the ocean, so Ram drinks up the ocean that is mundane existence.

5. The seven veils are earth, water, fire, air, ether, the cosmic ego and the cosmic intellect.

6. These are truth, compassion, penance and charity.

7. Parrots are caught with bait tied to a string, which is tied to a stick set in the ground so that when a parrot alights upon it, it revolves in such a way that the bird becomes confused and thinks it is tangled up in the string—it is not, and can fly away if it tries. Monkeys are caught with the help of a large jar with a narrow mouth. The jar is filled with grain and when the monkey puts his hand in and grabs a fistful, it cannot draw its hand out again and believes it is trapped—though it is not, for if it lets go the grain, it can draw out its hand and run away.

8. Waking, dreaming and dreamless sleep.

9. When the soul becomes one with the Universal spirit.

10. The birch tree allows even its bark to be torn off, to be used for paper etc., and constantly renews itself for the purpose.

11. For the stories of the prostitute Pingala, the Brahman Ajamil, and the elephant, see Balkand 26; for the story of the robber Valmiki, see Balkand 19, for the vulture Jatayu, see Balkand 24.

12. The five types of ignorance are mistaking the unreal for the real, the transient for the eternal, the painful for the pleasurable, the impure for the pure, and that which should be discarded as worth acquiring.